AGENDA FOR INSTITUTIONAL CHANGE

AGENDA FOR INSTITUTIONAL CHANGE IN HIGHER EDUCATION

Leslie Wagner
(Editor)
John Sizer   Tyrrell Burgess
Gerald Fowler   William Taylor   Brian Cane
Maurice Kogan and Christopher Boys
John L. Davies and Anthony W. Morgan
Burton R. Clark

SOCIETY FOR RESEARCH INTO HIGHER EDUCATION

Research into Higher Education Monographs

The Society for Research into Higher Education, At the University, Guildford, Surrey GU2 5XH

First published 1982

© 1982 Society for Research into Higher Education

ISBN 0 900868 85 6

Printed in England by Direct Printers, Butts Pond Industrial Estate, Sturminster Newton, Dorset DT10 1AZ policy issues in the light of the wider reaction. Stage six is the preparation of a final report. A seventh stage is of course intended, in which public authorities and institutions of higher education will take up the report's recommendations.

Publication of this monograph represents the conclusion of the first three stages in that part of the programme concerned with institutional adaptation and change. Consideration of these issues in a long-term perspective is particularly timely in the light of the many changes which are currently being forced on higher education institutions with, apparently, little consideration of their long-term implications.

Two previous volumes in the series have dealt with higher education and the labour market, and with access to higher education. In the former a careful review of the evidence suggested that there is little scope for any simple principle of manpower needs to replace the Robbins principle of student demand as a basic criterion that ought to determine the allocation of resources to higher education. However, there appears to be a good case for allowing subsequent employment opportunities to have a more explicit influence on the pattern and content of courses. There is convincing evidence that most students do expect their higher education to lead to improved job prospects and disappointment on this score was almost certainly largely responsible for the stagnating demand for higher education during the 1970s.

The volume on access to higher education starts from the view that current indicators give little hope of any significant increase in demand for the existing pattern of courses for many years. However, there is interesting evidence of considerable regional variation in participation rates and also evidence that the wastage of talent at sixteen through differential social class participation in post-compulsory education is no less than it was at the time of Robbins. The volume makes various suggestions for policies which might encourage significant increases in participation to the advantage of the higher education system and the community at large.

Five other main themes remain to be treated and these are summarized below.

THE RESEARCH FUNCTION

Universities are institutions whose function is teaching and research. In pursuing parity of esteem, many polytechnics have claimed equal treatment with regard to funding for research. However, there is ambiguity concerning the relationship that does exist, and that ought to exist, between research and teaching in higher education institutions. There is considerable disagreement, for example, about whether in practice, in the activities of academic staff, research is competitive with, or complementary to teaching. The actual and desirable relationship between 'research', 'scholarship', and consultancy activities is not at all clear. An unspecified proportion of the UGC grant to universities is normally deemed to be for research and

THE LEVERHULME PROGRAMME
OF
STUDY INTO THE FUTURE OF HIGHER EDUCATION

This is the third publication of a programme of study focusing info[r] opinion and recent research findings on the major strategic options lik[e] be available to higher education institutions and policy-making bodies i[n] 1980s and 1990s. The programme has been made possible by a gen[eral] grant from the Leverhulme Trust to the Society for Research into H[igher] Education, and is entirely independent of governmental or other orga[nisa]tional pressure. The present monograph arises out of a specialist semi[nar on] institutional adaptation and change held in September 1981 and chai[red by] Sir Alastair Pilkington. We are extremely grateful to Sir Alastair f[or his] chairmanship as well as for his considerable interest in the programme.

The fundamental question facing higher education is the extent t[o which] consensual arrangements and assumptions that generally worked well [in] the long postwar period of its expansion can cope with the muc[h more] stringent conditions likely to prevail in the 1980s and 1990s. [Is there] sufficient common purpose amongst the various institutions and [other] groups that constitute 'the higher education system' to per[mit the] development of viable long-run policy objectives or must higher e[ducation] policy become merely the outcome of a struggle for survival and d[ominance] among conflicting interests and ideas?

This is both a substantive and methodological question. Subst[antively it] will be faced squarely in the final report of the programme[.] Methodologically it will be tackled in the way the conclusions of [the] report are reached.

In brief, the study is an experiment in formulating long-term [policy] openly, taking into account the best available specialist knowled[ge of a] complex system, the legitimate interests of a wide range of [the] pressure groups, and wider public interests as perceived by d[isinterested] individuals with no direct day-to-day involvement in higher edu[cation. The] final recommendations will be the result of an iterative proce[ss in which] proposals are made, then discussed, then revised, then reconsid[ered. Stage] one is to commission research reviews by acknowledged exper[ts in the] specialist areas. Stage two is a seminar at which others w[ith direct] knowledge and experience of the area discuss these reviews. S[tage three is] publication of the reviews together with a report of the discussi[on and the] policy implications highlighted by it. Stage four is wider debat[e in print] and in specially convened conferences. Stage five is reconsid[eration scholarship. At the same time earmarked funds for scientific research are made available through the research councils. Increasingly, universities and polytechnics have undertaken contractual research for both public and private sector activities. The Rothschild Report of 1971 made various suggestions for rationalizing government-sponsored research, and an appraisal of the steps that have been taken to implement some of these recommendations is opportune. More generally a careful examination is needed of the place and organization of research in higher education institutions.

THE ARTS IN HIGHER EDUCATION
The role of the arts in education has for some time been a special concern of the Gulbenkian Foundation, which has made a special grant to enable the topic to be included in this programme. A consideration of courses in the arts (music, painting, theatre) raises a number of issues relevant to the future development of higher education as a whole. The nature of academic knowledge, the problem of assessment in activities that are at least partly expressive, the relationship between course provision and labour market opportunities are three of the generalizable issues that will be treated.

THE TEACHING FUNCTION
The largest task of higher education institutions is the teaching of students. In scope it ranges from training in specific vocational skills to the provision of opportunities for self-development in a wide range of general analytical and creative activities. Since 1960 there has been a huge increase in the curricular content of higher education; at the same time considerable attention has been devoted to the improvement of teaching, particularly through the use of new educational technologies. However, with rather few exceptions, of which the Open University is the most outstanding example, there has been little change in the ways in which the teaching function has been carried out. During the 1980s new problems are likely to emerge, particularly as the result of the aging of the stock of teachers and the lack of opportunities for mobility within higher education and out of it. The existence of a healthy higher education system in the 1990s is likely to depend at least as much on the attention that is paid to the content and methods of teaching as on external circumstances. This seminar will therefore give consideration to what is taught and how it is taught.

RESOURCES AND THEIR ALLOCATION
There are two levels of discussion about financial policy for higher education which ought to be brought together. The first is consideration of radical changes in present financial arrangements, such as greater dependence on private finance of various kinds and the replacement of student grants by loans. The second is whether the existing financial mechanism for disbursing public funds do in fact ensure an allocation of resources which is consistent

with public policy objectives. The tension between academic freedom and public accountability is one which needs to be kept constantly under review.

STRUCTURE AND GOVERNANCE
The Robbins Report recommended the establishment of what was in effect a unitary system of higher education dominated by the universities and regulated largely through the University Grants Committee. In fact a binary policy was established which aimed to give the public sector parity of esteem with the universities, largely through the concentration of advanced level courses in thirty polytechnics in England and fourteen institutions in Scotland. This policy has never been entirely satisfactory and there have been numerous attempts at improving the ability of the public sector to respond to changing social needs. The most recent development was the establishment in 1981 of a public sector national body for higher education. At the same time growing financial stringency has raised questions about whether the machinery of the UGC itself is appropriate for the likely conditions of the 1980s. The problem of co-ordination of resource and course provision between the university and public sectors is increased by resource stringency.

The reports on all eight of these seminars, together with comments on them from interested organizations and individuals, will form the basis for a final report setting out the conclusions and policy recommendations of the programme as a whole. This will be drawn up by the chairmen of the seminars and the editors of the accompanying monographs under the chairmanship of Lord Scarman, and will be published in June 1983.

The scope of the Leverhulme programme is very wide. The need for a major review of higher education has been recognized by informed commentators for some time and the financial stringency of 1981 has made it even more apparent. In its report *The Funding and Organisation of Courses in Higher Education* the Education, Science and Arts Committee of the House of Commons commended the Leverhulme programme of study and concluded, 'We believe that higher education is at a watershed in its development and that the time is ripe for a great national debate . . . .' The Leverhulme programme offers that debate both a structure within which the main issues can be considered and an assessment of the evidence on which future policy should be based.

Gareth Williams
Programme Director

FOREWORD

by Sir Alastair Pilkington

Change is usually the result of reaction to external forces. It is therefore an enlightened start to the introduction of change to get the right people together to discuss what the future should be and therefore in what ways it should be different. The SRHE/Leverhulme Programme of Study is a wholly commendable exercise and I am pleased to have played my own small part by chairing the seminar on institutional change.

I have to admit that I was surprised to find how objective and concentrated our discussions were. At no time did people fight for their own interests against others. The binary line did not seem to exist. The group struggled bravely and I think successfully not to allow itself to become obsessed with the problems of the present and to take a longer and creative view of the future.

Present problems do however offer some guidance as to future direction. Institutions and systems do not seem to be able to respond to the present situation in a way acceptable to those directly involved. This is most harmful, and shows a need to find a structure and method of working based on more partnership and openness. This approach was strongly advocated at the seminar and it is surely the correct one.

Another problem in any organization is to avoid the two extremes of too much centralization on the one hand and too little co-ordination and guidance on the other. The answer is partly a question of structure but more significantly one of leadership. I believe that the most important single task of someone at the top of a company or institution is to ensure a successful future. This means defining what success means in terms of all activities, defining main objectives, and identifying ways in which the efficiency of the whole and the fulfilment of individuals can be combined.

If the people at the top of an organization do not feel responsible for defining the future no one else will do it for them.

Higher education has been going along in a relatively undisturbed way for some time. Have the people at the top of the whole system and of each of the institutions been giving their minds to ensuring a successful future? Have they considered a definition of success as one of the most important parts of their job?

I believe that this whole exercise of considering the future of higher education is a task of great importance. It will make us all ask the most searching and difficult questions. It will compel us to define a successful future. Having defined it we may well fall short of it. But if we do not define it at all we do not deserve to succeed at all because we have failed to have any sense of direction and will not even know what we would like to achieve. The clearer our vision of what we wish to bring about the more likely it is that we shall design a structure and method of working to help it come about.

Alastair Pilkington
Chairman

CONTENTS

Introduction and Acknowledgements   1

Seminar Participants   5

AGENDA FOR CHANGE

1   The Challenge of Change   7
by Leslie Wagner
Introduction — Higher education and the political system —
The relationship between institutions —
Change within institutions — Mechanisms of change —
Recommendations

CRITERIA

2   Assessing Institutional Performance and Progress   33
by John Sizer
Introduction — Institutional Objectives —
Non-profit performance evaluation techniques —
'Partial' performance indicators — Future needs of society —
Portfolio analysis — Tests of appropriateness —
Institutional self-evaluation — Summary and conclusions

PROPOSALS

3   Autonomous and Service Traditions   70
by Tyrrell Burgess

4   Past Failure and the Imperative for Change   80
by Gerald Fowler
A failure to plan — The fallacy of seperate sectors —
Breaking the mould — Change is difficult: revolution
impossible — The need for systematic change

5   Change within a Contracting System   100
by William Taylor
Binary or beyond — Co-ordination, control and
academic imperative — Information networks for
co-ordination — The national body — The structure of the
academic profession — Summary and conclusion

6   The Contribution of the Public Sector   113
    by Brian Cane
    The contribution of the public sector —
    School-leaver participation —
    Course structures and insitutional management

IMPLEMENTATION

7   The Politics of Sectoral Change   127
    by Maurice Kogan and Christopher Boys
    Themes — The pattern of government and politics —
    Changes in British postwar higher education —
    Conclusions and possible policies

8   The Politics of Institutional Change   153
    by John L. Davies and Anthony W. Morgan
    Introduction — Institutions as organizations —
    Perceptions, expectations and restraints —
    The political nature of change in institutions —
    Resistance of organizational sub-units to the threat of
    contraction — Decision criteria —
    Generating effective policy — Building concensus —
    Centralization and participation — Conclusion

9   A Cross-National View   189
    by Burton R. Clark
    Structures of work — Structures of authority and
    modes of integration — The growing importance of
    federal organization

INTRODUCTION AND ACKNOWLEDGEMENTS

This book is the product of the third seminar in the SRHE Leverhulme Programme of Study into the Future of Higher Education, which was held in Bristol in September 1981. Drawing upon the whole seminar discussion, the opening chapter indicates what major long-term institutional changes are matters for serious consideration over the next decade. The other chapters are revised versions of the separate papers presented at the seminar and are grouped in three sections.

In the first section John Sizer discusses the assessment of institutional performance. The second section is concerned with the likely nature of the changes required to be made over the next decade. Here four personal views are presented by Tyrrell Burgess, Gerald Fowler, William Taylor and Brian Cane. The final section considers the politics of change, the mechanisms by which it can be brought about and the constraints upon it. Maurice Kogan and Christopher Boys focus on the relationship between different decision-making groups within higher education. John Davies and Anthony Morgan look at the problems arising from change within institutions of higher education, while Burton Clark provides an international perspective.

BACKGROUND

The horizon of the SRHE Leverhulme programme of study is 1990, not 1983 or 1984. Inevitably, however, recent and current events intrude. The seminar took place less than three months after the letter from the University Grants Committee to UK universities indicating what cuts in resources they would have to face over the next three years. Meanwhile the DES consultative document on two models for a national body for public sector higher education was published less than two months before the seminar and the merits of the respective models dominated the discussion in one session.

In so far as these recent events raise questions of longer-term impact they were legitimtate topics for scrutiny. The UGC cuts clearly call into question such issues as the role of the committee in relation to government decisions, the manner in which it takes its own decisions, the criteria it uses, and the relationship in higher education planning between the universities and the public sector.

This last issue is also raised by proposals for a national body for public sector higher education. These pose additional long-term questions about the role of local authorities in higher education provision and management, and the relationship between funding and validation bodies. It is important, however, to maintain a sense of perspective. For whilst current policy decisions will clearly have future impact there are other longer-term forces whose influence on higher education is likely to be even more profound. These include the relationship between higher education and the labour market and the problems of demand and access, the subjects of the first two volumes in this SRHE Leverhulme series.

The labour market volume does not in fact point to any radically new directions for change. It does not, for example, call for substantially more manpower planning to guide student selection or to change curricula, and it proposes that institutions should respond to their own perceptions of labour market needs. There is a proposal for better information flows between the labour market, higher education and potential students, which would be a particular function of government. All in all, however, it seemed that the pressure for institutional change was unlikely to come from industry and the labour market.

The second volume, on demand and access, raises questions of more direct concern. It points out that with an unchanged age participation rate the demographic decline in the 18-21 age group may lead to a fall in the demand for higher education by the early 1990s of up to 30 per cent.

However, the editor of that volume, Oliver Fulton, claims that the existing participation rate is 'undesirably low' both by international standards and 'in the light of economic, social and political benefits which higher education is said to confer'. Apart from increased participation from hitherto under-represented groups such as women, ethnic minorities and children of working-class parents there is, according to Fulton, a need and a scope for greater mature student participation. The legitimacy of seeking this wider participation, in terms of the benefits it would confer on the economy, society and the individual, is accepted by all the other contributors to the volume. There is less agreement about the methods by which such wider participation is to be encouraged, but Fulton stresses that it 'is not entirely dependent on factors external to higher education. Higher education itself can and should adapt in ways which will encourage greater participation.' Amongst the adaptations suggested by Fulton are changes in the structure, orientation and mode of courses, changes in admission policies, and changes in credit transfer arrangements.

So the higher education system and the institutions within it face change whatever their stance. If they do not seek greater and wider participation the demographic decline will produce a reduction in the number of students. No doubt some institutions will survive, and even prosper, while continuing to cater almost exclusively for the traditional group of entrants. Others will not, and the system as a whole will decline as falling student numbers are accompanied by reductions in funding and staff.

If institutions do seek new clientele both the search and its achievement will involve change, and this change will occur both within institutions and between them. The two approaches may well occur simultaneously, with some institutions seeking to encourage a new clientele and others concentrating on obtaining a larger market share amongst traditional students.

The mood of most participants at the recent seminar, on adaptation, was that change was both necessary and desirable. There was a determination to examine issues afresh, to grasp nettles such as political involvement and tenure which turned the meeting into what the Times Higher Education Supplement called 'a resilient and even gently radical occasion'. I am grateful to the authors for their papers and the participants for their contributions. Both have enormously influenced and informed my perception of the issues. Chapter 1, however, remains my own interpretation of the matters raised by the seminar. I believe it reflects the majority view in the discussions and that the conclusions and recommendations are consistent with the arguments expressed. Nevertheless the responsibility is mine alone and the proposals do not commit any of the participants.

The seminar provided a bridge between the external influences of the labour market and student demand and internal considerations of research, teaching, finance and structure which will be the subjects of later seminars in the series. Our discussion of the manner in which institutions need to respond inevitably touches upon these future concerns. We are thus taking the first step in their examination and setting part of the agenda for their later discussion.

ACKNOWLEDGEMENTS

A large number of people have helped me in the organization of the seminar and the preparation of this volume. My thanks go first to the authors of the papers, both for the excellence of their contributions and for their willingness to meet exacting deadlines. Gareth Williams, director of the programme, and Sir Alastair Pilkington, chairman of the seminar, have provided valuable advice, support and comment from our first thoughts about the seminar to the final stages of preparation of this volume. I am particularly grateful to Tessa Blackstone, Alf Morris, Sir Alastair Pilkington, Michael Shattock and Gareth Williams for reading the first draft of Chapter 1. Their comments have improved the chapter but I am sure they will be the first to concur with the usual statement that all responsibility for what appears there is mine.

Jenny Wagner typed and re-typed Chapter 1 under great pressure and with no visible effect on our domestic harmony. Betsy Breuer, the programme's administrator, provided her usual friendly and efficient service, as did Sally Kington in editing the final manuscript for publication.

Leslie Wagner
Editor

SEMINAR PARTICIPANTS

INSTITUTIONAL ADAPTATION AND CHANGE
Sir Alastair Pilkington (Chairman)
Prof. Leslie Wagner (Convenor) Polytechnic of Central London
Mr Christopher Ball, Keble College, Oxford
*Sir Kenneth Berrill, Vickers da Costa Ltd.
Dr William Birch, Bristol Polytechnic
Mr Richard Bird, Department of Education and Science
Prof. Tessa Blackstone, University of London Institute of Education
Dr Donald Bligh, University of Exeter
Sir Hermann Bondi, Natural Environment Research Council
+ Mr Christopher Boys, Brunel University
Mr Peter Brinson, Calouste Gulbenkian Foundation
+ Mr Tyrrell Burgess, North East London Polytechnic
Mr Peter David, The Times Higher Education Supplement
+ Mr Brian Cane, City of Liverpool College of Higher Education
+ Prof. Burton R. Clark, University of California at Los Angeles
+ Mr John L. Davies, Anglian Regional Management Centre
Prof. Lewis Elton, University of Surrey
Mr Rowland Eustace, Society for Research into Higher Education
Prof. Boris Ford, University of Bristol
+ Mr Gerald Fowler, Preston Polytechnic
Prof. David P. Gardner, University of Utah
*Prof. Ronald Glatter, The Open University
Mr Brian Gomes-da-Costa, Robert Gordon's Institute of Technology
Miss Harriet Greenaway, Bristol Polytechnic
Mr Trevor Habeshaw, Bristol Polytechnic
*Dr Edwin Kerr, Council for National Academic Awards
+ Prof. Maurice Kogan, Brunel University
+ Dr Anthony W. Morgan, University of Utah
*Mr Alfred Morris, Polytechnic of the South Bank
Prof. Roy Niblett, University of London
Dr Geoffrey Oldham, University of Sussex
Lady Pilkington
Mr Christopher Price, MP
Mrs Janey Rees, National Association of Teachers in Further and Higher Education
Mr Peter Scott, The Times Higher Education Supplement

*Mr Michael Shattock, University of Warwick
+Prof. John Sizer, Loughborough University
+Dr William Taylor, University of London Institute of Education
Prof. Philip Thody, University of Leeds
*Mr Peter Toyne, West Sussex Institute of Higher Education
Mr Phillip Whitehead, MP
*Sir Bruce Williams, Technical Change Centre
*Prof. Gareth Williams, University of Lancaster

+ Author of paper   * Discussant

THE CHALLENGE OF CHANGE

by Leslie Wagner

INTRODUCTION
The challenges faced by the higher education system over the next decade in terms of a possible decline in student demand and the need to respond to labour market requirements have been well documented in the first two volumes in this series. What changes at the institutional level are likely to be required if higher education is to achieve the twin goals of greater accessibility and greater responsiveness? Four areas of change can be highlighted: in the relationship between institutions and the wider political system; in changes both between institutions and within them; and in the mechanisms by which change can be facilitated. While the four are conceptually distinct they are also in practice inter-dependent. For example, the introduction of a more extensive credit transfer system between institutions is also likely to produce changes inside institutions.

HIGHER EDUCATION AND THE POLITCAL SYSTEM
The relationship between higher education and the state, while always a subject for discussion, has for many years been a relatively uncontroversial topic. In the university sector the establishment of the University Grants Committee in 1919, and its development, particularly in the period of rapid expansion in the 1960s, provided a model which was widely considered to be satisfactory. This model was designed to ensure, in the words of the Robbins Report, that 'measures of co-ordination and allocation that are necessary are insulated from inappropriate political influences' (para 727). The UGC was seen to provide this insulation through its membership, functions and procedures. Its membership consists largely of academics. Its functions involve advising governments on the total funds required by the university system and in allocating between universities such funds as the government provides. Traditionally its procedures included the principles of a quinquennial settlement and a block grant to each institution. As Burgess points out both those principles were designed to preserve the autonomy of the universities already enshrined in their individual charters. 'The quinquennial settlement reduced the possibility of pressure from year to year in response to changes of "policy" and government. The block grant kept decisions, and not just "academic" decisions, within each university. Any weakening of these principles would begin to introduce detailed external influence over academic matters in individual universities' (Chapter 3, p.74).

Until very recently during the whole of the postwar period these institutional arrangements were strengthened by two other factors. First, the resources available generally increased from year to year so that the nature of any 'political' interference was likely to be limited to questions of new developments which at the end of the day the universities would be able to resist if they considered them undesirable. The role of political bodies was seen as 'enabling' rather than 'compelling'. Secondly, the higher education community was confident that it had more influence than the politicians, a justified confidence as is shown by the fate of the thirteen points put forward by Shirley Williams in 1969.[1]

What has now come to be called public sector higher education did not have this conceptually neat model of autonomous institutions protected from political control by a self-governing, co-ordinating and resource allocating organization. Their historical links with, or more accurately their ownership by local authorities made this impossible. Yet here too, in the development of the polytechnics, the principle was established of as much separation as possible from political influence. The CNAA was developed, composed almost wholly of academics, particularly in its subject boards, to ensure that academic standards were maintained. As Kogan and Boys point out, in both the universities and the public sector 'the DES assumes that academics will themselves through such devices as the appointment of external examiners validate their own standards' (Chapter 7, p.130).

As far as the government of public sector institutions was concerned, while they were not given autonomous status, and remained in most cases in the ownership of their local authorities, the powers of their governing bodies and their internal governing structures were strengthened. On finance too, whilst the local authority continued to be responsible for polytechnic budgets, the pooling system ensured that an individual institution had relatively few financial constraints. Moreover, in the heady early days of upgrading and expansion the polytechnics appear to have felt, like the universities, that their influence over the politicians was strong enough to push policy in their direction.

Growing Dissatisfaction
As several authors in this volume point out, this general satisfaction with the relationship between higher education and the political system began to be challenged during the course of the 1970s. Doubts turned into anxieties and finally, by the end of the decade, into a crumbling of confidence in the existing arrangements. The increasingly severe financial constraints within which higher education has been forced to operate are a major factor contributing to this change. It is perhaps easy to forget in the gloom-ridden period of the early 1980s that less than a decade earlier the atmosphere was one of expansion and ultimately limitless resources. The 1972 White Paper was actually called *Education: A Framework for Expansion*. It reaffirmed the Robbins principle and expected full-time higher education places to grow from 463,000 in 1971/72 to 750,000 by 1981. The absolute expansion in the

number of places over the nine years to 1981 was expected to be greater than the increase that had occurred in the nine years since Robbins.

The reality has been very different. Fewer students wanted to come. Or, more precisely, the age participation rate having doubled in the decade following Robbins then began to decline. The effect on enrolment was mitigated by population growth within the 18-21 age group and continued growth in the numbers of mature students and overseas students which ensured some rise in overall numbers. Even this small growth was not fully funded. The dramatic rise in the price of oil at the end of 1973 and its exacerbation of the longer-term structural problems of the British economy resulted in a squeeze in public expenditure including the resources made available for higher education. The arms-length role of political authority which was possible in the period of plentiful resources was no longer tenable. In the public sector local authorities began to look more closely at polytechnic budgets to discover where funds could be saved. The universities experienced the collapse of the quinquennial system. Financial planning became a matter of trial and error. Subsequently, in 1979, the block grant principle was eroded as the UGC offered more and more detailed 'guidance' to institutions. The logic of these developments was the UGC allocation in July 1981 of the reduced funds provided by government. Not only did the committee share the cuts unequally between particular institutions, but its allocations were accompanied by detailed guidelines on the areas of academic study which it recommended should be reduced or withdrawn.

So the UGC became one focus of the university sector's discontent with existing arrangements. This might be viewed as an inevitable reaction to the much harder decisions incumbent upon the withdrawal of resources. Indeed some have argued that the UGC made the best of a bad job not of its own making and took some courageous decisions. Others, however, have cited the July 1981 decisions as final proof that the UGC is more of an arm of government than a buffer between universities and the government. What is certainly called into question is whether a body of twenty or so part-time members, led by a full-time chairman and with a small administrative staff should be making secret decisions followed by little public justification or explanation affecting forty-four institutions, some 25,000 staff and 300,000 students.

A further factor damaged higher education's confidence in the existing relationships. People in higher education suddenly realized that their political influence had waned. It might have been thought that if in the good times higher education had managed to receive more than its proportionate share of public funds then surely in the bad times academics and their supporters had enough political clout to ward off the worst effects. Sadly for higher education they did not. Neither the formal mechanisms of UGC and CVCP advice and pressure nor the informal mechanisms of college and clubland dining tables appear to be providing higher education with many friends at court. Or, as Kogan and Boys put it more formally, 'There are no active and strong political constituences with an interest in higher education, and with power to challenge the centre. . . . There are no external constituencies to whom appeal can be made and who are capable of applying electoral or other punishments to those who reduce the resources and the standing of higher education' (Chapter 7, p.140).

In the golden age of the 1960s when students were banging on the doors, and when higher education was seen as providing economic growth, social mobility and greater equality, there was no obvious need to cultivate a political constituency. It existed naturally. In the harsh climate of the late 70s and early 80s, when the students no longer queued and when disillusionment with higher education's contribution to economic and social progress was great, it was too late.

Changes

What are the changes required to improve the relationship between higher education and the political system? It is important not to over-dramatize the nature of government interference. As Kogan and Boys explain in their introduction, 'Hitherto the British system has sought to achieve a balance between respect for the inner life of higher education and the need to control its scope and purposes in the interests of the economy, or resource control and other social ends' (Chapter 7, p.127).

There has been little direct attack from outside on the 'inner life' of higher education. Internal research and teaching arrangements in terms of organization, curriculum, method and style are determined by academics. Peer group evaluation through faculty boards, senates, external examiners and the CNAA subject panels is used to maintain standards. Occasional mutterings about the importance of manpower planning and the need for a more vocational approach are as yet no threat to the sanctity of higher education's 'inner life'. Indeed the first volume of this series indicated that higher education could best meet its labour market duties by being allowed largely to continue its present 'inner life' arrangements, albeit enhanced by a more effective network of information.[2]

In order to preserve its institutional autonomy higher education has been happy to keep those with political power, nationally or locally, at arms length. This may no longer be possible. As resources become scarcer so the desire of those outside institutions to intervene more directly becomes greater. Far from seeking to block this outside intervention institutions may be better advised to harness it to work for rather than against them. The need to establish or re-establish political links and constituencies is urgent.

Some of the blame for the present situation must lie with the institutions themselves. Many have done little to foster the sympathy of whatever political friends they might have had. Universities have long claimed the right to be national and indeed international institutions. Their respected place in the local community has arisen largely from the prestige they brought to the town or city.

The local authority gave the university little money and had little influence in the national forums where the key decisions affecting the institution were made. In many polytechnics the same attitudes began to surface. To some extent it is understandable. In some authorities the legitimate interest of members and officers in finance and resources developed into a detailed control of expenditure and a threat to the 'inner life' of the institutions. The bureaucratic procedures within which such control was exercised sometimes induced despair amongst those trying to produce change or effectively manage such institutions. In these circumstances polytechnic directors could be forgiven for believing that national status was the modern equivalent of the Garden of Eden.

But it was in the Garden of Eden that loss of innocence and the Fall of Man occurred. In proclaiming themselves to be national and not local institutions, polytechnics effectively put themselves in competition with the universities for the allocation of national resources. And in an era of resource constraint, which is the only likely outlook for higher education, this may not be wise.

Local authorities can be important to higher education institutions in a number of ways. Despite the increasing pressures of central government they still have the ability to provide independent sources of revenue. Some polytechnics which took the view that their local authorities were not generous enough in the good times have found that they have not been too mean in the bad times. Furthermore, local authority representatives do provide links with the local community and, perhaps more importantly, have influence with the education committee. A local councillor who identifies with his polytechnic and college can be a tenacious defender of its interest when resource decisions are being taken.

So the local authority role in higher education is not to be derided. In Chapter 3 Burgess provides other valid arguments for a strong local authority involvement. These include accountability, responsiveness, facilitating links with further education and stimulating the local intellectual and economic environment. Burgess in fact argues that local authorities should also be responsible for most of the universities. But if polytechnic advocates of nationalization veer too much in one direction Burgess veers too much in the other. Higher education institutions do have national as well as local roles, and the need for some national co-ordination, if not planning, is clear.

A balance must be struck and various alternatives have been under discussion (DES 1981). Whatever form of national body emerges in the longer term for public sector higher education and whatever relationships develop between it and the UGC, both local and national authority interest must be represented.

Any new national arragements for the governance of higher education should allow for an enhanced role for local communities in all institutions in their locality. If institutions want their local communities to be supportive financially and politically they will have to be much more sympathetic to increased local involvement.

What form should this enhanced role take? Clearly local interests would need to be adequately represented on councils and governing bodies. Besides local authorities, these interests might include employers, trades unions, community groups, religious organizations, other local educational institutions, and so on. In many institutions such representation already exists. However, involvement should not be seen as simple tokenism of formal representation but as part of a genuine attempt to establish closer relationships between the institution and its local community. It will need to be supported by regular informal interaction.

A more radical step might also be considered, through involvement of the local community in the strategic planning of each institution. Present arrangements for such planning are varied. In most institutions where it takes place it is left to a committee of senate or an academic board, occasionally with a small council or governing body representation. What is proposed here is that such lay participation should be more overt and influential. Such a strategic planning group would be concerned with the institution's medium-term outlook, its objectives, the changes in direction it might need, and the ways in which it might find resources.

This would be a new depature for many institutions and will no doubt be considered by some to be dangerous. For it admits outsiders perilously close to the inner life of the institution. This may be risky but not necessarily dangerous. If higher education is to regain its political influence it will have to take risks. And one of those risks is to expose the inner workings of the system to a wider audience. The mysteries of higher education may once have contributed to the awe in which universities were held by those who had never experienced them, the great majority of the population. Those mysteries are now thought to be guilty secrets and are a source of suspicion.

Allowing people with influence and power within the local community to see what goes on and to identify with the achievements of their local university and polytechnic is more likely than not to increase their support, and in only isolated cases is there likely to be any attempt at improper intervention in academic affairs. The notion is outdated that institutions must remain politically neutered to be protected from undue political influence. The eunuch may still get raped. Adequate precautions are a better preventive measure.

Nor is this an impractical proposition. American participants at the seminar left no doubt about the value seen by institutions in the USA in involvement in political activity. State senators are used by state universities assiduously to challenge state government policies towards higher education. The institutions are directly involved in lobbying, manoeuvering and building coalitions. It is risky at times. Some votes are lost or the institution occasionally backs the wrong horse, but overall the effect appears to be advantageous for higher education.

National involvement in institutional management is more difficult to envisage. But one level of national support for individual institutions seems to have been surprisingly neglected by some. The local member of parliament has both a need and a duty to represent local interests at the national level. Yet in many cases he is called upon only in a crisis situation which often looks like special pleading. Here too a continuous relationship needs to be established through frequent normal contact between MPs and their local institutions. This should be formally enshrined in the principle that a member of parliament should have a seat on the governing body of all higher education institutions within his constituency.

Re-establishing its broader political influence is only one aspect, albeit an important one, of the relationship between higher education and the political system. Also of vital importance is the function of any central co-ordinating body. This will be considered by the seminar on governance and structure in late 1982, and will be discussed in the volume reporting that seminar.

It is possible however to discuss some general principles which might apply and to recognize at the outset that a tension exists between conflicting objectives. A theme that runs through many of the chapters in the present volume is the importance of diversity, pluralism, and de-centralization in the provision of funds and more general decision making within the system. A number of authors (Fowler, Clark, and Kogan and Boys for example) point to the need to allow institutions as often as possible to choose their own routes to salvation. Centralization, they argue, is to be avoided. Conversely, however, some co-ordination planning and overall resource-allocation is also required, and even in the market-oriented systems of the USA there is considerable statewide planning in the larger states.

However, institutions left to their own devices may not produce the radical changes required. It is not only the deadening hand of bureaucracy at the centre that inhibits change and prevents flexibility. Vested interests within institutions can be just as pernicious. Clarke and Kogan and Boys highlight the power within institutions of academic departments and the conservative influence of their preserving their economic and intellectual interests has often been commented on. More important, however, many of the changes discussed later in this chapter, such as a comprehensive credit transfer system and a more flexible approach to academic tenure, cannot be introduced effectively by individual institutions. A central co-ordinating role has to be performed somewhere.

The aim must be to ensure that any central body does not seek to impose uniformity. Instead its purpose must be to guide the system towards desirable change and to provide, encourage and maintain diversity in the system in terms of a variety of provision and a multiplicity of funding sources. Institutions must retain the ability to respond to their own perception of the need for change.

The experience of the UGC exercise of July 1981 and discussions about the future of a public sector funding body highlight another important issue, namely the extent to which resource decisions should be and can be informed by academic judgements. The problem arises even within institutions but is more acute at the national level, where adequate information is more difficult to obtain and to interpret.

Resource decisions clearly do imply academic judgements. The UGC, in imposing the largest of the 1981 cuts on Aston and Salford Universities, was at least in part making an academic judgement about those institutions. Any public sector body will face the same problem even if it tries to apply mechanical, across-the-board formulae such as unit costs. Such formulae involve academic judgements even if they are more heavily camouflaged in the weightings and equations used to arrive at the unit cost figures.

Academic judgements should not be denied or hidden; they should be made explicit. Moreover, the flow of information and influence between planning bodies and the institutions they are planning should be two-way. In particular, institutions should have a say in deciding the principles on which resource allocation decisions are to be made and any such decisions should be accompanied by a statement of the principles adopted. The UGC 1981 exercise in secret decision making should not be repeated if such bodies are to retain their credibility and the confidence of those affected.

In the public sector there is an understandable temptation to look to the CNAA (and other validating agencies such as TEC and BEC) in either a formal or informal way as the source of academic information on public sector institutions. The CNAA's authority in these matters is far greater than the UGC's in relation to the universities. A link between the validating bodies and a public sector funding body, possibly to the extent of making them a single organization, brings the danger of a monolithic approach where central decisions are based on a single source of information. The main principle to be established in any central body must be diversity. It should not apply a single set of criteria to the wide range of institutions it is funding. Moreover, even if the CNAA were to remain independent but provided the funding body with academic judgements about institutions' courses, it should not be the only source of information. In particular, the institutions themselves must be allowed to provide their own informational input into any decisions affecting them.

What is required is a greater degree of openness. Institutions must be more open to their local communities and planning and resource organizations must be more open to those affected by their decisions. Without this, the support necessary for institutions and planning organizations to function effectively may not be forthcoming.

THE RELATIONSHIP BETWEEN INSTITUTIONS

Binary Line
The subject of the binary line is raised in a number of chapters and a variety of views are represented. Taylor (Chapter 5) argues that the line has

sharpened in recent years. He attributes this partly to the continued existence of the two systems. The longer the distinction survives the sharper it becomes, he argues. Moreover, he anticipates that in a period of resource scarcity the temptation to withdraw from existing areas of co-operation will be great. However, it is possible to hold the opposite view. Hardship may well drive institutions into each other's arms as a means of mutual protection. Reports are already beginning to circulate about such co-operation.[3]

Cane (Chapter 6) not only accepts the division but sees some of its virtues in terms of the contribution that the public sector can make to institutional change. In a vigorous advocacy he argues that public sector institutions have shown themselves to be more flexible than universities in terms of access, mode of attendance, age of student, and length and structure of courses. However, he also indicates areas where institutions within the same region can co-operate across the binary line.

Burgess (Chapter 3) takes an opposite view to Cane, repeating his criticism of the 'academic drift' of public sector institutions. Fowler (Chapter 4) agrees in large part with Burgess that public sector institutions have tended to ape the universities. He puts the blame for this, however, on the shoulders of various governments since 1965 and contrasts government rhetoric about the importance of the supposed goals of the public sector with their operation of funding and control mechanisms, which have worked against them achieving these goals.

What then is the most appropriate relationship between the various institutions of higher education to develop for the end of the twentieth century? It is necessary to distinguish between relationships at different levels.

At the level of the individual academic, the centre of the internal life of higher education, much co-operation and association exists in professional committees, research organizations and validation bodies. The importance of these associations in influencing the values and behaviour of individual teachers should not be underestimated. Burgess might argue that the influence has been largely one way, from the universities to the public sector. This might be redressed if the suggestion in the next pages (20-21) for greater external peer review for universities is adopted and polytechnic and college staff are regularly included as members of the peer review group.

At the course, departmental and individual institutional level co-operation already exists and there is some evidence that the 1980s may see further moves in this direction. Such moves are to be encouraged for a variety of reasons. They may facilitate the objective of wider access. Joint courses, or at least courses which are jointly planned, may enable students to move more freely between institutions. Greater co-operation may enable unnecessary duplication to be eliminated and allow institutions to fill gaps in their own provision.

There is a certain cumulative effect in operation here. The more staff in different institutions are exposed to the modes of work of their neighbouring colleagues the less suspicion there is likely to be. The greater the understanding and mutual respect the greater will be the basis for future co-operation.

There is one final benefit to be gained from greater co-operation. The evidence from the experience of the Open University, and from CNAA validation is that the more course structures and content are exposed to outside view the greater the rigour with which they are prepared. There is an opposite view of course that the pressure is to greater conformity and conservatism. On balance, however, the effect is a beneficial one and may be a useful side-effect of greater co-operation between institutions in course planning and preparation.

All this leaves open the question of the formal funding and control relationship between the different institutions. Should there be one such body for all institutions (a Higher Education Commission?), and if so where is the line drawn? The Australian example was discussed briefly at the seminar and some of the benefits noted but no firm conclusioin was arrived at. Is the Burgess model of a small 'autonomous' sector with all the rest organized through local authorities the way forward? Most people thought not.

The position in the early 1980s seems to be that for historical, administrative and political reasons two reasonably distinct sectors are likely to remain for some time. However, if the emerging trends continued and the proposals made here were adopted then the distinction would become less and less sharp. In the near future the UGC is likely to continue with its more interventionist role and some national body for public sector higher education will come into existence.

Local authorities are likely to continue to have a role within this national body and in relation to their local college. If, additionally, universities offered an enhanced role to local authorities as advocated here, and agreed to greater external peer review (see below p.20) then in formal terms of financing and control there would be little to choose between the two sectors. The main distinctions would be that the universities through their Royal Charters would continue to have power to award their own degrees and might continue to receive an element of their research funding through the UGC.

How things might develop from this position can perhaps be left to a later volume in this series on resources and their allocation. An important question relevant to our own perspective is the effect of different structures on institutional change and adaptation. Here too there are differing opinions. Some argue that a unitary structure with all institutions in a single sector covered by a single planning body would inevitably lead to uniformity. Others respond by pointing to the Australian experience, where the existence of such a single body still allows diversity to be maintained. Moreover, it is argued that the binary system encourages uniformity. Having been differentiated formally, institutions then devote themselves to stressing their similarities and competing for the middle ground.

In the final analysis the form of any structure will be less important than the powers such bodies receive and the discretion they allow individual institutions. Whether the system is unitary, binary or trinary, the structures it creates must encourage initiative, responsiveness, and flexibility so that diversity in provision, access and institutional arrangements can be maintained and fostered.

Credit Transfer
One area in which co-operation between institutions could be improved is in the more ready acceptance by them of students who have completed part of their courses elsewhere. For all sorts of good educational and personal reasons an individual may want or need to leave an institution part of the way through his studies. The road to gaining access to another institution and receiving credit for studies already undertaken is strewn with difficulties. Partly this is a result of the variation of course structures and content that institutional autonomy inevitably brings about. But it is also caused by an unnecessary conservatism amongst staff. These difficulties and strategies to overcome them are well documented in the Toyne Report 1979. It is significant that at the time of writing, some two years after the report was published, progress has been slow and little initiative has been taken at governmental level to try to implement its recommendations.

This question is a good example of the dilemma faced by those who advocate minimal governmental interference in higher education. Credit transfer is an important element of a more responsive system. It can be fostered by bilateral agreements such as exist between the Open University and a number of institutions or by informal arrangements which create an information network amongst students and staff. This is essentially how credit transfer arrangements operate at present.

However, a network of bilateral arrangements is almost impossible to arrange and what is required is a national system, which can only be achieved through a more interventionist government role. How can this be reconciled with a less dirigiste approach which in other contexts is seen as the key to fostering institutional change?

One way would be for the government to see its role as encouraging and enabling rather than directing. The latter approach could not in any event work with credit transfer. Course structures and content which are clearly incompatible cannot be made compatible by central diktat. But that does not mean that there is no role for government. Essentially, government could operate in two ways, one passive, the other active.

The very least that is required is for a national information service on credit transfer possibilities to be established, independent of any existing institution. This was recommended by the Toyne report, which also stated that it was technically feasible to set up. More actively financial levers could be used to push and prod institutions in the right direction. Fowler shows in a number of areas how financial regulations concerning student grants, weightings for part-time study, and so on have influenced institutions in the type of provision they have organized. Institutional attitudes might change, for example, if the weighting system for calculating grants gave an increased weighting for those students who had been accepted through a credit transfer scheme. If sticks rather than carrots are seen as more effective then courses which did not accept credit transfer students could have their numbers for grant purposes lowered.

This is not particularly radical. The existing weighting system, while supposedly reflecting 'effort' or 'work-load', does contain powerful incentives and disincentives as recent official documents have admitted (DES 1980). The use of financial levers is a legitimate use of governmental power for it allows national priorities to be expressed while leaving institutions free to decide if they will respond to the rewards and punishments offered.

A national credit transfer system is an important long-term goal for the United Kingdom's higher education system. In more fully meeting student needs it would widen access. The dangers in terms of rigidity of course structures and content would have to be monitored of course. The balance of opinion of those who have studied the subject is that this is less of a problem than the inertia of the academic community. Skilled use of the financial levers of policy is one way for government to overcome this inertia.

CHANGE WITHIN INSTITUTIONS

The Two-Year Degree

There are many ways in which access to higher education might be widened: through, for example, more varied standards of entry, curricular structures and content, modes of attendance, and styles of teaching. These and other issues are fully discussed in the previous volume in this series and it is not intended to repeat them here. One issue which might be highlighted, however, is the traditional educational package offered to higher education students.

The three-year undergraduate degree course (and its sandwich-type variant) is still the norm of most higher education institutions. At postgraduate level a variety of certificates, diplomas, and degree structures are available, but the degree dominates undergraduate provision, particularly in the universities. The Diploma of Higher Education, now almost ten years old, has not attracted a great following, despite mandatory grants being available.

There is no shortage of proposals for alternative structures. Carter (1980) has proposed the introduction of more two-year courses, particularly to attract those who have reached an 'A' level standard of competence but are judged weak in their ability to complete a degree. He links this to proposals for institutional change whereby only a limited number of institutions provide first degree courses, the others providing 2-year courses.

One weakness of this proposal is Carter's own explanation for the existing pattern. 'A degree is an ancient and prestigious qualification, and the various diplomas and certificates below degree level carry no equivalent prestige: some are, indeed, liable to be interpreted as evidence of failure in a degree (Carter 1979). If this is so, how will the situation be improved if more non-degree courses are provided? Is there any evidence that these would be more attractive to potential students than the existing provision? Of course financial incentives could be provided to make the courses attractive, but there are deeper questions involved.

Why is the degree course so attractive? Is it because employers are wedded to the traditional bench marks of 'O' level, 'A' level and degree as indicators of intellectual competence and unwilling to consider alternatives? Does this perception feed back to prospective students and become the primary determinant of their choice? Or does the answer lie more with the academic community, which, having found a comfortable working structure in the 3-year degree course, sees no need to develop alternative structures?

The last reason is perhaps the key. Employer and student perception could be changed if higher education itself indicated that it took non-degree courses seriously. Their status at present is seen as inferior to, rather than an alternative to, degree courses.

It is because of this perhaps that Cane in a later chapter in this volume (Chapter 6) argues for a 2-year *degree* course, linking it to progress for the best graduates on into a 2-year Masters course. Such a proposal has many attractions. It provides the marketable element which most students are looking for as the end product of their studies; it would be cheaper to finance; it would provide an opportunity for those who find higher education's present offering unattractive as well as an alternative for those who at the moment take the 3-year course; and it would provide a further opportunity for curricular experiments.

Ah, but would it be a degree? The Independent University has so far failed to persuade validating bodies such as the CNAA that degree-level standard can be achieved in two years. This of course raises the question of what is 'degree-level standard'. The onus of proof or at least of argument should be on those who deny that a two-year degree is feasible.

One way some of their objections might be overcome would be to lengthen the academic year. At present this consists for the student of between 30 and 36 weeks a year even if the Christmas and Easter vacations are included as periods of study. Few students are required to study over the summer vacation. It would seem therefore that 90 weeks is thought to be the minimum time of study for a degree course. Why cannot this be compressed into two years, with the academic year running from early September to the end of July?

Of course there would be other problems to overcome. For example staff would claim that their research and study time would be prejudiced. This might be dealt with by more generous study leave arrangements, as exist at the Open University. Alternatively, such courses might be organized in institutions where research is not deemed to be a major activity. At the very least the CNAA ought to review its decision not to recognize 2-year degrees, and might encourage some public sector institutions to develop pilot schemes. And an enterprising university which does not need any one else's approval might also make a move in this direction.

Peer Review

A major binary distinction concerns academic autonomy. Universities have the power to grant their own degrees. Polytechnics and colleges require the approval of the Council for National Academic Awards who validate the courses and award the degrees. Within the universities senates have the ultimate authority in this area and typically they rely on internal appraisal and external examiners' evaluation. The CNAA on the other hand, whilst also receiving external examiners reports on existing courses, relies on external appraisal and detailed documentation for both new and existing courses.

The CNAA approach is criticized by some polytechnics because of the bureaucracy involved and the resources expended by institutions in preparing for CNAA validation. Others see the system as casting doubt on their academic maturity. The Council has attempted to meet both these objections in its recent proposals for 'Partnership in Validation' (CNAA 1979). In the 1980s the CNAA will be concerned much more with the re-validation of existing, if amended, courses rather than the validation of new courses. It is moving towards granting indefinite approval to many of these existing courses, subject to periodic progress review visits. In doing this, it will be much concerned with the effectiveness of an institution's monitoring and self-evaluation of its courses. The external peer review for existing courses is increasingly likely to take the form of a monitoring of the monitors.

The new approach to evaluation will bring benefits in encouraging institutions to establish mechanisims for regular appraisal of their courses. Such appraisal, apart from establishing quantitative data on drop-out, failure rate, level of attainment, and so on, should also highlight qualitative factors such as student satisfaction, and staff enthusiasm.

The key element is the external review of an institution's activity by an academic peer group, and it might be timely for universities to ask themselves if they might not benefit from such a procedure. Both the CNAA experience and especially that of the Open University indicate that knowledge that a course will be evaluated by a peer group of colleagues from outside the institution is likely to lead to more rigorous self-evaluation. It also enables the institution to obtain a wider variety of opinion about a course than might otherwise be available. And one longer-term spin-off is that it might raise the status of teaching in universities. At present, research activity is largely used as a criterion for promotion, partly because it is at least a visible element of an academic's work. If peer group evaluation became extensive then the teaching abilities of members of staff would become more widely known and could more easily be taken as a criterion for promotion.

This suggestion that universities should consider adopting external group review of their courses in no way challenges their right to award their own degrees. This right of senate would remain. What is suggested is that senates should agree to peer group review before they grant approval of new courses and renewed approval of existing courses.

In no way is the autonomy of the institution to make its own decisions compromised. Instead it is suggested that institutions might require a more comprehensive and rigorous evaluation of proposals before coming to their decisions. Indeed, in the long run this model might be applied to both universities and polytechnics. All such institutions would receive or retain the right to grant their own degrees. The CNAA would lose its formal powers of validation in relation to polytechnics and possibly some colleges of higher education but might retain it for the many other institutions of higher education whose courses it presently validates.

Mobility of Staff and the Principle of Tenure

No discussion of the internal changes facing higher education institutions can ignore the problem of academic tenure and staff mobility. It is very unfortunate that the financial problems of higher education in the early 1980s have made it difficult to conduct a rational discussion of these questions and their longer-term effects. As Taylor points out, '. . . immediate anxieties among staff about the nature of tenure and the possibility of redundancy mean that every proposal for re-structuring, whatever its long-term academic merits, is likely to be judged in relation to its short-term impact on jobs' (Chapter 5, p.108).

The principle of tenure is discussed at present in terms of whether it will or will not be an effective barrier against the loss of jobs as a result of financial cutbacks. Yet the much more important question for higher education over the rest of the decade is the effect of longer-term influences on staff mobility. The issue of tenure needs to be discussed in that context.

It is important to remember, in the midst of the present frenzied atmosphere in higher education that the problems likely to be thrown up by these longer-term developments have not suddenly become apparent. As long ago as 1974 Gareth Williams was reflecting on the twin effects of the rapid expansion of higher education in the period to the early 1970s and the less rapid expansion (as he saw it) over the next two decades. The rapid expansion of the earlier period provided much improved opportunities for appointment to higher education posts for recent graduates and post-graduates. The proportion of younger staff grew. In the universities in 1969, for example, 62 per cent of lecturers and 48 per cent of all staff were aged less than 35.

Williams predicted that 'from 1983/4 onwards there will be a sharp decline in opportunities and they are unlikely to recover again before the end of the century. . . . After the middle of the 1980s very few graduates indeed could expect to find academic jobs and indeed postgraduates who got one would also become a rarity' (Williams 1975). It must be remembered that Williams assumed a growth in the age participation rate of over 4 per cent per annum from the mid 70s onwards, whereas the reality has been stagnation and a small decline.

Therefore even if the cut in resources forecast for the first half of the 1980s were averted, and the decline in the 18-year-old population over the next decade were mitigated by attracting other groups, the outlook for staffing would be for a gradually ageing academic population with little infusion of new blood. This is a serious matter, not only for the young graduates denied employment opportunities, but for the future of higher education itself. It is not necessary to get into a sterile debate about the age at which people are at their most creative to recognize the importance of young academics in the higher education world. Without the stimulus of fresh thinking and of new approaches both to research and teaching a higher education institution stagnates. When the whole system is involved the danger is magnified. As one of the participants in the seminar put it, 'the worst crime those responsible for higher education could perpetrate over the next 15 years would be to bequeath to the next generation a system in which 80 per cent of the staff was over the age of 45.'

The task then is to find ways of increasing staff mobility and make employment opportunities available to the best young graduates. It is difficult to see how this can be done without some early retirement scheme for existing staff.[4] It is important, however, that such a scheme should not be devised or be seen as a hasty reaction to the need to make economies. It should instead be part of a longer-term development within higher education in which movement out of the system at an appropriate age might be seen as a natural process and in many respects a sign of career advancement and development.

There are other organizations in our society, such as the police and the armed services, where early retirement is regarded as natural and where only a limited number of staff continue beyond a certain age. Here comprehensive retirement schemes have been developed which provide a certain amount of financial security. In addition these institutions have established a strong organizational network with outside employers to enable staff to find alternative satisfying posts upon retirement.

Such a policy clearly needs a great deal of discussion, and negotiation with the unions, and cannot be introduced overnight. Apart from the need to change the attitudes of those already working in higher education, it would also be required to establish the sophisticated and comprehensive network of avenues to alternative employment, all of which would take considerable time.

In the first instance a less ambitious scheme might be more feasible in which early retirement might be linked to part-time work within the same institution. The attractions of academic life are not just the teaching and research elements but the intellectual involvement with colleagues, access to the library and laboratories, the status of the position, and the feeling of belonging to a community. All these could be retained by a part-time appointment. It should be possible to devise an appropriate scheme providing a reasonable amount of financial security to older staff, enabling them to maintain their links with their institutions and seek alternative sources of income, and at the same time releasing funds to enable an institution to employ younger academics.

In some cases the question of tenure is marginal to the question of staff mobility and the proposals outlined above. For if tenure were regarded as a fundamental principle it could still be retained up to the age at which the early retirement scheme came into operation. Given the age structure of staff it could still apply for the vast majority for some time to come. The proposal outlined above is not an attack on jobs. Its aim is to substitute young academics for older ones while keeping total employment numbers at the very least unchanged.

However, the issue of tenure cannot be avoided. Its importance in defending the freedom of academics from undue pressure both inside and outside the institution and in preventing arbitrary dismissal must be recognized. Moreover, this is a freedom not just to hold unpopular views against political pressure but to pursue scholarship and research wherever the imagination and expertise of the individual academic leads them. Advance in the sciences, social sciences and humanities, it is argued, has depended a great deal on this freedom.

Yet its importance can be exaggerated. There have been instances where tenure has not been an adequate defence against a strong-minded establishment. Moreover there are other ways, particularly through the reward and promotion system, whereby unpopular views can be and have been punished. It must be added of course that tenure only exists in the universities. In the public sector staff are generally covered by normal contracts of employment with a stated period of notice on either side. There is little evidence that staff in public sector institutions have been more inhibited by the absence of tenure in expressing their views or in deciding their teaching content or research activity.

So the advantages may not be so strong. Moreover disadvantages can also be cited. The security of tenure may stimulate some staff to fresh thinking. For others it is a cushion which enables them to ignore new ideas and reject fresh approaches. Also it effectively means that an institution's teaching programme is determined over a long period by the interests and needs of its staff rather than its students. Once a subject is part of a university and the staff are engaged, it must remain so, whatever student demand, until the staff leave or retire. Even if the total resources available to higher education remain stable, the need to cater for new subject areas will inevitably mean a declining need for the services of some staff. While retraining may be a possibility, tenure in this situation may block the university's ability to respond to new demands.

It is a great pity that the present financial cutbacks prevent a less heated discussion of the advantages and disadvantages of tenure. For any advocacy of a less tenured system is seen as an attack on jobs. It is not tenure which is a threat to higher education's health but staff immobility. In so far as tenure contributes to that, it should be questioned. However, the important task for higher education is to find appropriate ways with static establishment numbers for more young staff to be employed. Any funds available should be used for this purpose rather than for a more general attack on tenure.

MECHANISMS OF CHANGE

A number of major, if not radical, changes has been proposed in the previous pages (10-24). How can the higher education system best be induced to introduce them? This is not a trivial question, although it is too little discussed. Many have written about what should happen. Few have tackled the problem of how it should be made to happen. In this volume the problem has not been ignored and is covered particularly in the chapters by Davies and Morgan, Clark, and Kogan and Boys. The complexity of relationships and decision-making structures is evident from their contributions.

As they point out, higher education institutions do not conform to a single model of organization and decision making. Universities have developed generally from a collegial model in which formal authority over academic policy is given not to the vice-chancellor but to the senate over which he presides. The further education tradition from which the polytechnics developed is a more bureaucratic one. The principal of a further education college is formally in authority in his institution. The DES recognized this clash of tradition by issuing guidelines on the internal government of polytechnics in 1970. These were designed to protect the academic work of such institutions from undue interference not only from outside but also from autocratic directors. Some polytechnic directors have found this more restrictive role a little irksome. The last decade has seen the sometimes painful working out of appropriate relationships between the senior management of polytechnics and their academic decision-making bodies. Here again perhaps we have the coming together of practice on both sides of the binary line.

The existing system of decision making generally distinguishes between participative policy-making bodies and appointed leaders and officers. Committees at department, faculty and senate (academic board) level are paralleled by heads of department, deans and vice and pro-vice chancellors (directors and their deputies) supported by professional administrators. It is a system which has many advantages. It embodies the long-established collegial principle of higher education organization. It is also in keeping with modern developments of worker participation. Most of all, however, participation and appropriate delegation lead to better decisions being made. They provide both a wider input of views into the decision-making process and at the same time the means by which the consent can be acquired of those affected by decisions and those who will have to implement them.

Is it however the most appropriate system to produce necessary change? Some have argued the need for greater managerial discretion for the senior leadership of institutions. This would go hand in hand with a more bureaucratic organization best described, by Davies and Morgan in this volume, as 'a formal organizational structure, with specified roles, clear hierarchies and chains of command, pre-determined procedures and regulations' (Chapter 8, p.154). Others have taken the argument further and advocated a more 'entrepeneurial' leadership style, possibly on the model of some US college presidents.

Given that higher education will need to search for new clientele, fresh sources of income and thus new approaches, a certain element of entrepreneurship is not to be discouraged. Its limitations must also be noted however. Entrepreneurs typically cannot be bothered with committee and due processes. Sometimes it is necessary to act quickly and without consultation. Where an activity is a fringe element of an institution's concern, such as for example a consultancy service or a liaison with an overseas institution this may not matter unduly. Where the central activities become the focus of the entrepreneurial activity more care must be taken. This approach may lead to quicker decisions and enable isolated changes to be pushed through. It is unlikely to lead to better decisions or the wider acceptance of the need for change. An entrepreneur who seeks to produce change in the central activities of an institution by acting alone or with a small cohort of colleagues is unlikely to be successful.

It might be possible to strike a balance between participation and effective management by moving towards a consultative model of decision making. Here managers would have greater discretion to take decisions, and, certainly at the lower level, committees would have an advisory and consultative function. Senates and academic boards would retain their powers over strategic decisions but a greater managerial discretion, subject to consultation, would be allowed within the strategy. Whether or not this comes about, more skilled leadership will be required within institutions. Sizer mentions in Chapter 2 the need for 'managers of change'. What are required, he argues, are senior leaders in institutions with the political and man management skills to persuade colleagues to support change and participate in its planning and implementation.

But who are these leaders? At present leadership tends to fall on those who have reached a certain level of academic distinction. The general principle needs to be preserved, for those who aspire to lead and persuade their colleagues must do so from the safety of their own peer group standing. This is particularly important during a time of change. Academic staff are unlikely to support advancement into the relatively unknown territories of, for example, credit transfer, wider access, peer group review and varied course structures and lengths unless such proposals are advocated by those whose credentials they respect.

Academic credibility is a necessary but not sufficient condition for academic leadership. What is remarkable is that as far as the universities are concerned no systematic training is thought necessary or is provided for those who aspire or are appointed to leadership and 'managerial' positions. Polytechnics have the Further Education Staff College at Coombe Lodge but courses are optional rather than mandatory for institutional leaders.

The case study analysis by Davies and Morgan (Chapter 8) of a number of British universities and polytechnics indicates the importance of leadership style in the complex world of academic decision making. It may be that style cannot be taught but the adequate training of the leaders of institutions is a subject that requires immediate attention. Prescribing the basis for such adequate training is no simple task and is likely to occasion heated debate. But it is time for the debate at least to start.

Planning

One method by which change might be facilitated, which is discussed by one or two authors, is through appropriate planning. Sizer (Chapter 2) adopts a rationalist planning approach and examines the use of performance assessment, institutional self-evaluation and portfolio analysis in a dynamic planning process. Davies and Morgan (Chapter 8) stress more the behavioural implications of any planning system.

Some might argue that overt planning inhibits change in higher education. Given the diffusion of power and authority and the diversity of interests any attempt to set objectives and choose between alternative courses of action is doomed to failure. Those areas of the institution that are threatened can mobilize support and effectively veto decisions. Far better, it is argued, to proceed covertly without explicit policies, introducing change surreptitiously and by sleight of hand. If knowledge is power then the less those affected by decisions know about them in advance the better. Indeed it has been argued that the secret manner in which the DES managed the reduction in the provision of teacher education was a major factor in minimizing opposition.

There is no denying that this approach, however cynical, can work. Whether it is appropriate in the atmosphere likely to prevail in the 1980s is another matter. The immediate resource cutbacks and the uncertain demand outlook for the rest of the decade is creating a high level of suspicion. To attempt to change covertly in these circumstances is likely to be counter-productive. An open planning approach within institutions is more likely to succeed.

However, planning must not be conceived in terms of the preparation of grand plans, whether or not preceded by a consultative exercise. Its purpose must be to try to secure the institution's future by anticipating as far as possible and adjusting to changes in the external environment. In this context the planning function must be organized as an iterative process in which the effects of new situations on the institution are continually re-assessed.

Finance

Given the diffusion of authority that exists within institutions, and indeed, between institutions and government, the discretion available to even successful leaders is limited. Their prime task is to find and operate instruments that will influence behaviour. Of these instruments perhaps finance is the most effective.

There can be little doubt that the pattern of existing provision, student demand and academic behaviour has been affected by financing arrangements. Sometimes finance has been used overtly to affect provision and demand, as in the recent policy of full-cost fees for overseas students. In other cases the causal effect may be more indirect but still important. The low weighting given by the UGC and local authorities to part-time students in terms of full-time equivalents has for example been a factor in the relatively small provision of courses for such students. Demand by students for different types of courses has undoubtedly been influenced by decisions about course eligibility for mandatory grants. Generous compensation arrangements enabled the major reduction in teacher education in the 1970s to be implemented more smoothly than might otherwise have been the case. And is not the greater interest of many academics in research rather than teaching, particularly in the universities, strongly influenced by the reward and promotion system?

So to argue that financing arrangements and resource-allocating procedures can be used to induce change is not to advocate some radical instrumentalist innovation in higher education policy. Finance affects behaviour willy nilly. This should be recognized and acted upon so that its use becomes a systematic instrument of policy rather than producing haphazard sometimes contradictory results as at present.

Some suggestions have already been made on how finance might enable changes to be made in the area of credit transfer and tenure. Giving a larger weight to credit transfer students might be one way of speeding up the establishment of a credit transfer network. As with all pricing systems the weight to be attached to such students needs to be fixed at just the right amount. Too small a weight will lead to little change while too large a weight could have undesirable effects. But the risk is worth taking on a trial and error basis, for if such a network is considered desirable there is little else at present which seems capable of influencing its establishment.

This same principle of appropriate weighting can be applied to other areas of policy. The present biases against part-time students could be reversed by changing the system of grants both to students and to institutions favouring such students and the courses they take. More mature students might be encouraged to enrol if there were more generous maintenance grants. Similar treatment might be given to hitherto disadvantaged groups such as women and ethnic minorities. Here the principle would be a slightly different one however. In the case of mature students the larger grant could reflect the greater costs such students incur through giving up employment or having family responsibilities. This would not necessarily apply in the case of other groups. Any larger grant for women or for members of ethnic minorities would have to include an explicit 'incentive element' as part of a policy of positive discrimination in higher education.

Of course once an incentive element is included in the student grant it can be applied to a variety of different objectives, not all of which will be appropriate. For example an incentive grant might be used as part of an explicit vocationally-oriented higher education policy. Higher grants might be given for some courses rather than for others. It is for this reason that many have argued against differentiated student grants other than in relation to a student's income (or his parents'). They see it as a slippery slope and there is no doubt that dangers exist. But the point must be reiterated that the present financing system, supposedly neutral in its intentions, already produces biases in various directions. The courageous approach to the dangers of a differentiated policy is not to prevent it being established but to ensure that its biases are in the direction of the correct policies.

While these weightings will apply to national policy for bodies granting funds to institutions and students, they will also be relevant to resource allocation within institutions. If part-time or non-traditional students, variously defined, are given a greater weight in any calculation of departmental student numbers the incentive to recruit such students is obvious. Given the importance of the basic units it will be difficult for an institution to impose policy centrally. The best it may be able to do is to set some objectives and then use its control of finance to influence behaviour in their direction. At the more general level the UGC and any public sector funding body should overtly seek to encourage innovation through their disbursement of funds. For example, a sum of money equivalent to, say, 3 per cent of the funds available could be held back and made available for adaptation and change purposes on the basis of open bidding from any institution. It could for example be granted for staff development related to new course structures, innovative approaches to teaching, and wider access proposals.

In the days of plentiful resources it was of course much easier to use finance in this way. The extra finance needed to promote a particular policy could be added on to what already existed. The cake simply became larger. This is no longer the case. Higher education financing is now a zero sum game or indeed a negative sum game. Resources used to finance wider access cannot simply be added on to existing provision but must be taken from it. There will always be volunteers when resources are being handed out but few when they are being taken away. It is necessary to be explicit therefore and state that the resources required for adaptation and change will have to be taken away from certain existing areas. In the previous volume in this series (Fulton 1981) Fulton has already mentioned one of these areas, namely the level of the student maintenance grant.

However, saving resources to fuel change can be part of the process of change itself. One area of higher education that has been largely neglected in this respect includes new approaches to teaching. Of course new technology has been introduced, from the overhead projector to film, video and the computer. The main objective has been to improve the quality of the students' educational experience and the standards achieved rather than to reduce costs.

But new approaches to teaching do not necessarily require new technology. It should be possible to retain standard arrangements for lectures, seminars, tutorials and laboratory and experimental work yet organize matters in such a way that resources are saved without any deterioration in the standards achieved. At the beginning of the 1970s, when it seemed that resource constraints might inhibit the then planned expansion, some studies were published on the ways in which institutions could obtain economies of scale (for example Bottomley 1972 and Pickford 1975). However, during the 1960s and 1970s average costs per student in real terms hardly changed.

Yet there is no natural law stating that it should cost ten times as much a year to educate an undergraduate as it does a primary school pupil. It is easy to understand why many in higher education are reluctant to face this issue. In the present climate, with a government seeking resource cuts, any improvement in productivity is likely to be gratefully received as a method of reducing funds and employment rather than increasing student numbers or financing innovation.

A vicious circle thus develops. Innovations to increase access require funds. In a financial climate which at best will provide only level funding to higher education these additional resources can only be found through changes in other areas such as teaching methods which may in any event be desirable. However, as long as there is no guarantee that funds saved in one area will be used in other areas rather than clawed back no change is likely to occur. The giving of that guarantee is a governmental responsibility and can most easily be exercized through the provision of a special fund for innovation as mentioned earlier.

Thus the government could announce that the overall funds provided for higher education were being maintained in real terms but that a small proportion (3 per cent was previously mentioned) was not being immediately allocated. This would be available for bids from individual institutions which would be judged both on the innovation proposed and the contribution the institution itself might be making through changes elsewhere.

There is one change in policy which cannot, however, be financed by savings elsewhere, and which will need extra resources. The problem of tenure and staff mobility is too intractable to be massaged away by a marginal switch of funds from savings elsewhere. The seriousness of the problem for the long-term future of higher education and its complexity both technically and politically require a major policy initiative with specially earmarked additional funds.

It is appropriate to end this chapter by reiterating what was said in the introduction to the whole volume. Change is inevitable within higher education over the next decade because of the demographic outlook. If institutions do not react then change will take the form of an adjustment to decline. Evidence from other areas of the British economy, not to mention reactions to the present politically-determined reductions in higher education resources, indicates that the experience will not be a happy one. Change is also possible which anticipates decline and thus not only prevents it but also moves higher education more towards meeting both the needs of its potential clientele and of the economy and society.

It will require courage however. In part this courage must be displayed by politicians at all levels who must harness their natural and legitimate concern for finance to a commitment to and confidence in the higher education community. However, the major responsibility lies with the higher education community itself. Most of the changes advocated here can best (or indeed only) be brought about through the decisions of those inside institutions. There are some who believe that institutional leaders have neither the temperament, nor the political will for radical change. Time will tell. But it is encouraging to read the verdict of Davies and Morgan following their case studies of recent attempts at change in a number of institutions. 'We saw, even when early attempts had been unsuccessful, a determination to get things right but in ways which made sense in the historical development and character of the institution. Considerable learning and adaptation has taken place in a relatively short period' (Chapter 8, p.185). It is right to end on the optimistic note that this learning and adaptation process will continue apace during the 1980s.

RECOMMENDATIONS

1. *Any new national arrangements for the governance of higher education should allow for an enhanced role for local communities in all institutions in their locality.*
2. *This role should not only include adequate representation on governing bodies. Consideration should also be given to the establishment by each institution of a strategic planning group with joint lay and academic membership on which local interests would be represented.*
3. *The local member of parliament should have a seat on the governing body of all higher education institutions within his constituency.*
4. *The relationship between institutions and their fund-granting bodies should be improved. In particular, institutions should have a voice in deciding the principles on which resource-allocating decisions are to be made and any such decisions should be accompanied by a statement of the principles adopted.*
5. *Any public sector funding body must ensure that it receives information*

about institutions from a diverse range of sources, including the institutions themselves.

6   *While the binary line is likely to remain in formal terms, institutional co-operation across the line should be encouraged, particularly between institutions in the same locality.*

7   *The recommendation of the Toyne Report for the establishment of a national information credit transfer service should be implemented forthwith. In addition the possibility of using the grant system to encourage institutions to establish credit transfer should be seriously considered.*

8   *The establishment of a 2-year ordinary degree should be considered both by universities and by the CNAA.*

9   *Universities should consider subjecting their courses to external peer review at regular intervals.*

10 *A long-term early retirement scheme for academic staff is urgently required. While in the shorter term it might be linked to the substitution of part-time work in the same institution, in the longer term the aim should be to establish a network of links to other organizations which might provide suitable alternative employment. Such a scheme will require extra funds and its establishment is primarily a governmental responsibility.*

11 *Urgent consideration needs to be given to the type of training required by actual or aspiring institutional leaders. The provision of such training should be a matter of priority.*

12 *Institutions should adopt an open approach to planning. In the uncertain environment of the 1980s the planning function must take the form of an iterative process in which the effects on the institution of changes in the external environment are continually re-assessed.*

13 *Instruments of finance and resource allocation should be used as the most effective method of inducing change in higher education.*

14 *To encourage change, a small proportion of the funds available for higher education [eg 3 per cent] should be open to bidding from individual institutions with proposals for innovation.*

NOTES

1   At a meeting in September 1969 with representatives of the University Grants Committee and the Committee of Vice-Chancellors and Principals Shirley Williams (then Minister of State for Higher Education) put forward thirteen proposals on how universities might change their practices. Both groups considered but effectively dismissed the proposals which were not implemented.

2   The 'inner life' has of course been under attack from inside higher education. Fulton, in the previous volume in this series (Fulton 1981), proposes a number of changes in access and structure, and many of the authors in this volume advocate radical change in the activities and

organization of higher education.
3 See for example the report in the THES (23 October 1981) on proposals for sharing courses between the University of Leicester and Leicester Polytechnic and on tentative moves towards co-operation between the University of Sussex and Brighton Polytechnic.
4 The CVCP has indeed recently produced such a proposal.

REFERENCES

Bottomley, J.A. (1972) *University of Bradford: Costs and Potential Economies* Paris: OECD

Bragg, S. (1980) Inverting the system. In Evans, N. (Editor) *Education Beyond School* London: Grant McIntyre

Carter, C.F. (1979) Not enough higher education and too many universities *Three Banks Review* September

Committee on Higher Education (1963) *Higher Education* Cmnd 2154 London: HMSO

Council for National Academic Awards (1979) *Partnership in Validation* London: CNAA

Department of Education and Science (1980) *Continuing Education* London: DES

Department of Education and Science (1981) *Higher Education in England Outside the Universities: Policy, Funding and Management* London: DES

Fulton, Oliver (Editor) (1981) *Access to Higher Education* Guildford: SRHE

Pickford, M. (1975) *University Expansion and Finance* Sussex University Press

Toyne, P. (1979) *Education Credit Transfer: Feasibility Study. Final Report* Exeter

Williams, G. (1975) Academic tenure and the numbers game In Flood Page, C. and Yates, M. (Editors) *Prospects for Higher Education* London: SRHE

2

ASSESSING INSTITUTIONAL PERFORMANCE AND PROGRESS

by John Sizer

INTRODUCTION

This chapter reviews work that has been undertaken during the last decade and current thinking on the assessment of performance of institutions of higher education in Britian, Europe and the United States of America. It is written from an institutional and financial management perspective, and draws heavily upon the OECD/CERI Programme on Institutional Management in Higher Education. It provides a rationalist view of institutional management and should not be considered in isolation from the political, behavioural and organizational aspects, which are examined by Kogan and Boys, Davies and Morgan, and Burton Clark (Chapters 7, 8 and 9). In particular the chapter highlights:

i   The difficulties surrounding performance assessment in institutions which frequently do not have clearly defined objectives, which generate multiple inputs, outputs and outcomes, and within which sub-optimal behaviour tends to be the norm;

ii The changing nature of performance assessment in response to conditions of financial stringency, possible contraction and changing needs;

iii The managerial implications for adaptation and change.

The IMHE/AUPELF study (Hecquet and Jadot 1978) of financing and control systems and the IMHE State-of-the-Art Survey (Jadot et al. 1980) confirm that many institutions of higher education in Western Europe and North America have entered, or are entering, a period of financial stringency, falling real income per student, and perhaps actual decline in student numbers during the remainder of this century. They are increasingly being asked to justify their activities and account for their use of resources and their performance in terms of their effectiveness and their efficiency, not only to external financing bodies but also to other influential groups in society. For example, the House of Commons Education, Science and Arts Committee (1980a) has stated: 'We need a higher education system which is more accessible, flexible, accountable, and readier to undertake new and unfamiliar roles'. Furthermore, within institutions consideration has to be given to the efficiency of the various academic and service departments, decisions made concerning the allocation of resources, in some cases involving major cutbacks and reallocations. Managements need a sound basis upon which to arrive at and justify such decisions; in particular they need to develop and employ appropriate methods for allocating resources and for assessing the performance of the component parts of their institutions. Inevitably there is a demand for performance indicators which will aid (and possibly over-simplify) this process, and for relevant financial, quantitative and qualitative information for planning, decision making and control.

In the United Kingdom institutional performance assessment has to be undertaken against a background of: the long-term demographic trends; the requirement to charge overseas students full economic fees; a new policy focus and reorganization within the Department of Education and Science designed to achieve a capacity to plan a rationalization and collaboration across the binary line; statements from the chairman that the University Grants Committee will become more dirigiste; an influential report from the House of Commons Education, Science and Arts Committee advocating the replacement of the binary system with a plural system, rejecting the Department of Education and Science's concept of the 'broad steer', calling for greater accountability and highlighting amongst other things the unsatisfactory state of analysis of costs in higher education; DES proposals to establish a new structure for the management of public sector higher education; a call from the Committee of Public Accounts (1980) for the UGC to give more precise guidance on the causes of variations in costs from one university to another and from the Comptroller and Auditor General (1980) for more comprehensive reviews by the UGC of current staff student ratios for particular subjects or subject groups in universities; short-term plans to reduce significantly the level of government expenditure on higher education; and considerable uncertainty as to the level of long-term resource provision.

The IMHE State-of-the-Art Survey (Jadot et al. 1980) and the Final Report of the Carnegie Council on Policy Studies in Higher Education (1980) indicate that similar factors are operative throughout Europe and North America.

'The new tone of the advancing demographic depression is now more one of concern and even despair, of concentration on contraction, of avoidance or abandonment of telic reforms, of a single-minded emphasis upon survival.' (Carnegie Council 1980)

Within institutions there is a need to balance the pressure for increased cost *efficiency* and possible restrictions on student admissions in the short term with the actions that need to be taken if institutions are to be *effective* in the long term. For some British institutions, faculties and departments, survival is perceived as the name of the game.

What do we understand by the term 'effectiveness', should a distinction be drawn between *effectiveness* and *efficiency*, and what is their relationship with performance assessment? Is an organization *effective* if it achieves the objectives it has set itself? Is it *efficient* if it achieves those objectives with optimal use of the resources available to it in the long run? Coombs and Hallak (1972) have drawn a distinction between the education system's 'internal efficiency', ie the relationship between inputs and outputs, and its 'external productivity', ie the relationship between benefits/outcomes and inputs. As they point out, the relevance and appropriateness of an educational system's objectives and curriculum can have a major bearing on its 'external productivity'. Romney, Bogen and Micek (1978) regard institutional performance assessment to be the measurement or observation of the effective and efficient accomplishment of the expectations of the institution's constituencies. Romney, Gray and Weldon (1978) equate 'external productivity' with institutional performance assessment and argue that it is an examination of the goal (objective) achievement process which consists of at least four distinct stages in which goals (objectives) are set, resources are committed for the purpose of achieving these goals (objectives), committed resources are expended to achieve the goals (objectives), and outcomes result. Sizer (1980c) has suggested that indicators of performance be viewed in this context, and that the setting of long-term objectives for institutions is the most critical stage at present.

INSTITUTIONAL OBJECTIVES

Non-profit-making organizations exist to provide a service rather than earn a profit. Not only are services provided more difficult to measure than profits, so is the process of identifying, quantifying and agreeing an overriding objective in such organizations; developing a hierarchy of primary and secondary objectives that flow from this overriding objective; and subsequently measuring and comparing actual performance against these objectives. These difficulties, which are central to the process of performance assessment, are particularly acute in institutions of higher education.

Is an institution of higher education *effective* if it achieves objectives which are appropriate to the cultural, economic, socio-political, technological, ecological, and educational environment in which it operates? Should its objectives be congruent with the long-term needs of society? Many of those involved in the management of institutions would probably answer positively. However, would they be able to reach agreement on the long-term needs of society, the contribution their institution should make to satisfy those needs, and the objectives for their institution?

Norris (1978) has argued that:

'Until the goal question is resolved and meaningful priorities set for institutional policy as a whole, it is impossible to say what is really important for that institution, and hence where resources should be allocated.'

He asks whether the time has now arrived for setting and obtaining agreement upon objectives. A study of measures of institutional goal achievement conducted in 1976 by Romney (1978) for the National Center for Higher Education Management Systems is relevant to this question. Romney undertook a survey of 1,150 persons — faculty, administrators and trustees at forty-five American colleges and universities of six different types — which surprisingly indicated that faculty, administrators and trustees largely agreed on what their institution's goals should be. Respondents were asked to rate with respect to appropriateness for their institution twenty broadly stated institutional goal areas. While goal preference generally varied across institutional types (but not among trustees, faculty and administrators), within types only trustees in universities rated accountability/efficiency among the top seven goal areas.

However, even if agreement can be reached on the broad objectives for an institution, can these be translated into agreed quantifiable goals and desired performance indicators? What weighting should be given to the different objectives and how should conflict between objectives be resolved? If it cannot be, how can more detailed objectives and performance indicators be established to measure effectiveness and efficiency for the component parts of the institution? In some academic departments, particularly multi-discipline departments, is it unlikely that agreement can be reached amongst members as to what the objectives are for the department, for the courses offered by the department, and for the research programmes undertaken within departments? Therefore where do members of academic departments, heads of academic departments, and deans fit into the spectrum ranging from goal conflict to striving towards goal congruence within institutions of higher education? Does today's environment encourage goal congruence or goal conflict within institutions? Thus reflecting upon recent experiences at the University of Michigan in implementing the first phase of a planning and evaluation programme concerned with the development of department and programme objectives and priorities, and their integration and summarization into school/college and institutional objectives and priorities, Hinman (1980) has observed:

'The quandary of goals statements for universities is that, to be stated in a form which elicits widespread agreement, they must be ambiguous and monoperational; if concrete and measurable, they either provoke dissension or are too mundane to arouse enthusiasm.'

NON-PROFIT PERFORMANCE EVALUATION TECHNIQUES

Have attempts been successful in appling to higher education institutions non-profit performance evaluation techniques such as Programme Planning Budgeting Systems (PPBS) and Cost Benefit Analysis (CBA)? Both techniques attempt to relate costs to outcome assessments. They require the introduction of cost collection and allocation systems. While allocation of joint costs poses many problems, it is the measurement of outcomes that is the critical factor in their rejection. PPBS requires the specification of objectives which can be readily transformed into outcome quantities and statistics, and CBA the transformation of essentially non-monetary outcomes into monetary outcomes.

Drawing upon an extensive review and critique of PPBS in higher education undertaken with G.B. Weathersby (1972), Balderston (1974) observes that the specifics of measurement of the quantity and quality of results achieved are not very far developed; that a university abounds in multiple processes, and the analysis of costs and results in the presence of substantial jointness and inter-dependence is difficult; and that the problem of time horizons has proved to be, politically, the most serious of all, because funding sources were unwilling or unable to look beyond very short commitments — typically, the single budget year. Recent research by Gambino (1979) revealed that in almost all cases attempts at implementation of PPBS were facing serious obstacles. Phyrr (1973) has argued that Zero Base Budgeting (ZBB) can be used to reinforce PPBS. However, like PPBS, ZBB relies heavily on the quantification of outcomes which, as will be argued later, we still do not yet know how to measure. Balderston (1974) decides that:

> 'The most enduring legacy of the program budgeting experience of universities has been the development of a much more sophisticated analytic spirit, both within the university and in state and federal agencies.'

If PPBS, which aims at directing resource allocation according to the objectives of institutions, and subsequently comparing actual with planned performance, is not feasible, can this legacy be built on in the development of performance indicators for the various activities that take place within institutions of higher education? Balderston (1974) sees that the spirit of informed inquiry leading to more careful evaluation of alternatives and rational decision making, can be realized in *policy analysis* without 'the formal baggage of PPBS'. Thus he and Weathersby (1972) wrote:

> 'The approach of policy analyses is to bring careful analysis to bear incrementally in specific decision problems and build a planning and management "system" on a case law of precedent basis.'

Similarly in Sweden *activity evaluation* or *institutional self-evaluation* is seen as providing 'a starting point for the reappraisal and alteration of activities':

> 'Certainly the emphasis is on developing the institution's own capacity to critically examine its organization and activities, to reorder its priorities, to raise its effectiveness, efficiency and innovative capability.'
> (Östergren 1978)

Similarly, Romney (1978) suggests '. . . consensus building techniques can facilitate the selection of appropriate goals and measures within institutions'.

Thus we can see a logical development from quantitatively based PPBS and CBA techniques, to the increasing interest in quantitatively and qualitatively based participatory institutional self-evaluation, and consensus building techniques.

'PARTIAL' PERFORMANCE INDICATORS

Given the complexities and difficulties surrounding the objective setting and planning process, and the application of non-profit performance evaluation techniques and multi-dimensional analysis, it is not surprising that there is a tendency to recognize those parts of the institution that can be measured and monitored with a considerable degree of precision. While it may not prove possible to agree objectives, measure outcomes and develop performance indicators for an institution as a whole it often proves possible to do so for parts of the organization: ie to develop performance indicators that relate physical and monetary inputs to physical and monetary outputs and outcomes, and to build these into the planning and reporting system. However, do those who develop and employ such partial performance indicators always remember that optimizing the parts does not necessarily optimize the whole?

Sorenson and Grove (1977) have summarized the objectives and properties of various service performance indicators: availability, awareness, accessibility, extensiveness, appropriateness, efficiency, effectiveness, outcome benefits/impacts, and acceptability. From these Sizer (1979) has identified performance indicators for institutions of higher education (see Figure 2.1). Many of these partial performance indicators are traditional *process measures* of institutional performance, such as staff-student ratios and cost per FTE, rather than *outcome measures* or ones that substantiate *progress* towards achieving objectives. For example, in their study of performance indicators for the teaching function in higher education, Birch, Calvert and Sizer (1977) measured *response* to an institution's provision of learning opportunities: enrolment, pass and attrition rates; and resource utilization: class sizes, joint meetings, cost per student enrolled.

In his study concerned with measuring *effectiveness* in institutions of higher education, Cameron (1978) focused on organizational characteristics rather than goals, since it seemed unlikely that goals or outcomes were made operational in most institutions. This study employed an inductive approach in generating criteria of effectiveness, and the effectiveness indicators were best typified as *static* rather than *dynamic*. Approximately 130 variables emerged from a literature search, and they provided a framework within which interviews were conducted with members of the internal dominant coalition in six colleges and universities in the North-East of the USA. As a result of the interviews Cameron identified similar perceptions of effectiveness amongst internal dominant coalition groups. Nine separate groups of criteria of institutional organizational effectiveness emerged: student educational satisfaction, student academic development, student career development, student personal development, faculty and administrator employment satisfaction, professional development and quality of faculty, systems openness and community interaction, ability to acquire resources, and organizational health. Later in this paper it will be argued that *static* measures of effectiveness are not sufficient and that *dynamic* progress measures are also required.

Traditional process measures of institutional performance were widely rejected by almost all categories of respondent in the Romney study (1978). Objective measures pertaining to impacts of higher education such as satisfaction, ability to apply knowledge, publications, and value added were most preferred. Norris (1978) examines various outcome measures for evaluating progress towards institutional and departmental goals. However as Romney (1978) emphasizes in his conclusions '. . . much research is needed regarding the translation of institutional goals into measurable, observable objectives'.

No doubt Romney's respondents would argue that if an effective institution of higher education is one which achieves objectives which are appropriate to the environment in which it operates, its effectiveness should be measured in terms of the outcomes/benefits/impacts of its teaching and research programmes on society. There is a danger in using short-term input indicators of performance that sight might be lost of the long-term measure of the effectiveness of institutions: ie their contributions to the needs of society. Furthermore, questions concerning the quality of outcomes and their impact on society are bound to be raised by governments determined to get better value for public expenditure in higher education. In other words, short-term quantitative input and outcome measures and performance indicators are inadequate, and quality of outcomes and long-term impacts/benefits should be assessed. Thus, if the management of retrenchment is to preserve excellence, there *must* be some way to obtain quality assessments and use them for making selective priority decisions (Balderston 1979).

This argument is fine and logical but the difficulties involved in developing impact/benefit/outcome measures and incorporating them into management information systems should not be underestimated. It is likely that highly sophisticated research designs will be required, which will not only prove expensive but involve a degree of complexity which may be regarded as impractical, probably rightly so, by administrators. The fact is that the art of measuring the outcomes remains in a distinctly primitive state, and we know how to measure neither the quality of institutional research nor community-service outcomes (Romney 1978). Nevertheless, it may well be that the time is right in many countries to attempt to assess the quality of institutions and the social value of different disciplines.

It is not surprising that during the expansionary 1970s administrators and decision-makers tended to fall back on quantitatively based process measures even though they know these are inadequate measures of institutional effectiveness. Admittedly many of these measures (such as staff-student ratios and cost per FTE) are relevant to decisions regarding internal planning, control and resource allocation, and for measurement of efficiency as opposed to effectiveness. As Delany (1978) has pointed out, the function of control '. . . does not cover other aspects of policy making which deal with the quality of outputs'. It is concerned with the relationship between expected and actual inputs and expected and actual outputs. Furthermore, in discussing the role of government in institutional performance assessment, Hijmans (1980) has observed: 'Process-directed evaluation is probably less obnoxious to academe than the evaluation of

FIGURE 2.1
Properties of performance indicators in higher education

FOCUS OF MEASURE	CONCEPTUAL CONTENT	TELLS	EXAMPLES
AVAILABILITY	Amount and type of course, research facility, or central service provided	What can be obtained	List of services available in Careers Advisory Service; list of research facilities and opportunities available in academic department; number, capacities, and locations of lecture and seminar rooms
AWARENESS	Knowledge of user population of existence; range and conditions for entry or use of courses, research facilities, or central services	Who knows about what is available	Knowledge by prospective students of courses offered by an academic department; knowledge by prospective users of services provided by central computer centre
ACCESSIBILITY	Indicates if services can be obtained by appropriate groups	Ease of reaching and using facility	Availability of photocopying facilities; location of car parks; average waiting time for literature search by library information service; opening hours of medical centre
EXTENSIVENESS	Compares quantity of services rendered with capacity available and/or potential demand	'How much' but not 'How well'	Students enrolled on courses compared with course quotas; number of users of library; clients in medical centre; percentage of final-year students using careers advisory service; % utilization of lecture and seminar rooms
APPROPRIATENESS	Correct type and amount of service rendered, course offered, or research undertaken	Is quantity and/or quality of facility offered that is required?	Demand for courses; number and quality of applicants; mismatch between computing facilities required and available; comparison between class sizes and lecture and seminar room capacities

INSTITUTIONAL PERFORMANCE AND PROGRESS 41

EFFICIENCY	Compares resource inputs with outputs	How much resource was used, such as – how much did it cost per unit? – how much did it cost in total? – how much time did it take? – what grade of employee was used?	Cost per client service in medical centre Cost per FTE student by course Cost per literature search Cost per meal served
EFFECTIVENESS	Compares accomplishment with objectives (or what was intended) – Qualitative – Comparative	Characteristics Duration Content Effect Proportions served Variances from budgets, standards	Comparison of planned with actual; % utilization of lecture and seminar rooms; number of students graduating; number of graduates employed; ratio of actual to planned utilization of computer; comparison of budgeted and actual cost of central service; comparison of actual and planned cost per FTE for course; comparison of planned and actual course content; actual compared with planned wastage rate
OUTCOMES/ BENEFITS/ IMPACTS	Identifies social or economic benefit	Monetary effects Non-monetary effects	Increase in earnings arising from attendance at/graduating from course; benefits to society of successful research into previously incurable disease; benefits to local community of cultural programme; patents and copyrights registered
ACCEPTABILITY	Assesses match of service/ course/research outcomes with user/participant preferences	User satisfaction with services; student satisfaction with courses; client satisfaction with outcome of sponsored research	Demand for courses; number of complaints to librarian; course evaluation at end of lecture programme; repeat sponsoring of research

teaching or research itself, as it does not threaten academic freedom in a direct way.'

Romney (1978) considers institutions should concentrate, for the purposes of assessing institutional effectiveness, upon the development of measures that substantiate progress towards achievement in those few goal areas that constituencies consider appropriate; whilst in the context of the Swedish project on institutional self-evaluation Faxén suggests that 'If we cannot find good criteria (for assessing performance) let us start by sitting down and talking about what we are doing, why we do it and what we really would like to do!' (Faxén et al. 1980). Sizer (1980c) has argued that there is a strong case for developing *progress measures* of performance in addition to *process measures* and measures of *outcome/benefits/impacts*.

FUTURE NEEDS OF SOCIETY

Despite Romney's view (1978) that much research is needed regarding the translation of institutional goals into measurable, observable objectives, there is considerable pressure in many European countries for a concerted effort to be made to develop and obtain agreement within institutions on academic policy and objectives for the 1980s and 1990s. In response to demographic trends, should not institutions examine the environment in which they will be operating and attempt to identify the needs of its society?

Inevitably it will be argued that we are not very good at forecasting the needs of society, but surely it is better to attempt to identify future needs than to assume in a rapidly changing society that today's needs (frequently measured in terms of number and quality of applications from school-leavers) are the best and only indicators we have of future needs. The Carnegie Council and the Education, Science and Arts Committee both recommend the maximum constructive use of the student market to guide contraction. Students, it is argued, if they receive good advice, can probably make as good decisions, by and large, as can planners. Thus the Carnegie Council (1980) points out, 'Under the conditions of the next two decades, consumer sovereignty may well prevail largely undisputed in most institutions'. However, institutions should not lose sight of the fact that they help create the market place in which this consumer sovereignty is exercised. They should distinguish between selling and marketing: 'The road to survival now leads through the market place' (Carnegie Council 1980). The marketing concept focuses decision making on the consumer. Furthermore it is often argued in the United Kingdom that because we cannot plan very effectively in the short term at present, there is little point in attempting long-term planning; there are too many complexities and uncertainties. This argument confuses problems arising from short-term financial uncertainties with the need to examine the impact of long-term trends on an institution's portfolio of activities and to develop a strategy for the institution's long-term development: '. . . it is better to plan to meet the future effectively than just to fear it as a new dark age' (Carnegie Council 1980).

Consideration of the trends and factors which are influencing and will continue to influence significantly the environment in which institutions of higher education will be operating (Sizer 1980c) indicates that it is not simply a question of examining the impact of falling numbers on the higher education system, but that it is also necessary to recognize that society is likely to require a different mix of outputs. New courses and research priorities will emerge. It may be necessary to meet the needs of new groups of participants and new patterns of attendance may be required to meet individual needs. Some courses will face falling demand, others will disappear, while others will need adaptation to meet the changing demands of new technology. Thus not only will the system face falling total demand, but also changing demands. Furthermore, these changing demands give rise to questions about the types of course of higher education provided and the institutional structure we ought to create. Should all those who reach 'A' level standard be allowed to attempt a full degree course? Should degree work be removed from some polytechnics so that they can become part of a community college system and postgraduate work from some universities so that they become liberal arts colleges? There will also be opportunities for institutions to generate alternative sources of revenue from applied research, consultancy and continuing education opportunities. Thus Jochimsen (1979) argued from a German perspective that while

> '. . . a policy directed towards both preserving, and making the necessary improvement to, the standards of efficiency at universities can be implemented only if members, professors, administrators and students join in a new effort',

an essential pre-condition for such an effort is that

> '. . . policy-makers and society in general can really be convinced that such higher education institutions are not only willing to fulfil, but are also capable of fulfilling, the tasks required of them from the social aspect.'

If we accept Jochimsen's arguments, a key question is: who provides the scenario documents which attempt to identify the 'tasks required from the societal aspect'? Clearly government departments and agencies should undertake macro-forecasting as a basis for decisions about higher education systems. They should provide scenario documents for use by institutions, but in the end should each institution form its own view and discuss this with the appropriate financing body? Once financing bodies go beyond the provision of scenario documents questions concerning the autonomy of universities will naturally be raised; though the IMHE Programme's State-of-the-Art Survey (Jadot et al. 1980) and the IMHE/AUPELF study of financing and control systems (Hecquet and Jadot 1978) show that institutional autonomy has already been considerably eroded in a number of European OECD countries. The Carnegie Council (1980) has observed that higher education in the United States, including to a lesser extent education in the private institutions, has become subject to many forms of regulation and is taking on the status of a regulated industry. Furthermore, many financing bodies may not have the expertise or resources to provide scenario documents, and some governments are averse to new initiatives which necessitate public expenditure. Nor, given the difficulties involved in preparation, should we think in terms of a single, agreed scenario. If they can be mobilized, the expertise and resources required to develop scenario documents are likely to be available within institutions. As the Committee of Vice-Chancellors and Principals in the UK has argued (CVCP 1980a):

> 'Forty-five universities, each making its own informed interpretation of national needs, may well, between them, arrive at several valid versions of the best long-term pattern of research and teaching while the inevitable mistakes will not be on the grand scale of Government miscalculations.'

A view endorsed by the House of Commons Education, Science and Arts Committee (1980).

Institutions have to decide whether to develop their own scenarios. Sizer (1980c) has described an initiative taken at Loughborough University which he considers demonstrates the potential value of scenario analysis as a first stage in institutional self-evaluation and self-renewal. The School of Human and Environmental Studies established a working party under his chairmanship to consider the trends in society which are likely to make an impact upon higher education in the 1980s and 1990s and to examine the impact of these trends on the work of the school in future. Inevitably time constraints prevented the working party exploring in as great a depth as it would have wished all the issues involved in a consideration of likely future trends. Given the time constraints, the working party adopted the following approach.

1   A comprehensive list of issues and trends was drawn up after discussions within the working party and consultation with colleagues in departments with expertise in particular areas. A number of short papers relating to specific issues (for example, the impact of microprocessors) were prepared by some members of the working party.

2   An analysis of issues and trends identified six major broad trends: technological, demographic, environmental, social, political/ economic and educational. The implications of these six broad trends, and the complexities of their inter-relationships were considered in detail.

3   Departments were asked to respond to this analysis by indicating the relevance of their *current* activities to the likely trends and their implications, and to make suggestions for *new* initiatives at both departmental and school level.

The working party's report has provided a valuable input into evaluation of the school's current teaching and research programmes and helped in identifying opportunities for new initiatives in the future.

Certainly a consideration of the trends in society which are likely to affect higher education highlights the needs for institutions to recognize that they must plan not only for declining numbers but also for the need for *resource mobility* on the one hand and for research in anticipation of new course demands, research and consultancy opportunities, and services to the community on the other. *Therefore should the performance of an institution be assessed in terms of its responsiveness to these changing needs of society, and should appropriate performance indicators be developed to measure an institution's progress in developing and implementing its strategy for resource mobility and responding to these changing needs?*

PORTFOLIO ANALYSIS

One starting point in the process of responding to changing demands is to analyse an institution's historical and current performance. If such an analysis is combined with a continuous examination of the future environment to identify society's needs, it should initiate a consideration of whether the institution should sell existing courses and research facilities more effectively in existing markets; consolidate others; withdraw certain courses from the market; sell existing courses and research and physical facilities in new markets; develop new courses and research facilities for existing markets; and/or develop new courses and research facilities for new markets. Such an exercise would ultimately lead the management of the institution to identify its critical resources, and to ask which is the appropriate strategy, given its current and anticipated future resources; it should stimulate institutional self-evaluation.

Thinking along similar lines, Doyle and Lynch (1979) have applied the *product portfolio concepts* developed by the Boston Consulting Group to the analysis of a university's competitive position. They have modified the Boston Consulting Group's planning matrix (Figure 2.2) to distinguish between four types of courses.

'Props' (what the Boston Consulting Group calls 'cash cows'): A prop is a strong course in a weak area. These are programmes in which the university has a large market share of a small market. Doyle and Lynch consider such courses are good for the university's reputation, but there are limited opportunities for expansion without a sharp decline in entry standards.

'Dogs': These courses occur in small areas nationally and the university does not even get its share of those applying. It is suggested that such courses are not a good use for the university's small resources and consideration should be given to phasing them out in the long run.

'Problem areas' (what the Boston Consulting Group describes as 'question marks'): These degree areas are strong nationally, but the university's own courses are relatively unattractive to applicants. The general problem is a weak reputation in an attractive area for expansion. Doyle and Lynch suggest the problem is often caused by a university having a proliferation of courses and not concentrating on subject areas of greatest opportunity. If these courses are to be successful, they suggest the university must give them major investment priority and build up staff, research and support services. If, however, it has many courses in this quadrant there is almost certainly a case for rationalization.

'Stars': These are the university's strongest courses: in areas attracting a large number of applicants and where it has a strong reputation. Doyle and Lynch consider, in general, the university should give the highest priority to supporting the strength and reputation of departments offering these courses, and they should attract a disproportionate share of new resources.

FIGURE 2.2
University course portfolio

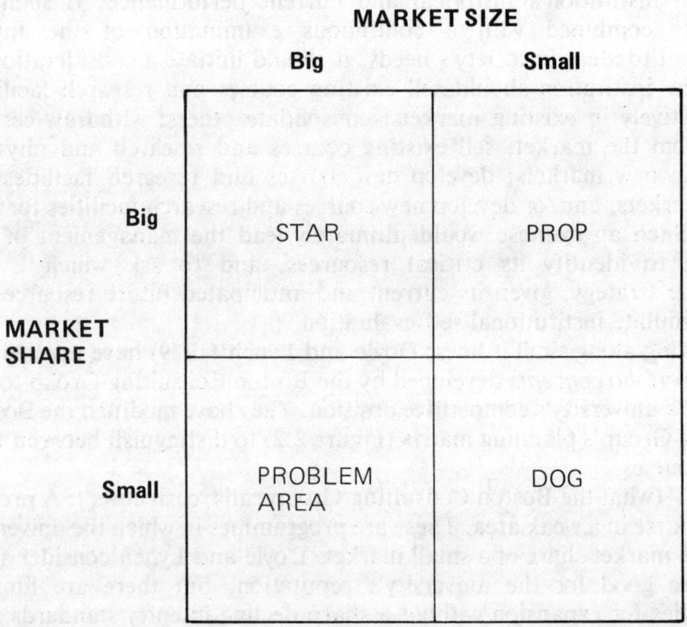

	MARKET SIZE	
	Big	Small
MARKET SHARE Big	STAR	PROP
Small	PROBLEM AREA	DOG

Doyle and Lynch argue that the model offers university administrators a tool to assist in assessing demand implications and testing the viability of alternative strategic priorities. Of course, they would accept that an analysis of an institution's current course portfolio is only a starting point in determining future strategies. Not only is it necessary to forecast future market growth rates to determine whether, for example, 'today's props' will become 'tomorrow's dogs', but also to assess the institution's critical resources to determine whether these can be employed to develop 'star' positions in emerging areas. By substituting *market size* in their matrix for *market growth rate* in the Boston matrix, Doyle and Lynch *do not differentiate between high growth, low growth and declining markets*. Their model is attractive in that it relates courses to markets, but it is a *static* one. Resources tend to attach to subject areas not courses, and by concentrating on subject areas, account can also be taken of research, scholarship and community service. Therefore, in assessing a university's performance potential, do we need to compare a university's *strengths* in various subject areas relative to other institutions with the *future attractiveness* of subject areas so as to identify priority areas for future growth, consolidation and rationalization? Such an analysis might provide a starting point for internal discussions on the institution's long-term strategy for resource mobility.

The directional policy matrices employed by large companies have been adapted by Sizer (1980c) for this purpose (Figure 2.3).[1] Individual universities and external financing bodies will define 'university strengths in the subject area' and 'future attractiveness of the subject area' in different ways. Subject areas may be single or multiple discipline. A technological university may view its role differently from a long-established civic university. Thus additions, deletions and changes might be made to the list of factors for assessing university strengths in the subject area and subject area attractiveness: eg service to the community, dependence on overseas students, service teaching to other subject areas, etc. It is important not to evaluate simply on the basis of the static analysis of the vertical axis.

The matrix could be developed at a number of levels: nationally by governmental and external financing bodies, regionally by groups of institutions, by individual institutions, and by faculties or schools within institutions. Presumably those governments that have regulated the size and type of overall intake by imposing formalized admission policies and criteria, consider they have the resources and expertise to undertake the evaluations incorporated in the matrix and so justify increased dirigisme in terms of societal needs. Should collaborative approaches to rationalization be welcomed by governments and external financing bodies and be seen by institutions as an alternative to increased dirigisme? In the United Kingdom the Committee of Vice-Chancellors and Principals (1980a) has recognized '. . . the need to face more boldy the prospect of inter-institutional arrangements designed to promote some rationalization'. In some countries institutions may well have to decide whether to compete or co-operate at the regional level. Dr Rhodes Boyson (House of Commons Education, Science and Arts Committee 1980b) has emphasized that co-ordination between national bodies across the 'binary line' would be essential in order to secure sensible rationalization, an optimum subject balance by area, and effective collaboration at regional and local level.

As the Swedes have recognized in their institutional self-evaluation activity (Furumark 1979), decentralized structures under conditions of

48   CRITERIA

FIGURE 2.3
University directional policy matrix

Criteria for University Strengths in the Subject Area:
- Size of department
- Market share
- Market position
- Number of applications
- Quality of student intake
- Graduate employment
- Cost per FTE student
- Reputation
- Quality & age of staff
- Research record
- Research capability
- Image
- Publications record
- Resources: availability and mobility
- Etc.

Criteria for Subject Area Attractiveness:
- Market size
- Market growth rate
- Market diversity
- Competitive structure
- Cost structure
- Optimal department size
- Demographic trends
- Scientific importance
- Technological trends
- Social/political and economic trends
- Environmental trends
- Government attitudes
- Employment prospects
- Cultural importance
- Etc.

University Strengths in the Subject Area	Subject Area Attractiveness — High	Medium	Low
High	Growth	Selective growth or consolidation	Consolidation
Medium	Selective growth or consolidation	Consolidation	Planned withdrawal & redeployment
Low	Consolidation or planned withdrawal & redeployment	Planned withdrawal & redeployment	Planned withdrawal & redeployment

financial stringency and possible contraction require institutions to study and evaluate themselves critically. Furthermore, the absence in the UK of many of the features of the US university system, ie the close interface with the political decision-making process, the role of laymen in university government and the management of higher education, the strength of local community links and the existence of well-recognized mechanisms for peer review, means that UK universities have to find *internal solutions to retrenchment*, ie self-evaluation. In other OECD countries the need has been recognized to find internal solutions to retrenchment if institutional autonomy is to be preserved or at least not eroded further. The evaluation of subject areas by the university is a first stage in this evaluation, employing the criteria incorporated into the directional policy matrix or similar criteria. A directional policy matrix (Figure 2.3) provides a *starting point* from which difficult managerial judgements can be made and for discussions on regional rationalization. The fewer the criteria the greater the gap that has to be bridged by managerial judgements. The decision-makers in the institution need to evaluate systematically the *trade-offs* between strong and weak areas, and the administrators and academics should provide the framework and information base for this evaluation.

The *growth, consolidation* and *withdrawal and redeployment* strategies in the boxes of the matrix are examples. Institutions may not wish to withdraw from all low strength, low attractiveness subject areas, but they should recognize the dangers and costs of not doing so. There is the obvious danger of increased government intervention if institutions are not prepared to put their own houses in order, or if they are not willing to co-operate regionally. The chairman of the UGC has stated to the Committee of Vice-Chancellors and Principals (CVCP 1980b): 'First, we want everyone to be good at *some* things, but we want you to concentrate on your *strengths*, and *not* support palid growths which are now never likely to reach maturity.'

A serious risk is that under conditions of stagnation or contraction the university will not be able to support existing developments and new developments in *emerging areas* which have high future attractiveness. *Emerging areas* can be supported out of incremental funds during periods of expansion, but not under conditions of stagnation or decline. Higgledy-piggledy expansion may have been acceptable in the past, but higgledy-piggledy stagnation or decline may not lead an institution to recognize the need to redeploy resources from low strength, low attractiveness areas into emerging and existing growth areas. 'The universities must not only adapt themselves to new needs and new tasks, which in fact they have always done, but they must be *seen* to be doing so' (CVCP 1980b).

However, despite the prima facie case for institutions redeploying resources from weak areas into emerging and existing growth areas, naturally, vice-chancellors do not like to face up to the prospect of closing departments! Whether a university needs to withdraw from some or all of its weak areas will depend upon the balance of its existing portfolio, in particular the number of such areas, the *resources* (not student numbers) attached to them, and the possibilities for rationalization and collaboration with neighbouring institutions. An institution with a strong portfolio may be able to support a limited number of weaker areas, particularly if they are not resource intensive and are seen as central to the life of the university. For example, consider the simplified portfolio in Figure 2.4 (in practice a university would have many more subject areas). Assuming the size of the circles is proportional to the resources deployed in the subject area, the university might decide to withdraw from subject areas (H) and (I) to support growth area (A), but decide to continue to support areas (F) and (G) because it has a number of strong positions in *consolidation areas*.

FIGURE 2.4
A strong portfolio

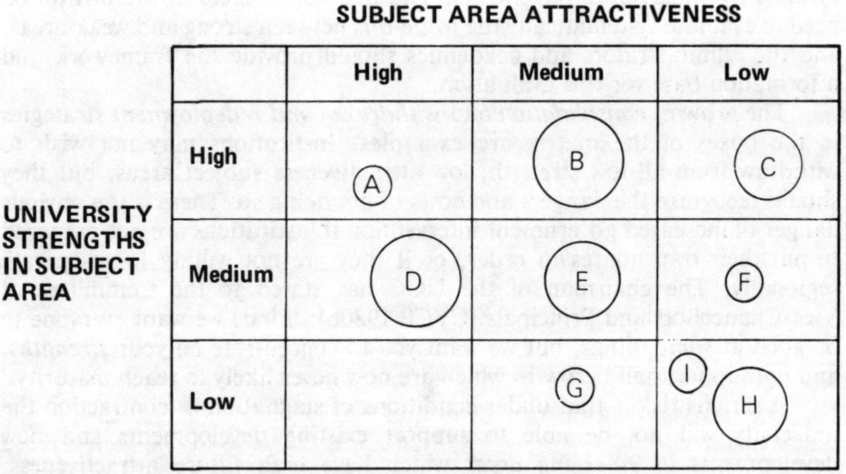

SUBJECT AREA ATTRACTIVENESS

	High	Medium	Low
UNIVERSITY STRENGTHS IN SUBJECT AREA High	A	B	C
Medium	D	E	F
Low		G	I H

◯ Proportional to resources deployed in subject areas

Consider now the position in Figure 2.5. This university has a much weaker portfolio, with many low attractiveness areas and few growth and consolidation areas. However, it has three relatively small *emerging growth* areas, (A) (G) and (M), in which few universities have yet established high attractiveness/high strength positions. Clearly the university must consider whether it can provide further support for these growth asreas, and, if they are resource intensive areas, it must consider withdrawing resources from a number of weaker areas. If the university faces increasing financial stringency the greater will be the need to develop a strategy for withdrawing resources from weaker areas to support emerging growth areas. The proportion of tenured salary costs to total recurrent expenditure and the age structure of the tenured staff will influence significantly the speed with which resource mobility can be achieved.

FIGURE 2.5
A weak portfolio

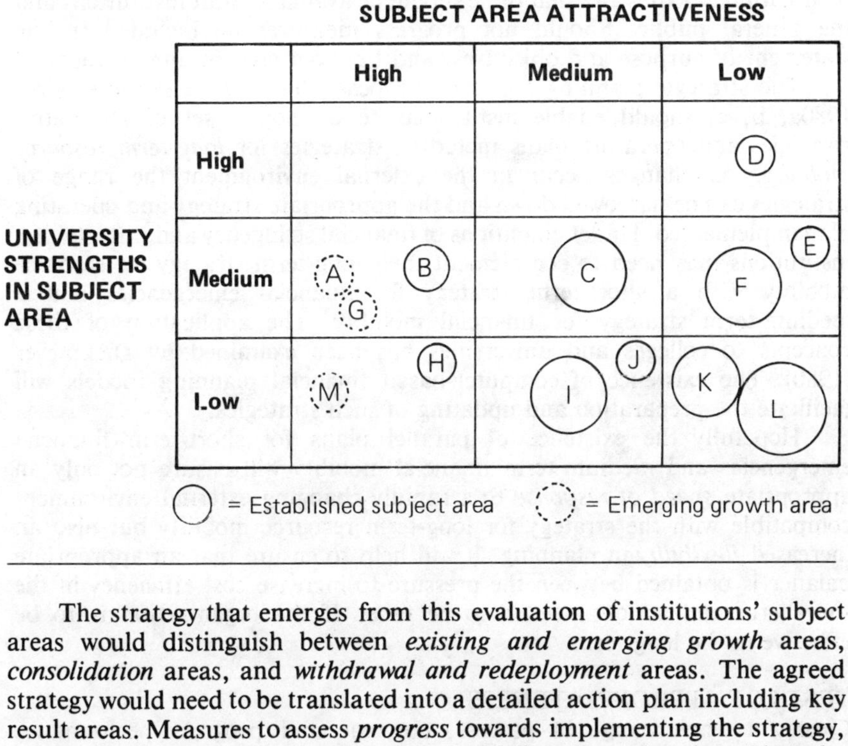

SUBJECT AREA ATTRACTIVENESS

	High	Medium	Low
High			D
Medium	A, G, B	C	E, F
Low	M	H	I, J, K, L

UNIVERSITY STRENGTHS IN SUBJECT AREA

◯ = Established subject area   ⋯ = Emerging growth area

The strategy that emerges from this evaluation of institutions' subject areas would distinguish between *existing and emerging growth* areas, *consolidation* areas, and *withdrawal and redeployment* areas. The agreed strategy would need to be translated into a detailed action plan including key result areas. Measures to assess *progress* towards implementing the strategy, particularly in these key result areas, would flow from the plan. Thus the Swedish National Board of Universities and Colleges considers:

'Every activity evaluation project should, we think, result in an action-oriented, preferably long-range plan for future activities, including indications of alternative ways to realize the desired changes.'
(Furumark 1979)

Should this long-range plan form the basis for detailed discussions with the UGC on a university's future development, ie a basis for agreeing a 'mission' statement for the university? Would the outcome be more palatable within a university, when the plan is not fully accepted, than more explicit approaches that threaten institutional autonomy? Thus it is interesting to note that the

House of Commons Education, Science and Arts Committee (1980a) recommends that all colleges, polytechnics and universities be asked to submit statements regarding their purposes and objectives: including types and levels of courses offered; study patterns and course structures; the profile of the students for which they are intended; the range of subjects covered; the balance between teaching and research, consultancy, etc.; and the relationship of the academic programme to the facilities available. They also recommend that institutions should subsequently make annual reports to their national bodies and that these should be available to all institutions and the general public. Should not progress measures be included in the statement of purpose and objectives, and be monitored in annual reports?

The strategic planning approach advocated here and elsewhere (Sizer 1980a, b, c) should enable institutions to develop a set of alternative strategies and operating plans including strategies for *long-term resource mobility*. As changes occur in the external environment the range of strategies can be narrowed down and the appropriate strategy and operating plan implemented. Under conditions of financial stringency and uncertainty, institutions may need to complement their long-term strategy for resource mobility with a short-term strategy for financial emergencies and a medium-term strategy for financial mobility. The application of these concepts to colleges and universities has been examined by Dickmeyer (1980). The existence of computer-based financial planning models will facilitate the preparation and updating of such strategies.

Hopefully the existence of parallel plans for short-term financial emergencies and medium-term financial mobility will ensure not only an appropriate *speed of response* to a rapidly changing external environment compatible with the strategy for long-term resource mobility but also an increased *flexibility* in planning. It will help to ensure that an appropriate balance is obtained between the pressure to increase cost efficiency in the short term and actions needed to be taken if the organization is to be effective in the long term.

TESTS OF APPROPRIATENESS

Clearly a whole range of process, outcome and progress performance indicators should be considered when establishing appropriate indicators for the research, teaching and central service functions within an institution of higher education. Given that higher education abounds with joint inputs and multiple outputs and outcomes, and the ultimate impact of many of the outcomes is long-term and extremely difficult to measure, what tests should be applied to various possible indicators to determine whether they are appropriate for the purpose intended? Sizer (1980b, c) has proposed tests of relevance, verifiability, freedom from bias, quantifiability, economic feasibility and institutional acceptability. It will be recognized that *trade-offs* frequently have to be made between standards. Space does not permit a full discussion of these tests of appropriateness, but aspects relevant to the theme of the chapter are examined.

Unit Cost Comparisons
One of the major problems facing those who wish to produce (for internal planning, control and resource-allocation purposes and for external comparisons either side of and across the binary line) financial performance indicators for research and teaching functions in higher education is the unscrambling of joint costs and of the central services that support them. It may be wise to recognize at the outset that it is not possible to unscramble the joint costs, and that any attempt to do so is riddled with assumptions that do not stand up to objective assessment and criticism. Most such attempts in institutions of higher education employ an absorption costing approach to produce full costs.

Do university administors who use such approaches to generate and supply financial indicators not only test their cost allocation procedures against the standards of relevance, verifiability, etc. but also explain the assumptions underlying the indicators, and the uses that can and cannot be made of them to those who receive and use the indicators? Do they always recognize:

i   There is no one way of apportioning joint costs to cost centres or absorbing joint costs into cost units. It is quite possible that two equally competent accountants working from the same basic data would arrive at different unit costs.

ii   In institutions of higher education a high proportion of the costs are fixed or period costs, therefore the average costs are unsuitable for determining either the *incremental costs* of extra or fewer students, changes in course design, etc., or the *avoidable costs* if a department is closed, a course no longer offered, etc. The system of 'tenure' creates rigidities in the cost structure not present in industrial and commercial organizations, and imposes considerable restrictions when developing strategies for resource mobility.

iii   Methods that allocate staff costs on the basis of diary analysis, timetable analysis, etc. do not answer the question 'If the lecturer was not lecturing to this course, what would he be doing with his time?' If the lecturer has to allocate his time to competing demands, is the cost of his meeting one demand the best alternative foregone, ie the *opportunity cost*, not the *sunk cost* of his salary which he will be paid regardless of how he allocates his time?

iv   Nor do such systems consider the *social costs* of higher education, such as the opportunity costs and benefits to society of students attending institutions of higher education.

It has been suggested that collaborative approaches at the regional level imply inter-institutional cost comparisons either side of and across the binary line. The Department of Education and Science was unable to supply the House of Commons Education, Science and Arts Committee (1980a) with a comparison of the cost of degree courses in different subject areas between the two sides of the binary line. The Committee of Public Accounts (1980) has suggested the UGC should give, if possible, more precise guidance on the causes of variation in costs from one university to another, based on their overall knowledge of costs in different universities. The Comptroller and Auditor General has called for a more comprehensive review by the UGC of staff-student ratios. The UGC and the Local Authority Associations are represented on a DES committee concerned with unit costs and their variations within and between institutions.

Clearly those calling for and undertaking such studies should be aware of the problems surrounding the unscrambling of joint costs, the distinction between input costs and outcomes and benefits, and the economic feasibility of establishing data bases. Inter-institutional cost comparisons may fail to distinguish between the costs of inputs and the quality of outcomes. The DES highlighted the limitations of crude macro average cost comparisons across the binary line in a memorandum to the Education, Science and Arts Committee (1980b). For the purposes of inter-institutional costs and staff-student ratio comparisons the UGC costs and other statistics published annually in the Department of Education and Science's *Statistics of Education: Universities: Volume 6* have a number of serious limitations. For example, the statistics are published for seventeen areas of study and not by individual departments. In some of these areas of study the composition of the group appears homogeneous and suggests reasonable inter-university comparisons can be made (eg Group B — Business Studies). In other areas such comparisons would prove more difficult (eg Group 12 — Physical Sciences, where 'large' physics differs sharply from 'small' physics) and in other areas it would appear quite impossible. For instance, Loughborough University's large and unique Departments of Library and Information Studies and Physical Education and Sports Science are included respectively in Group 16 (Other Professional Studies) and Group 1 (Education). Furthermore the basis on which the statistics are compiled by universities is not fully standardized and individual universities have a measure of freedom to decide, for example, how to calculate their student load. Furthermore there is room for variation in allocation of costs between departments and central services, and while UGC loads are spread over subject groups, costs fall as lump sums on individual departments.

To obtain accurate and meaningful inter-institutional comparisons either side of and across the binary line it is asked whether it is necessary for a central organization to:

    a   Establish and agree with participating institutions a detailed data element dictionary.

    b   Design and agree with participating institutions a methodology for collecting the data.

    c   Collect and check the actual data.

    d   Calculate, tabulate and circulate input and output measures and

performance indicators to participating institutions.
e   Assist the management of the participating institutions to interpret their data.
f   Undertake a continuous programme of education in the use of inter-institutional comparisons.

The need for a central organization to perform these functions was highlighted by Mertens (1978) on the findings of an IMHE group of six German universities on 'Cost Indicators for Institutions of Higher Education'. The project was concerned with ascertaining whether the idea of comparative indicators for enterprises could be applied to universities. Mertens points out that while the wide spread between the indicators suggests that there is scope for rationalization, many of the differences may be due to procedural defects. For example, the members of the participating universities' planning staffs collected the data and calculated the indicators, and the proejct leader had no means of supervising the data collection process. The impossibility of separating the joint costs of research and teaching proved very unsatisfactory and inter-departmental teaching load transfer was neglected. In the second phase of the programme the number of participating universities increased from six to twelve, and methodological changes were made. An initial list of 105 indicators was reduced to a system of twenty-nine which has been recommended for use within institutions.

Those advocating inter-institutional cost comparisons as a basis for resource allocation to and within institutions should consider carefully the methodological problems indentified by the German project, and its conclusions:

'— Indicators are, indeed, valuable instruments for the analysis and planning activities *within* a university or other institution of higher education. They are especially useful in the framework of a management information system, with reference to a management-by-exception concept.

'— The discussion of the methodological problems of operational comparison in higher education has revealed that it is possible to define indicators which are suitable for comparisons among institutions, by subject or by department. Indicators of this type necessarily (ie by definition) neglect departmental peculiarities and, therefore, are not useful for planning and resource allocation purposes within the individual institution.' (Elstermann and Lorenz 1980)

The various performance reports and indices generated by the type of information system advocated by Elstermann and Lorenz would prompt 'discerning questions' both on a 'management by exception' basis within institutions and, if inter-institutional reporting was introduced, across institutions; as should comparisons of 'frontier' and 'non-frontier' institutions. However, are any two institutions strictly comparable, and is there good reason why any institution in whole or in part should conform to national norms? Therefore, does a centrally organized inter-institutional

comparison scheme provide a more realistic starting point in the analysis of an institution's performance:
    a   relative to its own performance over time, or
    b   at a particular moment in time, relative to other institutions offering a smiliar mix of courses?

The comparison should enable the management to determine where and possibly *why* its performance differs from that of other institutions, but it will not necessarily tell it *how* to improve it.

Kronig (1978) went further than recognizing that inter-institutional comparisons stimulate 'where' and 'why' questions when he examined the possibilities of financing institutions of higher education on the basis of performance indicators. He recognized that it would be necessary to construct cost curves reflecting cost-volume relationships not for the university as a whole but in each case for particular performance areas: '. . . there is after all no point in trying to work out a single standard financing value for an imaginary average student' (Kronig 1978). Thus he makes the important distinction between financing based on average unit costs and financing based on cost curves.

The German Federal Ministry of Education and Science has sponsored recently a research project on financing universities on the basis of performance indicators. In their report Beckerhoff et al. (1980) recommend the use of indicators for the financing of universities for both teaching and research. As Elstermann and Lorenz (1980) point out, it is impossible to determine separate indicators for teaching and research which would be accurate enough to serve as a basis for an independent funding of teaching and of research. Because of this it is difficult to formulate a creditable and reliable process of quality assessment. On the other hand, to combine teaching and research in the financing procedure is likely to lead to an increase in teaching load leading to an inevitable increase in funds for research irrespective of its quality and relevance.

Management Information Systems
Having established appropriate performance indicators in the areas of teaching, research and support services, an information system has to be developed for reporting to responsible management physical measures of inputs and outputs and financial indicators, such as unit costs, and agreed measures of progress towards institutional objectives developed by consensus building techniques. However, will the cost of producing the performance indicator be outweighed by the benefit derived from its availability and use by decision-makers? Economic feasibility is part of the trade-off between relevance, freedom from bias and verifiability. Fortunately in institutions of higher education, as in other organizations, the costs of gathering, storing and presenting information have been declining rapidly in recent years, with the result that the standard of economic feasibility should encourage rather than deter requirements in information systems.

Balderston (1974) has argued '. . . universities will do well to install the best data systems they can afford and tolerate'. On the other hand, many would agree with Romney's view (1978) that 'Throughout higher education the potential for information overload is overwhelming'. While Somit (1979) has suggested that

> 'So long as universities enjoyed constantly increased funding, the fallacy that management decisions could be based almost entirely on "information", if only we have enough, remained unchallenged. When that era ended, the inherent limitations of data, and of the systems which provided them became all too apparent.'

In theory the manager of a responsibility centre, be it a service department, an academic department, or a research centre, should be required to agree objectives; to quantify targets; to evaluate and choose between alternatives; to plan and budget for the resources required; to organize, motivate and direct those resources; and to compare actual performance against the plan, and, when appropriate, take action on adverse deviations. The design and implementation of an information system to support this range of tasks is a demanding exercise even when objectives are clear-cut, the output is well defined, and input-output relationships are established. It is immensely more difficult in higher education '. . . given the intangible and inherently immeasurable nature of the values which pervade higher education and which, in the long run, determine our actions' (Somit 1979). Nevertheless, society and financing bodies are not prepared to exempt education managers from assessment in terms of their effectiveness and efficiency, and certainly they should be encouraged to assess their own performance.

Baldridge and Tierney (1979) have recently examined the values of management information systems (MIS) and management by objectives (MBO) and have considered whether these techniques really help improve organizational processes. They studied the impact of the Exxon Education Foundation's Resource Allocation and Management Program (RAMP) on the forty-nine private liberal arts colleges and universities receiving grants under the programme. A wide variety of projects were supported but two major types of activity predominated: the gathering and computerization of data through an MIS, and the improved use of data in planning through an MBO system. The development of an MIS was the most frequent project goal. Baldridge and Tierney '. . . judge that, by and large, MIS and MBO can make a significant contribution' to the management of institutions, and that they are economically feasible if structured in a lean fashion. Some of the specific findings which are discussed in detail in their book are very relevant to the theme of this paper. In successful projects the quality and quantity of the data improved significantly and the management innovations improved problem-solving capacities. Institutions with successful MIS projects reduced variations in per student expenditure among departments, and those with successful advanced MIS projects decreased their per student expenditure. MBO programmes have unique strengths in improving the planning process and when linked to an MIS programme they also capture the positive effects of MIS. Nonetheless, successful management innovations can have unanticipated and ambiguous consequences: adoption of an enrolment-driven MIS will cause departments to maximize enrolments; departments will try to minimize their indirect costs; departmental distrust may increase; and many management innovations will tend to centralize authority. The introduction of management innovations is a highly political process, and successful implementation involves a number of common features, including modest goals, a competent and well-trained full-time staff, support of top-level administration, effective funding, and widespread attempts to gain faculty support. Unsuccessful projects have common weaknesses including too high a turnover in project staffing, absence of administrative support, weak financing support, a scope too broad and grandiose, absence of faculty support, and a weak data base. One of the biggest problems of these management innovations is a failure to link planning activities with budgeting strategies.

Therefore, in the light of Baldridge and Tierney's findings and the discussion in this chapter (despite Romney's and Somit's observations), provided the information system meets the standard of economic feasibility, it is asked whether it should concentrate on:

a   Providing a base for planning and controlling *resource allocation and utilization*.
b   Monitoring the level of *response* to and *outcomes* of the institution's provision of learning opportunities, research facilities, and central services and expressing these responses in the form of non-financial and financial, quantitative performance indicators.
c   Monitoring agreed *measures of progress* towards institutional goals developed by consensus building techniques, so as to provide a meaningful starting point from which qualitative managerial judgements can be made.
d   Providing a base for inter-institutional cost comparisons.

Institutional Acceptability
Porter (1978) has argued:
'The measures of performance adopted may not themselves be the most reliable indicators of effectiveness or even efficiency but they could be justified if they lead to improved performance or decision taking even though they themselves may not be thoroughly sound intellectually. What is vital is that the people using the indicators should accept them, and the basis on which they are devised, as relevant and fair.'
Is Porter recognizing the political realities of institutions of higher education? As Argyris (1970) has pointed out:
'New developments for rational decision making often produce intense resentment in men who ordinarily view themselves as realistic, flexible,

definitely rational. Managers and executives who place a premium on rationality and work hard to subdue emotionality, become resistent and combative in the back-alley ways of bureaucratic politics when such technologies are introduced.'

Could 'heads of departments and units' be substituted for 'managers and executives' in Argyris' statement? Thus, is Romney (1978) right to argue, like Porter (1978), that consensus building techniques, such as those described in his study, can facilitate the selection of appropriate goals and measures within institutions? Will such approaches result in economy of information by concentrating on the few highly appropriate goal areas for which a consensus exists, rather than trying to document progress in every goal area that has been accorded some degree of appropriateness?

On the other hand, should we recognize that such consensus building might be more easily achieved when resources are relatively abundant than when they are relatively scarce? A study undertaken by Hills and Mahoney (1978) of the nature of budget decision making in a university is relevant. Their research indicated that relative abundance or scarcity of resources available for allocation is a significant influence in the budgeting process. They found that, while precedent was a significant influence in both situations, it was the *predominant* influence in the allocation of discretionary budget increments under conditions of abundant resources and a *secondary* influence under conditions of scarce resources. In this study the *predominant* influence during the period of scarce resources was externally based power represented by the existence of advisory boards; an influence not readily apparent during periods of abundant resources. Furthermore, a bureaucratic, or universalistic criterion, relative workload, was influential in the period of abundant resources but had little influence during the period of scarce resources. Hills and Mahoney (1978) consider their results suggest that

'... subunit budgeting is a process designed, in part, to ameliorate conflict and to maintain apparent harmony. This is accomplished by the allocation of discretionary resources according to accepted standards (workload) and a proportionate, or fair share, criterion during periods of relative abundance of resources.'

Hills and Mahoney's research suggests that during periods of scarcity of resources '... it is the powerful subunits that emerge to claim their resources at the expense of other subunits. Further it is the external ties that subunits have which they can use as this power base' (1978). Under these conditions, is 'cutting across the spectrum equally' acceptable, and should it be acceptable, to heads of powerful departments, and can institutional acceptability and consensus building withstand the pressures for self-preservation and survival?

INSTITUTIONAL SELF-EVALUATION
The need for institutional self-evaluation has been highlighted on a number

of occasions in this paper. Space does not permit a full discussion of the behavioural and organizational aspects of institutional self-evaluation which are examined by Davies and Morgan.

However, the author has led seminars and participated in discussions on experiences of institutional self-evaluation exercises which have been undertaken in Australia, Canada, Sweden and the United States. These experiences have highlighted a number of difficulties and issues at the interfaces between departmental, school or faculty, institutional and national systems evaluation:

i The conflict between the objectives at different levels giving rise to difficulties in obtaining reconciliation between department, school or faculty and institutional objectives. These difficulties arise with top-down approaches and bottom-up/top-down approaches.

ii The time perspectives for the self-evaluation exercises vary at different levels giving rise to further pressures. At departmental level self-evaluation is a time-consuming process because of the complex behavioural difficulties that have to be overcome if realistic and objective evaluations are to result. On the other hand political and financial pressures may give rise to requests at the system and institutional level that are not compatible with departmental and school or faculty time perspectives for self-evaluation, for example, the UGC three scenarios exercise was based on an unrealistic timetable.

iii Even if conflict between objectives at different levels can be resolved, the sum of the aspirations arising from these agreed objectives of departments may be greater than school or faculty resources can support; the sum of school or faculty aspirations may exceed institutional resources, and the sum of institutional aspirations may exceed national needs and resource availabilities. Institutional self-evaluation can create both unrealistic expectations and entrenched positions.

At the institutional level these pressures highlight the need for 'managers of change', who can help build consensus and resolve conflicts in the institutions. At the national level they lead governments and bodies such as the UGC to become more dirigiste.

SOME MANAGERIAL IMPLICATIONS FOR ADAPTATION AND CHANGE

Debates in the United Kingdom universities in response to a University Grants Committee planning exercise based on three possible levels of funding for a university for the quadrennium 1980/81 to 1983/84 (modest growth, no change, and modest decline) have highlighted the need to employ consensus building techniques and to avoid conflicts arising between the objectives, aspirations and self-perceptions of departments, schools and other faculty groups and the objectives of the institution. At the same time acceptance has to be obtained of the need for stronger central direction in universities than heads of departments and faculty have grown accustomed to. The debates have also highlighted the difficulties involved in consensus building, and the behavioural problems underlying institutional self-evaluation and self-renewal.

It is in this context that the question is frequently posed: Can you manage change and achieve resource mobility during a period when institutions are likely to be more concerned with coping with the pressures of revised student numbers and lower provision per FTE? In other words, will the senior academics and administrators, the managers of change, in institutions of higher education be so concerned with today's problems that they will not give adequate consideration, and make appropriate plans, to cope with tomorrow's problems, particularly when many of these managers of change may have retired before the 1990s?

Richard Cyert (1977), the distinguished organizational theorist and President of Carnegie-Mellon, has emphasized that the trick of managing the contracting organization is to break the vicious circle which tends to lead to disintegration of the organization, and that the management must develop counter forces which will allow the organization to maintain viability. Furthermore it is important to recognize that, although there are parallels with earlier periods of low growth in institutions, significant changes have taken place in the status and attitudes of university lecturers. They feel there has been a significant lowering of their status in society and they have been badly treated by governments. The House of Commons Education, Science and Arts Committee (1980a) has recommended that the government should examine the concept of 'tenure' in higher education, and a smaller proportion of future academic appointments should carry 'tenure'. Lecturers may face higher teaching loads at a time when their career opportunities have diminished significantly. Not only may they have less time for research, but, if there are few promotional prospects, they may well feel no motivation to undertake research of the type needed to cope with anticipated dynamic changes in society (assuming research grants are available). The unions that represent them may not accept, though they may recognize, the need for resource mobility and for lecturers' own retraining and redeployment. In the United States, which has already experienced contraction and retrenchment, Baldridge and Tierney (1979) found that when inflation rates are considered, the money spent on direct instruction has been steadily decreasing. Staff-student ratios have increased, the number of faculty has declined, senior faculty have been replaced by junior faculty and faculty salary increases have diminished. This decrease in institutional expenditure was apparent regardless of the type of management process the institution implemented. Given these motivational considerations, others have argued from different points of view, it may be less painful and damaging to close some universities and polytechnics and departments and faculties within institutions as the alternative to requiring some degree of contraction, and consequent stagnation, across the board.

However it is not sufficient to appoint 'managers of survival' who will balance the books, recruit the students and raise the funds (Carnegie Council 1980). Like Cyert (1978), Sizer has argued elsewhere (1980c) that there is a need to appoint high quality managers of appropriate academic standing, when the opportunities arise, who can overcome institutional inertia. These managers of change should not only be able to plan and control efficiently the allocation of resources to see their institutions through the short-term financial pressures, but also be able to motivate people to recognize the need for long-term change, and secure their participation in its planning and subsequent implementation. They have to persuade the university to decide, like the UGC,

'. . . that, in order to maintain the vitality and responsiveness of universities, resources must continue to be made available for necessary new developments, as well as for new appointments in fields of special importance.' (UGC 1981)

By gaining acceptance for phased withdrawal from some subject areas, they need to turn fixed costs into variable costs so as to release resources to finance new faculty and new initiatives in existing and emerging growth areas which are consistent with the institution's long-term objectives. They will recognize that innovations in response to new needs and new opportunities are frequently created through the initiative of individuals. If they are to break the vicious circle that leads to disintegration they have to create an environment which motivates individuals and fosters rather than frustrates such initiatives. They have to overcome resistance to change in circumstances when 'Preservation of the status quo may be the only possible rallying point for a consensus' (Carnegie Council 1980) and

'. . . too many denizens of the groves of academe believe themselves to be immune from the changes taking place in the rest of society, which they may regard as a temporary aberration in the long-term scale of university development, and many may have a feeling that they must refrain from (internally) and resist (externally) all *action* of an unpalatable kind.' (CVCP 1980b)

To support these managers of change, governments will have to accept that it will be necessary to develop an appropriate 'incentive structure' which will facilitate and not inhibit change: for example, more resources for staff retraining and development, generous early retirement schemes, etc. In her comparative analysis of US state agency procedures for initiating and implementing the discontinuance of academic programmes, Melchiori (1980a, b) found that the emergence of *obstacles* and neglect of *incentives* at various stages in the discontinuance process had a compounding negative impact on final implementation. The strategic employment of *copying mechanisms* between individual events proved to have an increasingly constructive effect on actual terminations.

However, while Cyert (1977) considers management '. . . is our major hope for the future' he also recognizes that '. . . academics resist being managed by expert managers and seek to have an academic in the top management position. Only rarely will this approach lead to an excellent manager' (Cyert 1978). It may be for this reason that an anonymous registrar of a British university (*The Times Higher Education Supplement* 28.12.79) has expressed the view that British universities find themselves without the apparatus for that efficient and effective deployment and management of scarce resources. He considers they are

'. . . hung up still on the medieval and almost superstitious fear of "management" within universities which leaves the resource allocation processes in many of them hardly able to stand comparison with an unsophisticated game of bingo.'

In Europe the Institutional Management in Higher Education Programme of OECD/CERI has made a significant contribution to breaking down this fear.

The Hills and Mahoney study (1978) suggests that university budgeting in the United States may be characterized in a period of abundant resources by adherence to arbitrary rules and historical precedents and by the maintenance of stable relationships between sub-units. It may be that during periods of scarcity of resources there will be greater competition for resources and questioning of arbitrary rules and historical precedents, but this may be resisted because of its potential disruptive effects upon sub-unit relationships. Do the decision-makers within institutions ask themselves whether their resource-allocation formulae are compatible with their long-term objectives and strategies? Could their resource-allocation processes be dysfunctional in this respect? Do the committees that take decisions about vacant posts take account of long-term strategies for resource mobility or simply concentrate on historical relative workload? Thus Baldridge and Tierney (1979) conclude that one of the biggest problems of MBO and MIS innovations is a failure to link planning activities with budgeting strategies. The information supplied by an MIS often came too late or was not used appropriately for budget decisions, and the planning processes of MBO sometimes had little impact on the budgetary decisions. Mertens (1978) has pointed out from a German perspective that '. . . there are a number of incentives which steer university decision makers in the wrong direction', and the Swedish Board of Universities and Colleges has recognized that 'If institutional assessment shall have any effect on decision making, we must tackle the problems of the incentive structure' (Östergren 1978b).

Over-emphasis by external financing bodies on *process performance indicators* that measure short-term effectiveness and efficiency at the expense of *progress measures* might result in incentive situations which are not consistent with the institution's long-term goals and objectives, towards which the managers of change are striving. (See for example examinations of formula budgeting and financing of public higher education in the United States, and of the operations of the Advanced Further Education Pool in the

United Kingdom). This is not to say that short-term cost efficiency is not important and process performance indicators are not relevant. It is a question of balancing short-term cost efficiency with long-term effectiveness. Certainly resource-allocation processes compatible with the institution's strategy to achieve long-term goals and objectives may be inconsistent with the achievement of improved short-term cost efficiency. Given that it is the nature of an organization to guard itself against change, at all events against changes which are not in accordance with the dominating internal value system of the organization, Östergren (1978b) asks:

> 'Can we change the incentive structure of a university so that rewards and punishments help universities to take the consequences of assessment? Or must decisions about more radical reallocation of resources be taken by authorities outside universities? That is a crucial *question* for the future authority of universities.'

If the resource-allocation processes in many universities are comparable with an *unsophisticated* game of bingo, would a strengthening of the application of management accounting concepts and techniques to the planning, resource allocation and performance assessment processes within institutions ensure at least a *sophisticated* game.' If the planning process is not linked with the budgeting process,

> '... the planning process is nothing more than a sham in which people spend time and energy but become extremely disillusioned. Budgets are useful only when they implement serious plans. The planning process is sensible only when it can be linked to real-world budgets.' (Baldridge and Tierney 1979)

SUMMARY AND CONCLUSIONS

It has been argued that during periods of contraction and under conditions of changing needs and financial stringency, high quality managers of appropriate academic standing should be motivating their institutions to strive to become effective in the long term through attempts

a To examine systematically the future environment in which it will be operating and to identify threats and opportunities.
b To understand and communicate the implications of this future environment to the institution's constituencies.
c To evaluate the institution's current subject area portfolio and critical resources.
d To agree through consensus-building techniques the goals and objectives (ie mission statements) for the institution and its constituent parts, and the *measures for monitoring progress* towards achieving these goals and objectives.
e To develop a set of alternative long-term strategies and action oriented plans including a strategy for long-term resource mobility; a strategy for medium-term financial mobility and short-term emergencies; resource-allocation procedures consistent with the

institution's long-term objectives; and a short-term planning and control system based on measurable information and performance indicators, possibly backed up by a nationally organized scheme for inter-institutional comparisons.

Within this framework it has been recognized that efficiency and effectiveness are elusive concepts in higher education. The problems of agreeing objectives, identifying and measuring the component parts of the institution, and evaluating performance and effectiveness suggest that only 'partial' measures of performance are possible, and that a proper balance has to be struck between qualitative and quantitative aspects. These 'partial' performance indicators provide a starting point for managerial judgements; and there is likely to remain in the foreseeable future a considerable gap that has to be bridged by such judgements. To achieve positive motivation institutions are having to recognize that faculty and administrators at all levels should participate in all aspects of performance assessment; hence the growing interest in institutional self-evaluation.

The 'managers of change' have to create an environment which will lead to positive responses to institutional self-evaluation. They should manage not for survival but for excellence, recognizing that qualitative innovation and growth should replace quantitative growth. However, it is to be asked whether institutions can attract such leadership when, as the Carnegie Council (1980) points out:

'... the tasks are grinding ones, the victories too often take the form of greater losses avoided, the internal constituencies are more likely to be united around doing nothing than doing something.'

NOTE

1   It is understood that a similar matrix has been developed and utilized by an American university which distinguishes between quality (high medium and adequate) and centrality (high, medium and peripheral).

REFERENCES

Argyris, C. (1970) Resistance to rational management systems *Innovation* 10, p.29

Balderston, Frederick E. (1974) *Managing Today's University* San Francisco: Jossey-Bass

Balderston, Frederick E. (1979) Note on Professor Sizer's paper *International Journal of Institutional Management in Higher Education* 3 (1) 76-77

Baldridge, J.V. and Tierney, M.L. (1979) *New Approaches to Management* San Francisco: Jossey-Bass

Beckerhoff, D. et al. (1980) *Hochschulfinanzierung auf der Grundlage leistungsorientierter Kennziffern* München: Gersback (Bundesminister für Bildung und Wissenschaft, Schriftenreihe Hochschule 33)

Birch, D.W., Calvert, J.R. and Sizer, J. (1977) A case study of some performance indicators in higher education in the United Kingdom *International Journal of Institutional Management in Higher Education* 1 (2) 133-142

Cameron, Kim (1978) Measuring organizational effectiveness in institutions of higher education *Administrative Science Quarterly* 23, December

Carnegie Council on Policy Studies in Higher Education (1980) *Three Thousand Futures, the Next Twenty Years for Higher Education* (Final report) San Francisco: Jossey-Bass

Committee of Public Accounts (1980) *Thirty-fourth Report: Session 1979/80* House of Commons Paper 783, London: HMSO

Committee of Vice-Chancellors and Principals (1980a) *Memorandum to the UK Government's Select Committee on Education, Science and Arts* 1st February

Committee of Vice-Chancellors and Principals (1980b) *A Slightly Shortened Version of the Address by the Chairman of the UGC to the CVCP on October 24th 1980*

Comptroller and Auditor General (1980) *Appropriation Accounts* Vol. 3 (Classes x-xv & xviii) 1979/80, London: HMSO

Coombs, P. and Hallak, J. (1972) *Managing Educational Costs* Oxford: University Press

Cyert, Richard M. (1977) *Academic Progress and Stable Resources* A lecture given at NCHEMS, Denver, Colorado, 7 November

Cyert, Richard M. (1978) The management of universities of constant or decreasing size *Public Administration Review* July/August

Delany, V.J. (1978) Budgetary control and monitoring effectiveness *Management Accounting* October

Dickmeyer, N. (1980) *Balancing Risks and Resources: Financial Strategies for Colleges and Universities* Paper presented to the Fifth General Conference of the Programme on Institutional Management in Higher Education, OECD/CERI, Paris, 8-10 September

Doyle, Peter and Lynch, James E. (1979) A strategic model for university planning *Journal of the Operational Research Society* 30 (7) 603-609

Elstermann, Gert and Lorenz, Wolfgang (1980) *Financing Universities on the Basis of Performance Indicators?* Paper presented to the Ninth Special Topic Workshop of the IMHE Programme, OECD/CERI Paris, 10-12 December

Faxén, Nils-Bertil et al. (1980) *Institutional Self-evaluation in Sweden* Paper presented to the Ninth Special Topic Workshop of the IMHE Programme, OECD/CERI, Paris, 10-12 December

Furumark, Ann-Marie (1979) *Activity Evaluation in Higher Education a Swedish Project* R & D Division of the National Board of Universities and Colleges, 1979-11-10, Stockholm

Gambino, Anthony J. (1979) *Planning and Control in Higher Education* New York: National Association of Accountants

Hecquet, I. and Jadot, J. (1978) *The Impact on University Management of Financing and Control Systems for Higher Education* Summary report of a joint project of the IMHE Programme (OECD/CERI) and L'Association des Universités Partiellement ou Entièrement de Langue Francaise (AUPELF)

Hijmans, Robbert (1980) *The Role of Government in Institution Performance Evaluation* Paper presented to the Ninth Special Topic Workshop of the IMHE Programme, OECD/CERI, Paris, 10-12 December

Hills, F.S. and Mahoney, T.A. (1978) University budgets and organizational decision making *Administrative Science Quarterly* 23, pp.454-465

Hinman, M.M. (1980) *Planning and Evaluation at the University of Michigan* Paper presented to the Ninth Special Topic Workshop of the IMHE Programme, OECD/CERI, Paris, 10-12 December

House of Commons Committee on Education, Science and Arts (1980a) *The Funding and Organization of Courses in Higher Education* Fifth Report 1979/80, Vol. 1 — Report, London: HMSO

House of Commons Committee on Education, Science and Arts (1980b) *The Funding and Organization of Courses in Higher Education* Fifth Report 1979/80 Vol. III — Appendices, London: HMSO

Jadot, J. et al. (1980) *Survey on the State-of-the-Art and Likely Future Trends* Report presented to the Fifth General Conference of the Programme on Institutional Management in Higher Education OECD/CERI Paris, 8-10 September. To be published in *International Journal of Institutional Mangement in Higher Education*

Jochimsen, R. (1979) Managing universities in the eighties: introductory remarks *International Journal of Institutional Management in Higher Education* 3 (1) 5-20

Kronig, W. (1978) *Performance-related Budgeting for Universities* Paper presented to the Fifth Special Topic Workshop of the IMHE Programme, OECD/CERI, Paris, June

Melchiori, Gerlinda S. (1980a) *Patterns of Program Discontinuance: a comparative analysis of state agency procedures for initiating and implementing the discontinuance of academic programs* Final Project Report, Centre for the Study of Higher Education, School of Education, University of Michigan

Mertens, Peter (1978) *Comparative Indicators for Institutions of Higher Education* Paper presented to the Fifth Special Topic Workshop of the IMHE Programme, OECD/CERI, Paris, 5-6 June; a translation of 'Kennzahlenvergleiche deutscher universitäten' *Betriebswirtschaftliche Forschung und Praxis [BFuP]* Heft 1/1978: 25-34

Norris, Graeme (1978) *The Effective University: a Management by Objectives Approach* Farnborough: Saxon House

Östergren, Bertil (1978a) *Some Comments on the Swedish Project 'Activity evaluation in higher education'* Paper presented to the Fifth Special

Topic Workshop of the IMHE Programme, OECD/CERI, Paris, 5-6 June

Östergren, Bertil (1978b) *The Swedish Project on Institutional Self-Evaluation* Paper presented to the Fourth General Conference of the Programme on Institutional Management in Higher Education, OECD/CERI, Paris, 11-13 September

Porter, Douglas (1978) *Developing Performance Indicators for the Teaching Function* Paper presented to the Fifth Special Topic Workshop of the IMHE Programme, OECD/CERI, Paris, 5-6 June

Pyhrr, Peter A. (1973) *Zero-Base Budgeting: A Practical Management Tool for Evaluating Expenses* New York: John Wiley & Sons

Romney, Leonard C. (1978) *Measures of Institutional Goal Achievement* Denver, Colorado: National Center for Higher Education Management Systems

Romney, L.C., Bogen, C. and Micek, S.S. (1978) *Assessing Institutional Performance: the importance of being careful* Paper presented to the Fourth General Conference of the Programme on Institutional Management in Higher Education, OECD/CERI, Paris, 11-13 September

Romney, L.C., Gray, R.G. and Weldon, H.K. (1978) *Departmental Productivity: A Conceptual Framework* Denver, Colorado: NCHEMS

Sizer, John (1979) Assessing institutional performance: an overview *International Journal of Institutional Management in Higher Education* 3 (1) 49-75

Sizer, John (1980a) *Performance Assessment in Institutions of Higher Education under Conditions of Financial Stringency, Contraction and Changing needs: a management accounting perspective* Paper presented to the Third Annual Congress of the European Accounting Association, Amsterdam, 24-26 March, and published in *Maandblad voor Accountancy en bedrijfshuishoudkunde*, Haarlem, April 1981; a revised and shortened version to appear in *Accounting and Business Research* Summer 1981

Sizer, John (1980b) Assessing the performance of institutions in the 1980s: a European perspective *New Directions in Institutional Research* San Francisco: Jossey-Bass, forthcoming

Sizer, John (1980c) *Institutional Performance Assessment under Conditions of Changing Needs* Paper presented to the Fifth General Conference of the Programme on Institutional Management in Higher Education, OECD/CERI, Paris, 8-10 September

Somit, Albert (1979) Management information systems: neither paradise lost nor paradise gained *International Journal of Institutional Mangement in Higher Education* 3 (1) 91-94

Sorenson, James R. and Grove, Hugh D. (1977) Cost-outcome and cost-effectiveness analysis: emerging nonprofit performance evaluation techniques *The Accounting Review* LII (3) 658-675

Times Higher Education Supplement (1979) *British Universities: What Next?* 28 December

University Grants Committee (1981) *Circular letter 8/81 from the Chairman to Vice-Chancellors, 15th May*

Weathersby, G.B. and Balderston, F.E. (1972) *PPBS in Higher Education Planning and Management* Report of the Ford Foundation Program for Research in University Administration, P-31, May

3
AUTONOMOUS AND SERVICE TRADITIONS

by Tyrrell Burgess

The British tradition of institutional change has been lovingly described as 'pragmatic'. Changes occur or are advocated in response to particular circumstances or perceived requirements. Rarely are they related to any explicit principles of governance or administration. This preference for pragmatism does not mean that principle is wholly absent: it stems rather from a reluctance to make principle too definite and clear cut. This has obvious advantages: it avoids debilitating and fruitless quarrels about theory, and it enables change to take place gradually and with general assent. It has the disadvantage, however, that valued arrangements may be undermined and lost by default, without anyone's having intended it.

It is the argument of this paper that institutional arrangements in higher education, particularly in its finance and control, have developed to the point where principle has become so weak that each new change can only add to muddle and ineffectiveness. It is important, therefore, to discuss the institutional future of higher education, not in terms of projecting past trends, or of meeting personal or social demand, of resisting financial stringency, or tinkering with present arrangements. The discussion should begin with renewed agreement about the principles on which a varied system of higher education can rationally be built.

In an attempt to contribute to this discussion I have in the past identified two traditions of higher education which I have characterized as the 'autonomous' and 'service' traditions. The first sees education, especially higher education, as an activity with its own values and purposes, affecting the rest of society obliquely and as a kind of bonus. The second explicitly expects education to serve individuals and society and defends it in these terms (Burgess 1977).

I have described the autonomous tradition as aloof, academic, conservative and exclusive. People and institutions acting in this tradition and with this view of their purpose think it right to hold themselves apart, ready if necessary to resist the demands of society, the whims of government, the fashions of public opinion, the importunities of actual or potential students. Many of us are glad that they do so. In totalitarian countries their stand may be heroic: educational institutions are often the first to be attacked by tyrannical governments. We can be glad of them in democracies, too. Democratic government can err. Popular demand my be foolish. Both can be arbitrary, unjust and capricious. A democratic society is a plural society, one in which criticism is welcome and alternatives possible. What is more, democracies recognize that there can be no certainty where human knowledge and understanding will next be advanced. Many of the greatest advances have been made against political oppression, popular indifference or worse. The creations of the human mind themselves achieve a kind of autonomy, imposing their own disciplines and creating their own problems, and it is right that there should be people devoted to following the disciplines and solving the problems. This is particularly true in areas where most people see little promise: you never know when a discipline may be urgently needed.

This aloofness is expressed in academic attitudes. Defenders of an autonomous tradition claim to be concerned with the preservation, extension and dissemination of knowledge — for its own sake. They speak of pursuing truth or excellence. They will, they say, follow the truth, wherever it may lead. However described, the activity is self-justifying. At least, it is not justified in terms outside itself, like meeting the needs of society. Academics derive their justification from a discipline or body of knowledge. They typically claim to spend half their academic time on research, because it is only by doing so that they can have anything worthwhile to teach.

Autonomous institutions are by their nature conservative. It is true that within them advances may be made at the frontiers of knowlege, though they are by no means the only places where such advances are made. On the whole, however, they are resistant to new disciplines. Science, technology, art have all had their battles for recognition as disciplines. It is hard to get new matter into undergraduate courses or to drop old matter. Interdisciplinary courses always fail. This conservation is defensible. It derives from the conviction that knowledge advances painfully by imposing order where previously there was chaos. Intellectual order is thus precious and vulnerable. Neglect of this may involve us all simply in attempts to teach chaos.

One important consequence of all this is that institutions in the autonomous tradition are necessarily exclusive. Given that what they do is self-justifying, they can responsibly accept as students only those who might 'benefit' from what they are doing. This effectively excludes most people. The exclusion is often defended in terms of maintaining standards, but since entry requirements are variable, this defence rings hollow. It is claimed, however, that the exclusiveness is neutrally 'academic'. It is effectively, if arguably incidentally, social. The processes of selection for higher education, which begin in the early years of secondary schools, enable middle-class youngsters to be over-represented in higher education and working-class youngsters to be under-represented. Expressions of the autonomous tradition are widely diffused throughout British higher education.

By contrast, I have characterized the service tradition as responsive, vocational, innovating and open. Institutions in this tradition do not think it right to hold themselves apart from society: rather that they should respond to its needs. They seek to place the knowledge that they have at the service of society. Indeed they believe that human knowledge advances as much through the solution of practical problems as through pure thought. It is important not to underestimate or vulgarize the service tradition. In seeking to serve it confronts very serious difficulties. In the first place there is the question of service to whom? Is it the student who is to be served, society as a whole, the government? There are many different interests — which is to be paramount? Can the institution serve more than one? The autonomous tradition settles this by asserting the priority of the discipline. The service tradition lays itself open instead to having serious human and political arguments. Clearly different interests are not always compatible. For example, the interest of an employer in further education may be that his workers should do their jobs better; the interest of the employee, by contrast, may be to get a better job. Neither may be very well aware of what society, as interpreted by an elected government, may require or want.

Second, it is not merely a paradox to assert that one of the services which educational institutions should render to a society is a serious and direct criticism of it. There are few countries where this is explicitly recognized: the United States is the only place I know where a formally constituted committee has actually recognized it (Carnegie 1973). But criticism is vital to a democratic society, and a service institution is failing it if it does not offer it.

All this raises the question of accountability. The challenge for service institutions is to work out forms of government which will enable them to do their work, including criticism, while responding to the society around them. It is not too much to say that this is one of the most serious problems democratic societies have to face, not only in education, but in all forms of social and political life.

Service institutions do not, on the whole, seek to claim that they are pursuing knowledge for its own sake. They are engaged explicitly in professional and vocational education — often in 'mere' vocational training. They attract resources because there are actual or potential students to be enrolled. Their 'research' is normally directed to some external problem, often in the form of consultancy. Apart from this they are typically teaching institutions, devoted to helping students towards some qualification.

There are many people who would feel that to call service institutions innovating is to be at best fanciful. But it is in their nature to be so: they must accommodate growth, must accept new kinds of students, offer them new kinds of courses, create new structures of study, pioneer new forms of governance, recruit new kinds of staff, and so on. When my colleague, John Pratt, and I contributed to an OECD symposium on innovation in higher education in Paris, it became clear to us that not only in England, but in many diverse systems, where institutions were prepared to accept the service view of purpose, they were indeed innovating in all these ways (Burgess and Pratt 1971).

Thus it is that service institutions have to be open. They cannot exclude students on the grounds that the latter are not properly prepared. Typically they accept 'maturity' or some such idea as an alternative to academic qualification as an entry requirement. Their students are as a consequence very diverse in themselves; they follow courses at many levels and by many different modes of study. They are the traditional route to high qualification for working-class people and their children.

It is important not to assume that these two traditions are found, pure and unmixed, in different kinds of institutions, though in England the universities are self-consciously in the 'autonomous' tradition and polytechnics were explicitly founded in the 'service' tradition. What complicates the issue is a process which my colleagues and I have described as 'academic drift' — which seems to be a world-wide tendency for 'service' institutions to seek to become more and more 'autonomous'. Thus we see that in England the polytechnics (like the colleges of advanced technology before them) have sought to resolve dilemmas of accountability through reducing public control, have chafed at external academic validation, have emphasized a commitment to research, have established subject departments and faculties, have transferred 'inappropriate' courses elsewhere, have rejected students they would have previously taken. This is academic drift at work.

There are many who explain 'academic drift' in institutional terms. They argue, for example, that it is natural for new or emerging institutions to ape those with established prestige. For a long time it was held that pay and conditions of service in 'autonomous' institutions were better than those in 'service' ones. There is of course also the general institutional point that any institution, however explicit the purpose for which it was founded, soon comes to have purposes of its own and indeed to act in ways which were not foreseen or intended. It is the institutions which are responsible day to day for what happens. Their staffs have their own goals. There may be directives and regulations, there may be a powerful board of governors or trustees, there may be all manner of devices for implementing the original policy — but these must in the end be powerless against the minute-by-minute, hour-by-hour, day-by-day activity of those actually in the institutions.

The existence of academic drift, and attempts to halt or reverse it, are often presented in terms of a conflict between the two traditions. The purpose of distinguishing them, however, is not to present them as alternatives but to assert the importance of both and to find institutional arrangements which will preserve them. One question is what should be the balance between them, both within institutions and in the system as a whole. Another is a serious theoretical one about the compatibility of the autonomous tradition with education (Burgess 1979). The immediate problem, however, is that the institutional expression of both traditions in Britain has broken down, so it is urgent to ask whether and how it can be re-established.

The institutional expression of the autonomous tradition is the University Grants Committee. Universities themselves have autonomy enshrined in their individual charters. Hitherto the autonomy has been preserved, even though universities get most of their income from the government, via the UGC. The committee is composed largely of academics, and is staffed by civil servants. It has had a dual task: first to advise the government on the total money provision to be made for the universities; second, to allocate the total provision between the universities. In carrying out the first of these functions the committee is advisory in the strictest sense: the decisions are taken by the government in the light of the committee's advice. In the second function, however, the UGC is only formally advisory, because the convention has been established that the government does not inquire into or question the committee's recommendations about allocation between universities.

Two principles governing the UGC's work were established from its earliest days. The first was the principle of a quinquennial settlement and the second was that of a block grant. This combination of principles was held to facilitate the planning of academic development and give the universities a great measure of financial autonomy and responsibility.

Both principles were designed to preserve autonomy. The quinquennial settlement reduced the possibility of pressure from year to year in response to changes of 'policy' and government. The block grant kept decisions, and not just 'academic' decisions, within each university. Any weakening of these principles would begin to introduce detailed external influence over academic matters in individual universities.

It is clear that these two principles have indeed collapsed. There simply are no longer qinquennial settlements. The universities get their grants from year to year and are thus vulnerable to external pressure. Lip service is still paid to the block grant principle, but in practice it is ineffective. Ever since the early 1960s the apparently passive function of the UGC as a buffer between universities and government has been changing. The Robbins Committee noted that the UGC was not passive in regard to the policies of particular universities (Robbins 1963). Block grants were made after examining and discussing with each university the national and regional background. By 1967 the UGC's Manual of General Guidance included not only the 'various factors' which had been taken into account in deciding about university development generally, but also a statement of its attitude to the development of particular academic activities (UGC 1967). It was at that point that the colleges of advanced technology discovered that moving from the 'service' to the 'autonomous' arrangements balked them for the first time of an academic development that they wished to undertake. Since that time the 'guidance' to individual universities has become more and more explicit. The effect of the decisions made by the UGC in 1981 will be not only to destroy the capacity of the worst affected universities for rational academic development but will discourage other universities from independent planning in the future.

As much as seven years ago John Pratt showed how the UGC had come to operate in ways that were indistinguishable from those of a department of state (Pratt 1975). The controls which it exercises resemble those of the Department of Education and Science in the public sector. For a time university people comforted themselves with the thought that since the committee was composed of academics, it must be intrinsically different from a department of state; but it is not the composition of the committee which is significant, but the job it is required to do. A committee which operates as a bureaucracy will not cease to do so because it is not staffed by bureaucrats: indeed this may mean only that its bureaucratic activities are done less well.

Much of the present collapse of the autonomous institutional arrangements derives from financial stringency, but decay had set in long before. The change in the character of the UGC was almost certainly not deliberate. Rather it was attributable to the growth of the number of institutions for which it was responsible and of the amounts of money dispensed. This particular device for recognizing and preserving autonomous institutions can simply not be operated if the number of institutions is very large. In other words, the old relationships have become impossible. If the autonomous tradition is to be preserved and indeed strengthened, its institutional arrangements must apply only where they are apt. This means very greatly reducing the scope of responsibility of the University Grants Committee.

A similar collapse has occurred in the institutional structure of the service tradition. Under the Education Act 1944 powers and duties are so distributed as to make higher education in the 'public sector' responsive to personal and social demand. In particular the local education authorities are established as providing bodies, with the duty to see that there are adequate facilities for further education (including higher education) in their areas. This local responsibility is designed to ensure that in every area there is a varied and comprehensive educational service. The means by which these duties were to be performed were set out in the Act. The local authorities were to produce 'schemes' of further education, showing what provision the authorities proposed, and submit them to the Secretary of State. The Secretary of State was to approve the schemes, modifying them perhaps after consultation with the authority concerned. There was provision too for the schemes to be changed in the light of circumstances.

This simple device could have secured the development of responsive higher education in the service tradition in every local authority area. It would have been properly based on local consideration and local initiative, moderated only as appropriate by the Secretary of State. After a good start, however, the system fell into abeyance. The local authorities stopped producing schemes, and the Secretary of State stopped considering and approving them.

In its place there grew up a system of national initiative and direction, in which the responsibilities of local authorities were persistently neglected and undermined.

In particular an entirely false division was established between further education and 'advanced' (or higher) further education. Local authorities were prevented from developing the latter by a series of central decisions. In 1956, for example, it was decided to establish eight, later ten, colleges of advanced technology, where advanced work was to be concentrated. Within a decade these colleges had been taken from the local authorities.

In 1966 it was centrally decided to create 30 polytechnics, in which advanced work would again be concentrated. Ever more elaborate arrangements for funding these institutions have been evolved, to the point where local authority interest has almost collapsed and where it seems inevitable that yet another quangoid growth must be established to administer them.

Of course, it has always been argued that these national decisions are needed for 'co-ordination'. Substantial FE institutions, for historical reasons, are unevenly spread, so they cannot be a matter for local administration.

Neither of these arguments will do. Thirty years of national co-ordination has left some places with more advanced further (or higher) education than they well know what to do with and others with almost none. It is not a paradox to assert that real local responsibility for providing the service would have produced a better and more co-ordinated spread than the series of national decisions we have actually had.

It is important to realize that the institutional arrangements for both the autonomous and the service traditions have been under threat from the same source: a powerful centralizing tendency which was resisted longest in education but now seems well established there. The University Grants Committee is no longer a 'buffer': it is an instrument of central control. The powers and duties of local authorities in higher education will be effectively removed by the proposals in the recent Green Paper on public sector higher education. If a working party of civil servants and local officials has its way, the provisions of the 1944 Act will be repealed. Other recent pressures have included that from Lord Rothschild which would place more research in a 'customer contractor' relationship with central government departments.

These tendencies must be questioned and reversed. It simply cannot be shown that centralized decisions, either by the UGC or by central committees dominated by the Secretary of State, lead to better and more rational outcomes. The health of higher education, like the health of society, depends on reversing centralization and placing responsibility where it can properly and sensibly be exercised.

The key lies in recognizing that both the autonomous and service traditions are weakened if institutional arrangements appropriate to one are imposed upon the other. In particular it must be quite clear that undergraduate education on the scale that exists in Britain now is a service and not an autonomous function. It is no longer an anomaly or an enclave: it is a stage of education, and part of a recognizable system accommodating everyone from toddlers to adults. It must be responsive to personal and public demand. It should be part of a varied and comprehensive education service in every area.

The local education authorities, then, should be responsible for education up to first degree level. They are already legally responsible for this in their own institutions, and the responsibility should be made real again. There must be no quangoid growths for central control, and both the advanced further education 'pool' and regional advisory councils should be abolished.

The immediate objections to these proposals constitute the original arguments for centralization and pooling: that higher education is a national rather than a local matter, that some authorities have more substantial institutions than they 'need', and others have none at all. But however potent these arguments may have been in the past, recent events have invalidated them.

In the first place, there has been the reorganization of local government. This means that we now have about 100 large local authorities. Few of these lack substantial institutions which either already offer enough places for local people or could readily be developed to do so.

The idea that there are large numbers of authorities which do not or could not provide higher education is based on ignorance. If each local authority had an 'institute' of higher education, that would give us about 100 of them — which, with over forty universities, would seem reasonable for a country of this size.

In the second place, public sector higher education has been reorganized too, creating larger institutions through the amalgamation of colleges of education or through joining colleges with polytechnics and other colleges. Not only is there a local administrative base, but a local institutional base as well.

Third, under the proposals advanced here, undergraduate education in universities would be part of the local authorities' provision. The simplest way in which the local authorities could secure this provision is by making grants to universities under Section 84 of the Education Act 1944. Happily the need to secure the approval of the Secretary of State for doing this was specifically abolished in the Education Act 1980.

The existence of widely dispersed institutions of higher education shows that the argument that higher education is a 'national' matter is spurious. Education as a whole is a national concern, but we have decided it should be provided locally. The arguments for doing so (accessibility, self-government, responsiveness) apply to higher education.

There are, of course, positive arguments for seeking to ensure that each local authority has its own higher education. There is its potential effect locally as a centre of intellectual activity. There is the advantage of returning the administration of all further and higher education to the same body —

so that work of all levels can be equally accommodated: academic drift and the neglect of lower level work can be resisted. There is the saving on student residence at 'national' institutions and the retention by authorities of the spending power of their students.

There would be some problems — most of them problems of transition. An authority with insufficient places, or with too many, would need to collaborate with other authorities until the balance was adjusted. But the terms of this collaboration would be for the authorities to decide for themselves. It might involve a joint education committee or a form of recoupment (as for school places) instead of the present elaborate nationally determined scheme.

A long-term problem might be the need of the individual student requiring a course which his authority did not provide. This problem would be acute only if an authority genuinely fell down on offering a reasonable variety of higher education: the pressures for it to do so would be the same as those on it to provide decent schools and would be at least as effective. But the individual student with a genuine need to go elsewhere could be supported at the authority's discretion on a recoupment basis — or could himself meet the same recoupment charge if he wanted the place that much. (Mandatory grants for maintenance are a different question and could be settled independently of these arrangements.)

The proposal itself would not only strengthen the service tradition: it would also preserve the autonomous tradition. Most obviously it would remove from the University Grants Committee huge responsibility for undergraduate education which it is ill-equipped to carry. The UGC would be a body supporting postgraduate work, wherever it occurred, and institutions devoted to postgraduate work alone. Its object would be to fund the preservation, extension and dissemination of knowledge for its own sake, in contrast to undergraduate education on the one hand and the particular support of research councils and government departments on the other. This task would be entirely within the compass of a central body, acting as a 'buffer' between the funding authority (the government) and the funded institutions.

It may be argued that an increase in postgraduate work is required, even that some universities which now accommodate undergraduates should turn wholly to postgraduate study. There is no need to be hidebound on the question: but experience suggests that the number of institutions making this change should be very small indeed.

It has been the argument of this paper that institutional change in British higher education has been piecemeal and thoughtless — to the point where important principles are in danger of being overlooked and lost. It is important to recognize that valued arrangements are no longer working as intended, that their consequences are now the opposite of what they are meant to be. In these circumstances it is important to return to an understanding of the principles involved and to establish new institutional arrangements which will preserve what is best in our traditions of higher education.

REFERENCES

Burgess, Tyrrell (1977) *Education After School* Gollancz and Penguin

Burgess, Tyrrell (1979) New ways to learn *Royal Society of Arts Journal* February 1979

Burgess, Tyrrell and Pratt, John (1971) *Innovation in Higher Education: Technical Education in the United Kingdom* OECD

Carnegie (1973) *Priorities for Action: Final Report of the Carnegie Commissioin in Higher Education* McGraw-Hill

Pratt, John (1975) The UGC Department *Higher Education Review* Spring 1975

Robbins (1963) *Higher Education: Report of the Committee Appointed by the Prime Minister under the Chairmanship of Lord Robbins* Cmnd 2154, HMSO

UGC (1967) *Memorandum of General Guidance* University Grants Committee

4

PAST FAILURE AND THE IMPERATIVE FOR CHANGE

by Gerald Fowler

A FAILURE TO PLAN

The Robbins Report,[1] whatever its many merits, did one great disservice to the development of higher education in Britain. That was the establishment of the 'Robbins principle' that places should be provided in higher education for all those qualified for and seeking them. As a result much discussion of the future of higher education has been demography-led, especially in official publications.[2] Thus a peaking of the 18-year-old age group in the early 1980s, followed by a decline in the late 1980s and early 1990s, suggests a series of alternative strategies, one of which is 'tunnelling through the hump' (the strategy of the present government), and another of which, arising primarily out of the logic of the demography, is the attraction of new client groups.[3] It is significant that whatever may have been said on the sidelines,[4] the attraction of new client groups was not proposed by government as an end in itself, but rather as a means of utilizing effectively the resources already provided within the system to cope with a larger 18-year-old group.

The weakness of basing planning on the Robbins principle, at a time when the age participation rate is failing to increase, and indeed is declining, is apparent; Britain will remain the Western developed country with the lowest participation rate in higher education apart from Portugal and Ireland for the foreseeable future, and may be passed by them before too long. That may be right, or it may be wrong; the case has to be argued. It may be that, pace OECD studies of the 1960s, there is no connection between educational investment provision for higher education in Britain and the country's poor economic performance. But that too is a proposition which remains to be demonstrated, and which, in the light of complaints about shortages of skilled manpower even at a time of high unemployment, seems implausible.

The Robbins principle always had several inherent weaknesses. The first was that there was no coherent definition of what counted as higher education, and hence of what qualified a student to partake in it. It is conventional to define higher education courses by their terminal point — taking that to be a point more advanced than GCE Advanced level. That tells us precisely nothing about the starting point. This problem becomes clear when we look at the varying basis upon which projections of higher education numbers have been made since the time of Robbins. Some of the 'error' in the earlier projections was not error at all, but stemmed simply from the fact that the assumption was made then, and is not made now, that entrants to teacher education courses would be larger in number than they are and would have a lower level of qualification (five 'O' levels, rather than the current requirement of two 'A' levels and passes at 'O' level in mathematics and English). The decline in the participation rate in higher education in recent years is principally explicable by the reduction in provision of teacher education and the new level of qualification required for entrance to it.[5] As for degree-level education, there is not the slightest evidence that even in the British system five passes in the General Certificate of Education, of which two shall be at 'A' level, is either a necessary or a sufficient condition of success. Students without this level of qualification, albeit of more mature years, succeed; some students with this level of qualification fail despite intensive teaching and mandatory maintenance awards; and in some subjects there appears to be no clear correlation between 'A' level grades and the class of final degree.[6] Further, the establishment of this as the basic level of qualification seems to have led to a social downgrading of courses, with a lower entry requirement, but nevertheless at higher education level. Numbers on Higher Diploma courses and above all on part-time courses of higher education, have showed even less buoyancy in Britain in the 1970s than those on degree courses; yet in the United States and in Europe these areas of work continue to develop, and it is arguable that we in Britain have a shortage of technicians.[7]

Worse, the maintenance of the Robbins principle has become an article of faith to which the academic community attaches more weight than successive governments. It was tacitly abandoned by government a decade ago, when the 1971 PAR Study of Higher Education stated that the then projections would require a level of 210,000 to 225,000 under-21s entering higher education in 1981, but that to provide places for 200,000 entrants would not 'wholly deny the principle' (whatever that could conceivably mean).[8] Similarly, the 1975 Public Expenditure White Paper[9] made financial provision for a lower number of students in 1981 than strict observance of the Robbins principle would have suggested. None of this mattered. The decline in the proportion of the age group who were both qualified for and sought places in higher education made unnecessary these attempts to 'come off Robbins' by sleight of hand; governments were saved by the unpredictable behaviour of young people. But governments do not learn; enjoying luck, they try their luck again. Without announcement, the Robbins principle has now been finally abandoned, with the 'capping of the pool' for public sector higher education,[10] and the establishment of tight cash limits for university expenditure.[11] Cash rather than qualified demand is now the sole determinant of the number of places to be provided. In short, there is *no* principle whatsoever behind the planning of higher education provision in Britain.

The principle was always more observed in the breach than in its maintenance, if one looks to the *balance* of provision within higher education. In 1976 a Prime Minister complained that there were 30,000 unfilled places in science and technology.[12] No one ever explained the figure, but if accurate, it reflected governmental policy over the previous decade. For the 1967-1972 quinquennium the balance set for the universities was 55 places in science and technology to 45 in arts and social sciences. For the following quinquennium the balance changed to 53:47. It is now near to parity. Planning took place on the 'carrot' principle: if places were provided in particular disciplines, young people would come forward to claim those places. They did not, and in consequence were censured by idiot politicians, seeking a scapegoat for their own mistakes. For a long time the expanding teacher education system was the cushion which absorbed the shock of governmental planning errors, taking up students qualified for study in the arts and social sciences for whom there were no places on degree courses. Its decline to 25 per cent of its 1971 level (initial teaching education places outside the universities) means that it can no longer be so. Compensation has come in the form of new arts or 'general' degrees in the colleges of higher education formed largely from the old colleges of education, but (quite forgetting the incursions into the Robbins principle made by manpower planning in respect of medical and as well as teacher education)[13] any match between the places available in higher education and the qualified demand, taking 'qualified' to mean qualified for study in particular disciplines, is partly an accident.

In this context, planning for the development of higher education in Britain can be seen to have become increasingly schizophrenic. Government consultative documents — the 1978 'Brown Paper', the present government's paper on post-experience continuing education in a vocational context, and the MSC document *An 'Open Tech' Programme* — assume the utilization of spare capacity in further and higher education in exactly those areas where there is little evidence of increasing student demand.[14] On the other hand there is an implicit assumption that the ability to profit from higher education (that is, by normal definition, to achieve a first degree) is usually, although not always, to be measured by the level of achievement in an examination set for 16 and 18-year-olds, which is itself designed (and here enters an element of circularity) to permit the successful achievement of a degree in one discipline or a combination of 2/3 disciplines in 3/4 years, with favourable staff student ratios and (by international standards) intensive teaching. This is the Robbins principle, alive, well and unargued. Even one of the two degrees in independent study extant in Britain, that at Lancaster University, observes it.[15] The evidence of the other degree by independent study, at North East London Polytechnic, as well as the success of the Open University, suggests that this is not a sensible planning assumption.[16]

Also implicit in the planning of higher education in Britain is the belief that it must rest upon the existence of a large number of institutions which are 'autonomous', not only in the sense of freedom from direction by the state, but also in their ability to operate independently of their peer institutions. The universities are here the model. Nevertheless, the polytechnics and the CHEs have sought to follow it.[17] Controls exercised by central government upon the development of public sector institutions are largely negative.[18] We thus have the problem that the individual autonomy of institutions leads to a questioning of their collective autonomy, which ought to be beyond question.[19] Put another way, it is the failure of the institutions to plan their provision collectively which is likely to provoke intervention by the state. In 1981 this is already occurring, with UGC allocations to the universities based upon subject preferences, and with the publication of a government consultative document suggesting a mode of financing polytechnics related in part to the 'vocational' content of their courses (whatever that means).[20] The irony is that individual autonomy of institutions is a hollow facade, in that in respect of full-time courses at least each institution apes its equals or betters. We can detect here the influence of validating bodies, staff from the academic community, academic peer groups in particular disciplines, and governmental 'arms-length' agencies largely staffed by academics.[21] The clearest evidence comes from the new CHEs, and their failure to provide new part-time or mixed-mode courses.[22]

We thus have a system of higher education which is based upon a principle which is no longer observed, was incomprehensible when first stated, was always denied by governments in their desire to secure an accretion to the stock of qualified scientific and technological manpower, and which runs counter to the principle of the individual autonomy of institutions. That of itself suggests that a new approach may be required.

The Fallacy of Separate Sectors
Successive governments have mistakenly perceived the problem as one of the financing and control of institutions. Hence they have attempted to establish new sectors of higher education, separate from the universities. Yet, it is alleged, these institutions always become mini-universities, in defiance of the intentions of government. The history of the CATs, which did become universities, is instanced as the best example of 'academic drift'.[23] They rapidly shed part-time and sub-degree work, and tried to achieve an academic subject balance in their provision which denied their purpose of providing applied and vocational courses. It is in part the growth within them of traditional non-applied studies, perhaps less well done than in some older universities, which has led the UGC in 1981 to single out some of them for discriminatorily harsh financial treatment.[24]

The CATs having been received into the bosom of the UGC, the then government went back to the starting point, and set out again along exactly the same road, with the creation of the polytechnics. This time however they were to be denied permanently the prospect of university status.[25] Despite this, they too have been charged with 'academic drift'.[26] Worst of all, many of the new CHEs of the 1970s, formed from colleges of education which have little expertise in the physical or applied sciences, have diversified into 'general' higher education (the strange DES term for non-teacher education) heavily orientated towards the arts and the social sciences. They contribute little to the provision of courses in business, management and the applied sciences, and those of them which did not have an FE college as one of their precursor institutions make little provision for part-time or sub-degree work.[27]

It is my thesis that this has happened because government has grasped the wrong levers of control. The positive argument for this view is that, whatever the dicta in White Papers about the need for applied studies or 'relevant' work,[28] the actions of government on more detailed technical matters have a precisely opposite orientation. Thus, the Woolwich speech which delineated the polytechnics was made in 1965, but it was not until a decade later that the law was changed to ensure mandatory grants for HND students. The DES Permanent Secretary of the time argued strongly against this move, on the grounds that to extend the mandatory principle to any course which did not have an entry requirement of two 'A' levels was to 'set one's foot upon the top of a slippery slope'. Thus, mandatory awards for DipHE students were acceptable, although it was already obvious that few DipHE courses would have an applied or vocational bias, but they were not acceptable for HND or HD students, and certainly not for those taking any other form of sub-degree vocational qualification. There has been no further extension of the mandatory principle. Similarly, within the public sector, part-time students are converted into full-time equivalents by a formula which downgrades part-time courses.[29] The present government expresses an interest in the development of resource-based learning, including distance learning; yet pure distance learning students within the system are non-persons, having no FTE equivalent at all.[30] Work is graded into five categories, with all sub-degree work graded lower than all degree work, and the relative renumeration of staff is then related to this grading. The student who is qualified to enter a full-time degree course has no incentive to begin his higher education with part-time study, for which he will receive no financial support from public sources, or with a sub-degree qualification; it remains impossible, save in a few instances, to carry credit forward from sub-degree study at higher education level to a degree course. Even the Open University mysteriously awards only one credit for a HND, normally deemed to be only a year's work short of a degree, although equally mysteriously giving three credits to those who possess a teacher's certificate, provided that they follow the approved course of studies. The government itself has been silent for nearly 2 years on the subject of the Toyne Report on credit transfer, the implementation of which would be the first tentative step towards making the higher education system 'progressive', with sub-degree study leading to higher qualification through the accumulation of credit.[31]

The negative side of the argument is best illustrated by the weakness of the reasons adduced by Crosland in support of local authority control of the polytechnics, said to be designed to ensure 'social responsiveness'. He suggested that the universities could not meet the rapidly rising demand and need for vocational, professional and industrially-based courses of higher education, some of them at below degree level and some part-time.[32] The argument is clearly valid if he meant that the *existing* universities could not meet that demand. But it is not obvious why thirty institutions, given a charter which precisely specified their objectives, and financed in accordance with those objectives, could not meet them just as well as thirty institutions under the control of local authorities.

Crosland went on to argue that to remove from further education all degree-giving institutions must depress morale in the further education system. Again, it is unclear why morale in a local FE college should be more depressed if the degree-giving institution along the road is a university rather than a polytechnic under the control of the same LEA. The policy of concentrating full-time and sandwich advanced work in the new polytechnics (subsequently of course denied by the reorganization of the colleges of education into CHEs, and in some areas never applied rigorously by the department in any event)[33] gives the lie to this argument. Nor did Crosland show clearly why 'social control', designed to ensure 'social responsiveness', must mean local authority control.

In this context, Crosland claimed that 'it is further desirable that local government, responsible for the schools and having started and built up so many institutions of higher education, should maintain a reasonable stake in higher education'. This sentence is to me incomprehensible. The responsibility of LEAs for the schools seems to be quite irrelevant, not least because the principal qualification offered by the schools, the GCE, is validated by the universities and not by any public sector institution. The schools have been the subject of repeated charges that they do not prepare pupils well enough for the demands of industry and commerce — ie that their work is biased towards theory rather than practice and application.[34] Further, we must ask what is a 'reasonable' stake for the LEAs in higher education? That local education authorities should be responsible for higher education courses meeting a purely *local* need (mainly part-time) does indeed seem reasonable.[35] Beyond that, it is impossible to attach any sensible meaning to the word. If we judge by the experience of chief education officers, not one of whom in England has to my knowledge any direct experience of administering an institution of higher education, then the LEA 'reasonable' share would be nil. It is certainly true that LEAs have 'started and built up' institutions of higher education; many of them have long since become chartered universities.[36] I assume therefore that Crosland's arguement, even if drafted by a civil servant, was purely political. Some LEAs had been offended by Circular 10/65 on Comprehensive Secondary Education, others had been offended by the transfer of the CATs to direct grant status in 1962, and others again were about to be offended by the Weaver Report on the Government of Colleges of Education, which weakened direct local authority control of these institutions but was partial compensation for the failure of the government to implement the Robbins recommendations with regard to the colleges.[37] To remove all regional colleges of FE, and some area colleges, from LEA control would thus have been too much. Further, there existed no national or regional mechanism of control for the new institutions: to create one was more difficult than to leave them with the LEAs.

There thus never was any coherent justification for local control of institutions offering courses serving a regional, national, or international need. Initiatives have come from the institutions themselves, not from their LEAs, and LEA control has in general been purely negative — sometimes (but rarely) refusing to give an imprimatur to proposed new course development, or in recent years restricting or reducing the finances of the institution, under pressure from central government.[38] In general, it is the negative nature of control over the public sector of higher education which gives rise to most concern. The UGC has been able to encourage developments in universities, and to back them with finance.[39] In so far as anyone has performed this role in the public sector, it has been Her Majesty's Inspectorate, which has operated a new version of the doctrine of advice and consent. They will give their consent if you take their advice. It is no criticism of HMI to point out that very few of them have themselves direct experience of teaching in or administering higher education. Nor do they have acess to any blueprint for meeting national manpower requirements which is not available to the institutions themselves.

The central problem lies in the very phrase, 'the public sector of higher education': For it suggests that there are sectors with distinct purposes, which are served by distinct methods of funding and control. It is indeed possible to categorize institutions of higher education by their functions.[40] But the division between universities, polytechnics, and other colleges of higher education in the the English/Welsh system does not correspond to any such categorization. The government suggests that PSHE should have a 'vocational' bias. There are two weaknesses in this. The first is that many university courses have a vocational bias and always have had (medicine, the law, etc.). The second is that vocationalism is in part, like beauty, in the eye of the beholder; whether a course is vocational or not depends upon the use to which the indivdual student subsequently puts it. If we were to ask which course, historically, had been the vocational preparation for senior administrators in the Civil Service, we should have to answer Greats at Oxford. It is certainly not obvious that, for example the University of Bath has a less vocational orientation than Bristol Polytechnic. It is worth remembering that degree courses in fine art, which must be accounted the least vocational of all courses, are primarily located in the polytechnics. Some CHEs, which still have teacher education as their main concern, are heavily vocational, even if their graduates now find it increasingly difficult to obtain employment in their chosen vocation; others, which have diversified widely, are among the least vocational institutions within the higher education system.

We must therefore ask whether it makes sense in the long run to maintain separate *sectors* of higher education, as opposed to funding a diverse range of institutions, each with its own defined function, with public financial support for the performance of that function. Put another way, the fundamental question to ask is how long two separate university grants committees, one called by another name, can co-exist. That Oxford University, Preston Polytechnic and Bulmershe CHE should not have the same purposes and the same pattern of courses is right and proper. It is not clear to me that the first should be funded through one mechanism of national control, and the other two, which are quite as different from each other as they are from it, should be funded through another.

We are then back to the fundamental question of determining by what mechanism government can ensure that institutions or groups of institutions perform the functions assigned to them by government on the basis of strong evidence, weak evidence or no evidence of national need. My thesis is that this has little to do with the ownership of institutions, or the mechanisms through which public funds are channelled to them. It has a great deal to do with the value accorded by government to particular types of course, particular modes of learning, to part-time as opposed to full-time study, to sub-degree as opposed to degree and post-graduate work, to research as opposed to (or as complementary to) teaching, and to the creation of a set of interlocking escalators through credit transfer rather than the maintenance of a set of fireman's ladders rising from the tender and ending marginally nearer to the sky but connecting with nothing. It is therefore to these questions that I turn in the next section of this paper.

BREAKING THE MOULD
If any reformed system of higher education is to operate efficiently, as well as in an innovatory manner, then institutions must be trusted adequately to perform the tasks laid upon them by their funding and managing bodies. The same proposition may be expressed in another way: funding bodies must base their decisions about what to support and what not to support upon an evaluation of the academic and educational value of existing or proposed activities. There can be no place for a permanent split between funding agencies and validating agencies. At present the UGC decides in what areas each university is, in its view, competent, providing that for which there is a national need; the university is then free to provide it, the shape of the package being in accordance with the academic judgement of its members. In the public sector, by contrast, HMI may suggest the provision of a course, an institution may propose it, the Regional Advisory Council may approve it and so may DES, and validation may then be refused by the CNAA, or by TEC or BEC or some other external body. The problem is further compounded by the judgement of the professional bodies in respect of 'vocational' courses; it is in their interest to restrict entry to the professions in order to maintain shortages of specific types of highly qualified manpower

and thus salary differentials. It is not in the national interest. Thus a course approved regionally and nationally, and validated by the CNAA, may not be accredited by a body such as the Institution of Electrical and Electronic Engineers, which is accountable to nobody save its own existing membership. Both rational planning and innovation thus become doubly difficult to achieve.

The government's proposals for the funding and management of the public sector of higher education entail the creation of a national body whose members are appointed by virtue of their expertise in higher education, or their knowledge of industry, commerce, or other sectors of employment. Its membership must therefore logically be indistinguishable in character from that of the CNAA, as well as overlapping that of the UGC. It may even overlap with those memberships in respect of particular appointees. Its task will be to distribute funds according to its own judgement of national need and institutional capability. It would therefore seem to be a work of supererogation for the CNAA, or other validating bodies, to do its job for it all over again, in respect of the validation of new or revised course proposals which fall within the basic framework established by the validating body in question. One could even have the embarrassment of the same person making different judgements when wearing different hats, through his membership of more than one body. In short, while existing roles may be maintained in respect of the provision of courses designed to meet local needs at what are locally oriented institutions, those institutions falling within the remit of any new national body must become essentially self-validating. It does not necessarily follow that they should award their own qualifications. Here, the CNAA document 'Partnership in Validation'[41] might be held to point the way forward to a system of national awards the standard of which was essentially guaranteed by the institution offering them, operating within defined ground rules, and periodically scrutinized by the academically competent body which supplies its funding. Unfortunately, no one, least of all the CNAA itself, seems certain of the precise meaning and intention of 'Partnership in Validation'. Numerous proposals have been called, but few are chosen.

Such a system clearly demands that recognized institutions of higher education should collectively determine what credit weighting to attach to each other's offerings, which may be parts of courses as well as whole courses. We return here to the thesis of collective autonomy rather than individual autonomy as the key to change within the system. This seems to me to be a matter for institutions themselves, although it may well be that there will be little movement, not least from the universities, without governmental pressure. The American analogy certainly suggests that institutions should collectively organize their own credit transfer arrangements, rather than look to some public body. The logic of that argument is that the 'credit transfer bank' suggested by the Toyne Report should itself be funded by institutions of higher education, their public financial support taking account of this additional commitment. Once such a system were established, there would be no good reason why any institution offering courses at higher education level, even if purely on a part-time basis to a local clientele, should not join the credit transfer consortium. It would of course be essential to ensure that such a consortium was not dominated by traditional university interests, with the effect of downgrading sub-degree work for credit purposes, as much of it is by the Open University.

There is nothing strikingly radical about such a proposal. In mediaeval and renaissance Germany wandering between universities was the norm rather than the exception. In the United States precisely such a credit transfer system operates. It is only in Britain that such proposals are regarded as dangerously innovatory. That is because of the view, normally unstated but almost universally held in Britain, that it is the single unified course which is the keystone of higher education. The autonomy of the course is more important than the autonomy of the institution.[42]

This doctrine clearly has more than one root. One is the belief that higher education is an activity undertaken in youth, and designed in some sense to qualify the partaker for a specific place in employment and life. It must therefore beam in on a narrow focus, with each element of the course a linear extension of what has gone before. Indeed, the same is true of courses which lead to qualification for entry to higher education, which are perceived as preparatory to degree courses. The *General* Certificate of Education in nothing of the kind. To my knowledge, no credit is given for expertise in plumbing, or in electrical maintenance. Students who wish to work in these areas should take CGLI or TEC courses — their qualifications then going unrecognized by most universities. Yet there is no evidence whatsoever that a student who has 'majored' in English literature at school, and has studied as a subsidiary plumbing and electrical maintenance (were such a creature to exist), would be a worse student of English literature at degree level than one whose subsidiary work was in history or in French. He might incidentally be a better householder, husband, and citizen, but those are questions which we normally disregard in education.

Another root of the dominance of the coherent single-subject course is the belief that the structure of academic disciplines reflects the 'real' world. It is not my purpose in this paper to discuss the structure of knowledge. Suffice it to say that this view has been widely questioned in recent years.[43] The only impeccable defence of the traditional single-subject Honours degree is that it has no vocational value, but is a training of the mind through exercise in the intricacies of a single academic discipline. (We are back to Oxford Greats and the Civil Service, not perhaps accidentally.) This is of course a denial of the vocational relevance of any course. Yet the demands of mature students reveal that vocational relevance must be different for each individual — the principal manifestation of this phenomenom being degrees by independent study.[44] The areas of study chosen by mature students in their final year of work for such a degree normally reflect their work experience hitherto, and their expectation of the demands of work thereafter. The government now accepts that mature continuing education students may require a different type of course and a different mode of teaching from the conventional undergraduate, and no one any longer questions the validity of the Open University credit-based degree. The pattern of 18-year-old teaching remains, however, essentially unchanged.

A further root of the difficulty lies in the belief that the 3-year Honours degree is the 'normal' mode of higher education, although peculiar to the United Kingdom and not even to all parts of that (granted the Scottish system). Institutions offering 2-year qualifications are common in other countries, both Francophone and Anglophone.[45] Four-year systems of two + two, are implemented in other countries. In Britain, an attempt to introduce a general 2-year course of higher education (as opposed to the vocational HND or HD) was the inception of the DipHE. It was determined that it should have the same entry requirement as that of a degree course, and it was thus killed stone-dead, except as a drop-out course for those who could not succeed on a degree whatever their initial qualifications, or in institutions which manifestly 'misused' the new course and abused the DES determined rule.[46] Yet nothing in the experience of other countries suggests that those entering 2-year courses with an entry qualification which would not qualify them for admission to a degree course may not contain a substantial proportion of students who will ultimately succeed in such a degree course.[47] Further, the reorganization of the colleges of education in Britain into CHEs was carried through on the principle that they should become mini-universities, offering the same range of courses, without the same range of academic expertise. They were the models of what might have been 2-year institutions, and most of them should become so, within a system which through credit transfer permits the progression of their students to other institutions and higher qualifications.

The arguments of the preceding paragraphs immediately suggest to any self-respecting politician the question 'How do we effect this change?' This is a serious question, since it is not obvious that either HMI (with most of their experience outside higher education) or administrators within DES (normally with no experience whatsoever of teaching in or administering higher education) could exercise informed judgement. Decision must therefore be left to an appointed body, largely composed of experts in the field. It cannot, however, sensibly be left to two separate bodies — the UGC, and a new national body for PSHE. In any event, initiative must come largely from the institutions themselves. There seems no good reason why a single national body should not invite proposals from all institutions as to their own future, with a verdict given upon them within a 3-year period. Equally, it is hard to see why it should not offer to institutions the option of running 2-year courses with a lower entry qualification than that currently demanded for degree courses, although if this were to be done sensibly it would demand a reform of 16-19 education to permit the accumulation of credit points rather than qualifications in specific disciplines.[48] Nor is there a convincing argument why proposed schemes should not include the merger of existing institutions, or the establishment of consortia formed from several existing institutions, or collaboration between institutions, with some serving of 'feeder' colleges to others. The alternative, if traditional course patterns persist, and as the traditional client-group declines in size, must be the closure of colleges; to share a declining number of students among the same number of competing institutions can make neither economic nor academic sense. For those working within institutions which survived, this might seem a viable policy; but this would be to neglect the national interest, since we are here discussing a national resource. It would therefore seem more sensible to rejig the system, on the basis of suggestions emanating from it, than to close parts of it, thus bringing us further out of line with international patterns of higher education.

In short, it seems to me desirable that we should move to a pattern of 2- and 3-year institutions, 3- and 4-year institutions and 4-year-plus institutions, on a principle of voluntarism, each institution proposing its own role, with a single national body ratifying that role and providing appropriate finance.

Within that system there can be no financial discrimination between types of institution. except as is appropriate to the expense of varying activities. At present such discrimination occurs not only between universities and other institutions, in respect of background support for research, but also between departments within institutions (the 'level' of work) and between individual members of staff (again 'level' of work, but also mere length of tooth, unrelated to its ability to tear academic and educational meat). Sometimes the provision of a subsidized home for a principal is no more than unexamined tradition, handed down from a precursor college. That is to say, within the present system reward is not directly related to the perceptions of utility which the organs of government have, judging by their stated priorities, less than coherent though these may be. In the end it is they and the public they represent who pay the piper. This is the hub of all the problems facing higher education in the 1980s. It is of course about value for money, and here the record can be made to look excellent, as every vice-chancellor will demonstrate. But it is also about money for changing social values, and their embodiment in institutional activities. Only a varied, flexible, and perhaps constantly changing pattern of institutions and of educational enterprises within them, can guarantee continued and ungrudging financial support.

The validity of this argument is clearest if we look at the relationship between course patterns and their varying entrance requirements, and institutional structures and the grading of staff with institutions. Here the universities are liberated, in the proper sense of the word. But in the public sector a department which concentrates upon part-time and sub-degree work has less opportunities for promotion, whatever the excellence of its staff, than one whose teaching record is less than good but which conducts a substantial amount of research and postgraduate work. Its head will be accordingly paid less. If it be national policy that certain sub-degree courses should run in the national interest (the HC or HD), then it cannot make sense that those teaching them should be paid less than those teaching postgraduate students, merely by virtue of the 'level' of work. The national interest is indivisible. It is time that the higher education system came to terms with this.

The national interest and perceptions of it change from time to time. New arrangements for the funding of higher education must therefore avoid the danger that the system might take on a new shape, but then ossify in it. Our successors in the twenty-first century may find a 1980s pattern of provision as deficient and unsatisfactory as many now find that created in the 1960s and 1970s. This danger may be avoided if there is, and is expected to be, a continuing dialogue between individual institutions and the national body (or bodies) and any sub-committees it may establish for subjects, types of course, or geographical areas. It is not steady evolution which is the enemy of excellence in higher education, but the imposition from above of half-planned but far-reaching change at irregular intervals. While the academic grass is not always greener the other side of the Atlantic, the American system of higher education does have the virtue that some part of it is always in a state of Heraclitan flux, responding to new need and demand. Contrast Europe: if we neglect the British experience, the French post-1968 'reforms', the German attempts to create comprehensive universities, and even the Swedish reforms of the last decade all suggest that an imposed once-for-all change of direction brings in its wake unforeseen difficulties and undesired consequences as well as predictable resentment. In America, evolution comes largely, though not wholly, in response to 'market forces'. In Britain, the dominance of government as the source of finance means that steady change can only be achieved if there is constant dialogue between the centre and the periphery, as well as between institutions and their potential clients. This cannot eliminate problems, of which staff tenure and the unwillingness of old academic dogs to learn new tricks are obvious examples; but at least it can ease their handling.

CHANGE IS DIFFICULT: REVOLUTION IMPOSSIBLE
Lest this paper appear starry-eyed, I must summarize briefly the obstacles to the reform of our system of higher education.[49]
1   Central government has a poor record of imposing change on the system, except either by addition to it (the creation of the polytechnics, etc.), or where it or its agencies or local government is/are the sole employer (the foundation of new medical schools, the contraction of teacher education), or where it has provided a positive financial incentive to change.[50]

2. The internal politics of institutions, where power normally resides with élites based on existing structures, inhibit change.[51]
3. The system of academic tenure and the absence of any comprehensive exchange/retraining facilities, stemming from the independence (autonomy) of each institution of higher education frustrate the redeployment of staff (contrast the USA).[52]
4. The diffusion of power between several levels of control in the British HE system has a conservative effect, because of the tension between the several organs of control. The best instance of this problem in recent years is the failure to resolve the problem of the control and funding of PSHE, which is now a long-running saga worthy of Hollywood.[53]
5. The links of the academic community, and especially of the universities, with Whitehall and the political parties also favour conservatism in the development of the higher education system, although the higher education lobby is now weak by comparison with the 1960s.[54]
6. 'Academic drift' blunts the edge of innovatory schemes, of which perhaps the best example in recent years is the failure of the CHEs to develop a character other than that of mini-universities, as has been pointed out earlier in this paper.[55]
7. Economic recession and the tight control of public expenditure restrict the introduction of innovatory schemes which are initially expensive — resource-based learning, distance learning, etc.[56] If the Open University had not been founded in 1969, it is likely that it would never have been founded at all.
8. The autonomy of individual institutions and the autonomy of the teacher (sometimes called 'academic freedom') also inhibit innovation — such as the spread of credit transfer, the supplementation of examinations by student transcripts, or the collective development and use of resource-based learning materials, and hence both the optimization of resource use throughout the system and a shift in the age pattern of students in favour of adults. Again, collective or collaborative autonomy (the freedom of institutions and of those teaching with them from direction by the state) may seem more important than individual autonomy, but that is not the tradition of the British system.

THE NEED FOR SYSTEMIC CHANGE

The reform of higher education is impossible without a reform of the educational system as a whole. Thus, attempts to extend the participation of under-represented client groups in higher education (adults or 'working-class' students)[57] raise fundamental questions about the relationship of HE institutions to the rest of the educational system (entry requirements, selection mechanisms, and the pattern of examinations/assessment/credit), and the financing of school, FE and HE institutions (funding cannot be divorced from control, nor the character of institutions from client demand, in a system where the client provides any substantial part of institutional finance). It is not the purpose of this paper to discuss these questions. Nevertheless, proposals for changes in the system, in the character of institutions, or in the pattern of courses cannot be divorced from them. The reform of HE made little progress in the 1970s precisely because no one envisaged the need for systemic change. In the 1980s reform must be comprehensive if it is to be reform at all.[58]

NOTES
1. Committee of Higher Education (1963) *Higher Education* Report of the Committee apointed by the Prime Minister under the chairmanship of Lord Robbins 1961-63; Cmnd. 2154; London: HMSO; esp. paras. 31-33 and Ch. VI.
2. *Higher Education into the 1990s, A Discussion Document* (1978) London: DES and SED. Layard, R., King, J., and Moser, C. (1969) *The Impact of Robbins* Harmondsworth: Penguin; chs 2 and 3. *Student Numbers in Higher Education in England and Wales* (1970) Education Planning Paper No. 2; London: HMSO. *Education: A Framework for Expansion* (1972) Cmnd. 5174; London: HMSO; paras. 114-128.
3. *Higher Education into the 1990s* (op. cit. 2 above) paras. 30-34
4. Houghton, V. and Richardson, K. (1974) *Recurrent Education* London: Ward Lock; esp. pp.123 seq. Schuller, T. and Megarry, J. (Editors) (1979) *Recurrent Education and Lifelong Learning* World Yearbook of Education 1979; London: Kogan Page. McIntosh, N.E.S., with Woodley, A. and Griffiths, M. in Pike, R.S. et al. (1978) *Innovation in Access to Higher Education* New York: ICED; pp.151-218.
5. Hencke, D. (1978) *Colleges in Crisis* Harmondsworth: Penguin.
6. Daniels, M.J.M. and Schouten, J. (1970) *The Screening of Students* London: Harrap/Council of Europe. Perry, W. (1976) *Open University* Milton Keynes: OU Press; esp. pp.135-198. McIntosh, N.E.S. (1978) *op. cit.* (4 above) and (1977) *Selection and Certification in Education and Employment* Paris: OECD; pp.44-58.
7. The IUTs in France run 2-year, purely vocational courses, and Junior Colleges in the USA 2-year, largely non-vocational courses. Canada has a mixture of institutional patterns. There are enough models from which to choose. Cf. *Short-Cycle Higher Education* (1973) Paris: OECD.
8. *Higher Education* (1972) Report by DES and SED (unpublished).
9. *Public Expenditure to 1979-80* (1976) Cmnd. 6393; London: HMSO; of which para. 10.8 (p.87) speaks of 'some increase in competition for entry in some subjects compared with recent years . . .'.
10. Hitherto the pooling system for AFE meant that everyone paid what everyone else spent. In 1979/80 (Education Act 1980), the pool was 'capped'. the metaphor revealing it to be not a pool, but an uncontrolled gusher; s. 32 and Schedule 6.
11. Cash limits were first imposed in 1973/74; by July 1981 they had become the weapon of fundamental restructuring of the university system; UGC

letter to university vice-chancellors, 1 July 1981.
12 Speech of the Rt. Hon. James Callaghan, MP, Ruskin College, Oxford, 16 October 1976. Cf. *University Development 1962-67* (1968) London: HMSO; paras. 331-335 and Appendix 12. *Education: A Framework for Expansion* (1972) London: HMSO; para. 136. *Op. cit.* (8 above). Gannicott, K. and Blaug, M. in Ahamad, B. and Blaug, M. (1973) *The Practice of Manpower Forecasting* Amsterdam/London/NY; pp.240-260.
13 Ahamad, B. in Ahamad, B. and Blaug, M. (1973) *op. cit.* (12 above) pp.261-309.
14 *Op. cit.* (2 above) *Post-Experience Education in a Vocational Context* (1981) London: DES. *An 'Open Tech' Programme* (1981) London: MSC.
15 Percy, K. and Ramsden, P. (1980) *Independent Study* Guildford: Society for Research Into Higher Education; Ch. 2.
16 *Op. cit.* (15 above). Perry, W. (1976) *op. cit.* (6 above). cf. Burgess, T. (1977) *Education After School* Harmondsworth: Penguin; pp.147-167.
17 For the modern university system and its origins see Green, V.H.H. (1969) *The Universities* Harmondsworth: Penguin; esp. pp.127-143. On the doctrine of 'autonomy' see Moodie, G.C. and Eustace, R. (1974) *Power and Authority in British Universities* London: George Allen and Unwin; esp. pp.45-47, and Berdahl, R.O. (1977) *British Universities and The State* New York: Arno Press (reprint of 1959 edn.); passim. 'Academic drift' (aping the university model) is documented for the ex-CATs in Burgess, T. and Pratt, J. (1970) *Policy and Practice* London: Allen Lane, and for the polytechnics (presciently) in Burgess, T. and Pratt, J. (1971) *Technical Education in the United Kingdom* Paris: OECD; pp.89-103, and Burgess, T. and Pratt, J. (1974) *Polytechnics: a Report* London: Pitman. A somewhat different view is taken by Venables, Peter (1978) *Higher Education Developments: The Technological Universities 1956-1976* London: Faber and Faber, who looks for a 'characteristic but not exclusive orientation of functions' in different groups of institutions (p.248), with which cf. Brosan, G., Carter, C., Layard, R., Venables, P., and Williams, G. (1971) *Patterns and Politics in Higher Education* Harmondsworth: Penguin; esp. pp.116-164.
18 Fowler, G.T. in Bell, R., Fowler, G.T., and Little, K. (1973) *Education in Great Britain and Ireland* London: RKP; esp. p.183. Cantor, L. and Roberts, I.F. (1972) (2nd edn.) *Further Education in England and Wales* London: RKP; Ch. 2. Cantor, L.M. and Roberts, I.F. (1979) *Further Education Today* London: RKP; Ch. 2.
19 Mannerkoski, M. (1979) The collective autonomy of universities *International Journal of IMHE* Paris: OECD; p.295.
20 The UGC letter of 1 July 1981 to the universities, and the consultative document *Higher Education in England outside the Universities: Policy,*

Funding and Management (1981) London: DES; esp. paras. 9-12.
21 On the operation of the CNAA, see Corbett, A. (1973) Degrees of esteem; in Bell, R., Fowler, G.T. and Little, K. *op. cit.* (18 above). A detailed study of the influences conducing to homogeneity of university provision may be found in Lockwood, G. (1981) *The Planning Process of the University of Sussex* Unpublished PhD thesis of the University of Sussex. Innovation and barriers to it are examined more generally in Kogan, M. (1978) *The Politics of Educational Change* Glasgow: Fontana/Collins; Ch.8, and in Becher, A. and Kogan, M. (1980) *Process and Structure in Higher Education* London: Heinemann; esp. pp.142-147. For the attitudes of the academic community and their effect upon institutional activities, see Halsey, A. H. and Trow, M. (1971) *The British Academics* London: Faber and Faber, with which compare Whitburn, J., Mealing, M. and Cox, C. (1978) *People in Polytechnics* Guildford: Society for Research into Higher Education, which reveals (for example) that already by 1972-73 32% of polytechnic academic staff 'considered that the polytechnics would become increasingly like universities' (p.38).
22 The government's consultative document *op. cit.* (20 above) reveals voluntary colleges in particular to be almost entirely concerned with FT degree-level work.
23 Burgess, T. and Pratt, J. (1970) *op. cit.* (17 above).
24 In the UGC letter of 1 July 1981 (11 above), Salford, Bradford and Aston Universities, all ex-CATs, were singled out for discriminatorily harsh cuts. On the details, cf. *THES* 25.9.1981, p.9.
25 This was clearly implied in the White Paper *Polytechnics and Other Colleges* (1966) Cmnd. 3306; London: HMSO, and in ministerial speeches, such as those of the Rt. Hon. C.A.R. Crosland at Woolwich Polytechnic (April 1965) and Lancaster University (January 1967), in which the new polytechnics were defined *by contrast with* the existing universities.
26 Burgess, T. (1977) *op. cit.* (16 above) esp. p.83; cf. on the general process Jencks, C. and Riesman, D. (1977) (Phoenix Edn.) *The Academic Revolution* London and Chicago: University of Chicago Press.
27 Cf. (22 above), and the statistical appendix to the government's consultative document of 27 July 1981 (20 above).
28 The word 'relevant' was used in the 1972 White Paper (12 above), which spoke of 'knowledge and skills related more directly to the decisions that will face them (students) in their careers and in the world of personal and social action' (para. 108), which if not vacuous is scarcely clear and precise.
29 Cf. the DES consultative document of 27 July 1981 (20 above) Table A: PTD students count as 35% and PTE as 10% of FT students, whatever effort goes into teaching them. Burgess (1977) *op. cit.* (16 above)

THE IMPERATIVE FOR CHANGE 97

protests that this undervalues part-time study (p.224).
30 The problem is recognized by DES in *Continuing Education* (1981), but not by MSC in *An 'Open Tech' Programme* (1981) (14 above).
31 *Educational Credit Transfer: Feasibility Study* (1979) Final Report, Exeter, Peter Toyne (Project Director).
32 Speech of the Rt. Hon. C.A.R. Crosland at Woolwich Polytechnic on 27 April 1965.
33 It is less surprising that in 1981 about 20% of all non-university HE students were outside the 90 or so colleges which were already centrally funded or were maintained colleges which were predominantly engaged in higher education or made major national provision in certain specific subject areas or provided initial teacher training, than that 15% of *full-time and sandwich* advanced students were in other colleges 15 years after the 1966 White Paper: see the government's consultative document of 27 July 1981 (20 above) para. 33.
34 Not least in the 'Great Debate' which began with the speech of the Rt. Hon. James Callaghan at Ruskin College, Oxford, 16 October 1976; cf. *Education in Schools: A Consultative Document* (1977) Cmnd. 6869; London: HMSO; para. 7.1.
35 It was the failure to distinguish such courses and the colleges offering them from those meeting a national or regional need which was a fatal flaw in the Oakes report *Report of the Working Group on the Management of Higher Education in the Maintained Sector* (1978) Cmnd. 7130; London: HMSO.
36 One, Loughborough, is more a monument to Principal Herbert Schofield than to the LEA, which he often led by the nose: cf. Burgess and Pratt (1970) (17 above) pp.31-33.
37 *Report of the Study Group on the Government of Colleges of Education* (1966) London: HMSO. On this and the link with Robbins, see Niblett, W.R., Humphreys, D.W. and Fairhurst, J.R. (1975) *The University Connection* Windsor: NFER; Ch. 11.
38 FECL 1/80 (1980) insisted that a course proposal must be supported by the maintaining LEA before the Regional Advisory Council or DES could consider it; changes in the allocation of the 'Pool' to LEAs followed the 1980 Education Act (10 above) and further restrictive change seems likely in 1982, with standard unit costs becoming the basis of funding.
39 See for example *University Development 1962-1967* (1968) (Report of the University Grants Committee) Cmnd. 3820; London: HMSO; Ch.V.
40 See Adelman, H. (1973) *The Holiversity* Toronto: New Press; pp.44-45; and Brosan, G. in Brosan, G. et al. (1971) (17 above) pp.116-122.
41 *Partnership in Validation* (1979) London: CNAA. Note that the CNAA's Committee for Institutions, which considers 'partnership' proposals, already undertakes the scrutiny of colleges which will be an essential part of any new national body's work.

42 There are of course exceptions to this rule: see Perkin, H. (1969) *The New Universities in the United Kingdom* Paris: OECD, and compare the many 'modular' degrees in the polytechnics and CHEs.
43 For example, Young, M.F.D. (Editor) (1971) *Knowledge and Control* London: Collier-Macmillan.
44 *Op. cit.* (15 above).
45 *Op. cit.* (7 above) Watson, C. (1973) *New College Systems in Canada* Paris: OECD. Markiewicz-Lagneau, J., Netter, M. and Lorieux, J. (1973)*Les Etudients des Instituts Universitaires de Technologie en France* Paris: OECD.
46 On the entry qualification, see *Education: A Framework for Expansion* (1972) (2 above) para. 112, which argues that the same entry qualification for a degree is necessary if DipHE courses are to be 'no less demanding intellectually than the first two years of a course at degree level'. Yet at North East London Polytechnic many students without the conventional degree entry qualification (sometimes of more than normal student age) succeed on the DipHE, and then proceed to complete a degree; cf. Burgess, T. (1977) (16 above) pp.147-159. This poses questions about both the value of GCE 'A' levels as a preparation for a degree, and the evaluation of the 'intellectual demand' made by a course.
47 But doubts are expressed by Bowman, M.J. and Anderson, C.A. (1974) *Mass Higher Education: Some Perspectives from Experience in the United States* Paris: OECD; p.16. They point to a constant attrition rate in the first two years of higher education in the USA, and lack of evidence that junior colleges provide an effective route into senior colleges for the socially disadvantaged.
48 No official body in Britain has yet made such a proposal, although at the end of 1981 it seemed likely that the Labour Party would shortly publish for discussion proposals for the reform of 16-19 education which might point in this direction.
49 Cf. the works cited in 17 and 21 above.
50 A good example of the operation of financial incentives was the creation in several *universities* (not polytechnics) in the late 1960s of Centres for Tribology, the money coming from the Ministry of Technology, not the UGC. The argument that there is no necessary connection between the title, status, and control of an institution and its willingness to perform the 'service function' is developed by Fowler, G.T. (1974) *Relations Between the Structures of Higher Education and the Service Function in University and Society: Towards a European Policy of Higher Education* Bruges: de Tempel; pp.113-146.
51 Cf. Lockwood, G. (1981) *op. cit.* (21 above).
52 In Britain the problem emerged in an acute form in 1981, when it was estimated that it would cost £250m to £400m to compensate tenrured staff declared redundant as a result of the cuts announced in the UGC

letter of 1 July 1981 (11 above).
53 *Polytechnics and Other Colleges* (1966) (25 above) was overtaken by the crisis in teacher education, resulting in *Education: a Framework for Expansion* (1972) (2 above), *Circular 7/73* (1973) London: DES, and the diversification of the colleges of education which followed. 'Pilkington numbers' of the 1960s, designed to ensure economy by eradicating 'weak' courses, had to be supplemented in the 1970s by 'Delany norms', fixing target staff: student ratios; but were temporarily undermined by the 'general approval' given by DES for new diversified courses in CHEs (1975). The Oakes Report (1978) (35 above) rightly provoked controversy, recommending as it did that parts of some 400 colleges should come under the aegis of two national bodies (for England and Wales), and the 1978 Education Bill, implementing it, fell with the 1979 general election. Since then the 'pool' has been 'capped', course approval has been tightened, and the government is again consulting about a national body (10, 20 and 38 above). There is much talk of 'unit costs' (38 above). Meanwhile, the caravan trundles on across the desert.
54 Kogan, M. (1975) *Educational Policy Making* London: George Allen and Unwin; esp. p.44. Becher, A. and Kogan, M. (1980) (21 above), pp.26-43 and 142-144.
55 Cf. 17, 21, 33, and esp. 26 above.
56 'Resource-based' teaching materials have a high initial production cost (not least in respect of staff time consumed), which must then be divided by the likely number of annual student enrolments multiplied by the number of years the course can run without substantial revision, with the resulting sum added to the genuine 'teaching' cost per student, before a sensible economic comparison can be made between traditional and non-traditional teaching methods.
57 Cf. esp. *Higher Education into the 1990s* (1978) (2 above) paras. 30-34.
58 The problem is well illustrated by Simon, B. and Taylor, W. (1981) *Education in the Eighties* London: Batsford, which deals with few of the problems which are the subject of this chapter, and none of the systemic *relationships* mentioned in this paragraph, despite its sub-title 'The Central Issues'.

5
CHANGE WITHIN A CONTRACTING SYSTEM
by William Taylor

To focus single-mindedly on institutional development as the barometer of change in higher education is significantly to misconceive the nature of educational processes. The shaping effect of institutional forms on behaviour is more evident and direct in some places than in others. The structures of universities and colleges tend to be what is fashionably described as 'loosely coupled'. They are capable of accommodating a great deal of movement in social process, in modes of control, curriculum, pedagogy and assessment, without changing in outward form. On the other hand, there is no guarantee that altered organizational arrangements will have corresponding effects at every level of internal operation, least of all within individual departments. The effect of a new name, a new legal status, new sources of funds, different modes of course approval and validation, even a changed clientele is sometimes not very evident in the daily practice of lecture hall, laboratory, tutorial room and departmental meeting.

Important changes take place in the content of higher education within apparently unchanged institutional structures. As the research findings appear, the books are written, the conferences take place and the beneficiaries of sabbatical leave return to their posts, so intellectual paradigms are modified, content and methodology are adapted, syllabuses and examination papers revised.

This continuous process never makes the headlines, seldom forms the subject of even a chapter in the report of a committee of inquiry. The curriculum of higher education is a sadly neglected area of study. But without some measure of political understanding of and sympathy for the internal dynamics of change in higher education, the best intentioned institutional reforms may fail to achieve their purposes.

Our political and administrative concern with form rather than content allows the discussion of change in higher education to become dangerously over-simplified, in terms of conflicts between traditionalists and progressives, conservatives and reformers. Too much of the energy left over from teaching and research is wasted on debates conducted within a framework of sterile positions labelled élitist and democratic, relevant and academic, theoretical and practical, open and closed, terms which facilitate our discourse at the cost of trivializing our understanding.

During the 60s and early 70s, when internal changes were called for, these often took place by means of addition rather than reorganization. Faculties of social science and of education were set up, multi-disciplinary and professional centres and units created alongside the existing structure of departments, schools and faculties. Only in some of the new foundations, where structures could be devised ab initio, was there anything like a sustained attempt to devise radically new academic and social frameworks and processes.

In conditions of growth, both within institutions and in the system of higher education as a whole, there is generally speaking an absence of threat to existing roles, statuses and identities, and a great deal of opportunity for the creation of new ones and the satisfaction of personal ambition. Even those who have viewed many aspects of growth with distaste ('more means worse'), or who disapproved of the introduction of particular courses or the setting up of new schools or complete institutions, were able to deal with the late-comers either by labelling ('Mickey Mouse courses'; 'third rate degrees') or by ignoring the new presence.

These mechanisms will not suffice to handle rationalization and contraction. Becoming smaller, shedding certain subjects and levels of work, responding to new needs without the lubrication provided by growth (Taylor 1980) will impact upon individual institutions rather than simply on the system. The consequences for morale, for styles of institutional and system management and for individual careers are already visible.

There is no *intrinsic* reason why demographic decline should lead to institutional rationalization and contraction, especially in relation to an age participation ratio of only 12.4 and (if we exclude the Open University from the calculation) modest growth in numbers of part-time students. The current trend towards restricting the range of work undertaken by some institutions, of reduction in size, and the lack of institutional innovation, have more to do with:

Public expenditure policies

A rejection of the claims of higher education to contribute significantly towards a healthier economy, a more responsible polity and a more equal society

The failure and abandonment of many of the *ideas* concerning future structures that fuelled expansion, such as mass higher education, recurrency between education and work, the comprehensive university.

A reassertion of the importance of 'standards', a resurgence of the latent anti-intellectualism that characterizes British society and of fears about the subversive influence of some staff, students and unemployed or under-employed graduates

A lack of confidence in forecasts of the future and in the direction of the impact of new technologies on both pedagogy and employment

The changes that take place in academic and social structures and process in the eighties will occur in a context of threat and defence against threat. If the cuts in targets and income are sharp enough, the volume of institutional change might be considerable, just as it was in the colleges of education during the seventies reorganization. Indeed, the amount of institutional, as distinct from system adaptation may need to be much greater than in earlier periods of growth (Taylor and Simon 1981).

Although it has been stated that rationalization will involve differential treatment on the basis of academic judgements, rather than simply relying on the market or sharing out losses equally, such a policy will inevitably provoke sharp academic and political responses, and it seems likely that in the event all three elements — judgement, the market, and the principle of equal misery — will play some part in the outcome. This is particularly likely when decisions affect the balance of activity in work between the sectors. In some subjects there is no justification on grounds of quality for closing or running down university departments when the same subject continues to be offered in polytechnics and colleges. There may be other relevant arguments, such as maintaining institutional viability in regions and localities, local or vocational need, or sharing out job losses among members of more than one trade union — but these have nothing to do with standards of work or the quality of the staff and students involved.

BINARY OR BEYOND

Many of the issues that currently feature in arguments about the future co-ordination and control of higher education in the United Kingdom have been on the agenda for nearly twenty years. They remain unresolved because they raise thorny and politically sensitive issues about the relations of central and local government, about institutional autonomy and public accountability, and about academic status and course control.

The Robbins Committee wished to preserve the distinction between university and non-university institutions, although they would have brought the then 'third sector' of teacher education under university management and permitted a continuing process of transition from non-university to university status. This was rejected in Anthony Crosland's so-called 'Woolwich' Speech in 1965, although ministers and officials were subsequently at pains to argue that the notion of a binary system embodied no assumptions about hard and fast boundaries between the sectors, and tried to argue for *pluralist* rather than *binary* images (Crosland 1974).

Over the years ministers of both political persuasions have repeatedly restated this testament. Arguments that all degree work was properly a concern of the universities soon faded away. A few academics retained a belief in and wrote about the virtues of the comprehensive university (Pedley 1969) and some members of parliament and councillors of a radical persuasion continue to raise from time to time the possibility of bringing the whole of higher education under local control (most recently in discussions included in the 5th Report of the Education, Science and Arts Committee of the House of Commons in December 1980). Even they have not gone so far as to advocate the redesignation of existing universities and polytechnics.

The discussion of change has largely been limited to modifications in finance and control *within* the university and non-university sectors, and although, if implemented, these could have important long-term effects for the relations of institutions across the sector boundaries, there is still no really serious direct challenge to the binary principle as such.

For binary the system remains. Despite very great institutional diversity within each sector, the pluralist image never caught on. Whatever similarities there might be, following the Weaver Report, in styles of institutional government, and however hard the DES might work to ensure that residential provision, building standards or student awards for similar courses are the same, irreducible differences remain between universities and the rest.

Prominent among these differences are the freedom of institutions to spend the money available to them as they see fit, the ability to offer new courses and programmes of study, and the right to assume responsibility for academic standards. Other contrasts, such as salary scales and research opportunities are either secondary or, like questions of status, public standing and attractiveness to students, derive from these central issues.

There is of course a great deal of co-operation across the binary line, much of it informal and individual rather than institutional and collective. There are plenty of examples of joint course planning, the sharing of teaching resources, inter-departmental research activities, the exchange of examiners and supervisors and the validation of academic and professional awards. On the non-academic side, there is co-operation on computers, libraries, careers advisory services, residence, student health and sports facilities.

Nonetheless, it could be argued that the binary line has hardened in recent years. In part, this is a function of its longevity. We have grown used to the system. Many heads of institutions and senior staff have grown up with it. Some twenty-five per cent of places on CNAA boards and committees are filled by university men and women, although the proportions tend to vary somewhat between levels and particular committees. The staff of universities on the one side, and polytechnics and colleges on the other, are members of different trade unions, which do not always see eye to eye on matters of policy or procedure.

Some of the first generation of polytechnic directors previously held university posts of one kind or another. Several had been professors. At least one came straight from a fellowship at an Oxford college. Many of this generation of directors are still in post. But newcomers are taking over, most of whom have served their apprenticeship as administrative and academic leaders within polytechnics, few ever having held a post in a university (Taylor 1981).

Why not? There is nothing sacrosanct about having had university experience and much to be said for offering opportunities for progression to the highest ranks through the public sector itself. But given the nature of the system, such trends will inevitably reduce the possibilities of real sympathy and understanding across the binary divide.

In a year or two there will be fewer public sector colleges validating awards through the universities, another kind of link that, for all the criticism levelled at it, has had its uses as a form of cross-binary connection.

In conditions of declining demand, the institutional co-operation at local level that has been urged on universities and polytechnics from so many sources in recent years seems unlikely to feature high on staff agendas. Although students may find it difficult to find places in first-choice institutions for the next year or so, as the demographic trough deepens there is likely to be sharper competition for the available trade. Some polytechnic people have already expressed chagrin at the way in which university autonomy permits their neighbouring institutions to start up new courses and options without what they see as the rigmarole of local authority, regional council and DES approval. Such feelings will be expressed even more forcibly when the survival of departments, faculties and whole institutions is at stake.

One of the happier aspects of co-operation has been the participation of college, polytechnic and university staff in the work of numerous disciplinary and professional associations, voluntary bodies that receive nothing by way of subsidy, and which depend upon the willingness of members and officers to organize national, regional and local meetings, to edit newsletters and to do all those other things that facilitate voluntary association.

CO-ORDINATION, CONTROL AND ACADEMIC IMPERATIVES

The freedom of universities to maintain such teaching and research as they see fit, to offer whatever courses they like, to open and close departments and units at will, has always been circumscribed by the realities of quinquennial funding and the dual support system. On the whole, although they may huff and puff, vice-chancellors, finance committees and senate can see the writing on the wall as well as anyone else (after all, some of them helped to put it there). There have always been enough scandalous examples of advice ignored, property acquired and 'unnecessary' courses maintained to keep happy those who like nothing more than raking muck around in Augean stables. For the most part, however, the network of connections between administrators, institutional authorities and academics has kept a more or less responsive and workable pattern of initiatives and decisions in being, of a kind that certainly does not justify the suggestion that universities have been at liberty to pursue their own selfish ends, without reference to 'social need', 'community welfare' or those other ill-defined imperatives which critics readily trot out as evidence of their own superior perspicacity and altruism. When ministers and bureaucrats align themselves with such criticism we should be daft not to listen. But given the kind of political arrangements under which we live — and which it is one of the important functions of higher education to foster and protect — agents of the state have no necessary monopoly of wisdom in such matters.

For every academic who vows to fight to the death the alleged dirigism of the UGC and to resist every attempt to limit freedoms that for the most part have never existed in pure form, there are two, three or four others who find wisdom in the equally facile notion that 'he who pays the piper calls the tune', and who by so doing appear to contract out altogether from the political processes by means of which the choice of tune is decided and the level of payment fixed.

If we try to avoid being dazzled by the illuminated wording of university charters, by the lack of formal requirements for the external approval of course proposals and guarantees of academic quality, what do we find?

In most subjects there exist networks of information and influence, contributed to by the existence of scholarly associations, by the holding of conferences and meetings, by the activities of external examiners, and through the journals and publications of the trade. These 'spontaneous orders' (Hayek 1976) generate and make available for use far more information than could possibly be produced by administrative process. Judgements of quality and promise made within such networks influence staff and student choice, help shape the biographies of individuals, colour the responses that funding bodies make to requests for research support. To a greater extent in the future than in the past such judgements will play a part in the recommendations that the UGC's specialist subject committee make to the parent body.

Academic judgements have always influenced resource distribution between as well as within universities. Hitherto, such network-generated judgements have been reflected in budgets mainly through student choice — growth conscious institutional and departmental heads established their resource claims on the basis of bourgeoning student demand and worsening ratios — and external research support.

Such mechanisms are appropriate to growth, less suitable as a way of managing contraction. Where the making of judgements embodies a threat to resource levels — even to institutional existence — their basis will be challenged. There will be demands that criteria be made explicit. The links — informal, conventional but nonetheless real — that have bound together finance, the initiation of new courses and the maintenance of academic standards will come under strain. It is important, not least for universities themselves, that they should not be allowed to snap. For it is the separation of finance and control, course approval and academic validation that has bedevilled improvements in the co-ordination and effectiveness of public sector higher education, and which none of the recent proposals for a new national body for non-university higher education are likely to solve.

INFORMATION NETWORKS FOR CO-ORDINATION
To be effective in relation to purpose, institutional decision making not only needs to take place within an appropriate framework of governance and to be able to count upon adequate support, both material and moral, it also requires larger quantities of comparable information that are unlikely to be avail-

able from its own resources and which cannot be obtained in printed form.

Co-ordination between and within institutions is dependent on access to information generated by networks that cut across institutional boundaries, and which, although they may have a formal or quasi-formal character, also operate informally, in transmitting, sieving and sorting facts, interpretations, judgements, reputations and rumours.

If decisions about closing departments, merging institutions or rationalizing teaching are to give due weight to all the relevant considerations, including academic quality, they must reflect the full range of information that circulates within these networks, and avoid giving undue prominence to the views of the better organized interest groups. There are those who complain that the present policies of the UGC and the likely approach of a national body for the public sector transgress the rights of institutions to make their own academic judgements. They may be overstating the extent to which institutions act rationally and in the general interest. But such protests serve to remind us that only *within* institutions and awarding bodies will academic considerations be given due attention. The emphases in external decision making are more likely to be political, administrative, managerial or employee-focused.

Given the way in which higher education is currently financed, complete institutional autonomy or total reliance on market forces is out of the question. This being so, the capacity to establish criteria, make judgements and reach decisions on the basis of something more than political, administrative, managerial and employee-focused considerations (important though all of these may be) is an essential desideratum of mechanisms for co-ordination and control. This is not achieved by treating resource control and academic control as separate processes subject to different kinds of rule. It is by means of resource distribution that academic judgements are made to stick. It is through academic judgements that resource distibution is legitimated. Neither can stand alone.

THE NATIONAL BODY

A split system of course approval and academic resource approval worked reasonably well in conditions of growth, when there was plenty of scope for the addition of new courses, and institutions could present their funding bodies with bills for academic resource approval — improved staffing, more library resources, enhanced administrative back-up — with the virtual certainty that these would be met. These conditions no longer exist.

When resources are scarce, decisions need to be informed by kinds of academic judgements that arise from within subject and professional networks, and which at present facilitate the work of panels and boards of the CNAA. There are insufficient means whereby on the one hand course approval decisions and on the other academic resource acceptability can be related each to the other. Formal mechanisms for this purpose do not exist. The informal ones are inadequate.

CNAA have the task of approving or withholding approval from institutions as suitable locations for the teaching that leads to the council's awards, and accrediting the courses and programmes of study for such awards. But it has no control over the resources available in support of such courses. If through inability or unwillingness to devote the necessary funds, a maintaining authority makes it impossible for an institution to meet the council's requirements, academic approval can be denied or withdrawn. This could rapidly lead to the closure of courses or of the whole institution. So far it has not happened, although there have been one or two close shaves. The decisions of the funding body are taken independently of the relevant academic and professional considerations, and are uninformed by any assessment of national need or the existence of alternative provision.

But perhaps today the emphasis should not be on the difficulties that present arrangements make for the approval of new courses but on their inadequacies in coping with unilateral course discontinuation. Institutions do not have to seek approval to close courses down. The decision is likely to be made by the polytechnic's or college's academic board or planning committee, and to turn on such considerations as the pattern of staff retirements and resignations, short-run student demand, the possibility of useful savings, and opportunities to protect existing jobs. As happened on more than one occasion with the former colleges of education, the effect of many separate decisions concerning under-recruiting courses can be to reduce total provision below that needed to meet, for example, requirements for teachers in a particular specialism, and even to cut the number of places below the total of qualified candidates in that subject.

There are at present no formal mechanisms in the public sector whereby proposals of this kind can be made known and discussed before decisions are taken, and the informal networks whereby information on these matters can be circulated and acted upon are in some subject areas not sufficiently well developed to fill the gap.

The arrangements which emerged in November 1981 as agreed between the DES and local authority associations did not deal adequately with this question. They failed to give representation to institutions or validating bodies at the highest level (known as the 'Committee for Local Authority Higher Education') and provided for only one CNAA member and no university representation whatsoever at the second level ('Board for Local Authority Higher Education'). No formal structure of academic advisory committees was proposed. Instead ad hoc groups would be established to examine particular fields of academic provision. The proposals made no mention of how teacher education, an important area of provision in which both universities and public sector institutions are heavily involved, might be managed, although discussions in the Advisory Committee for the Supply and Education of Teachers (ACSET) suggested that DES was moving towards the establishment of some kind of transbinary machinery for the closer monitoring of courses and recruitment.

THE STRUCTURE OF THE ACADEMIC PROFESSION

If significant institutional change could be brought about by a simple renaming of departments and units, by drawing up new regulations and drafting fresh ordinances, it would be expeditious and easy. Because it has to do with the identities, roles, statutes and group participation of people, it is difficult and often very slow.

Even during the working lives of many serving academics, there has been a considerable shift in the extent to which staff are prepared to accede to institutional changes. In Venables' (1973) words, we have moved from required assent to voluntary consent, from 'compliance perforce' to 'consent perhaps'.

With staff accounting for seventy-two per cent of total spending, there are few institutional changes that do not have implications in terms of disestablishment of posts and redundancy on the one side or additional expenditure on the other.

The chance of changes in the structure of the academic profession featuring on the agenda of institutional change for the eighties and nineties is diminished by expenditure implications which in the current climate are unlikely to be acceptable. Furthermore, immediate anxieties among staff about the nature of tenure and the possibility of redundancy mean that every proposal for restructuring, whatever its long-term academic merits, is likely to be judged in relation to its short-term impact on jobs.

The larger number of grades in the career structure of the Burnham Further Education scales has to be seen in relation to the great variety of kinds of work to which such scales apply. In universities there are effectively only three grades. The lecturer scale extends over seventeen points, the senior lecturer/reader scale over eight. Professorial salaries are fixed in relation to a minimum and an average, institution by institution. Universities do not have staffing establishments such as those found in polytechnics and colleges, but at present not more than forty per cent of their staff may occupy positions on the senior lecturer/reader scale or as professors. The current proportions of university staff in each grade are professors thirteen per cent, senior lecturers and readers twenty-six per cent, and lecturers sixty-one per cent.

Criticisms of current arrangements include:

Anxiety about the shortness of the period of probation

Progression up the scale is largely a matter of seniority and gives little incentive for the display of or recognition of merit

Absence of flexibility

The effects of the erosion of differentials, specially in the case of professors

Difficulty in coping with the very uneven age distribution created by rapid growth followed by stagnation of recruitment

Union opposition to making three- or five-year term appointments, and the consequent tendency in the face of resource cuts and uncertainty to recruit larger numbers on one-year contracts

Difficulty in giving adequate recognition to the rather different kinds of contribution represented by teaching, research and administration.

It seems unlikely that these problems will be overcome until the overriding issue of tenure has been dealt with. Tenure is often defended on grounds of academic freedom, when the chief motivation is in fact job security. Attacks on it on the grounds of inflexibility often disguise feelings that it constitutes an outdated privilege, appropriate to a period when scholars were also gentlemen, but out of place in the context of contemporary industrial relations, and perhaps offering publicly financed shelter for some kinds of dangerously subversive opinions and activities.

There *are* grounds for linking tenure with academic freedom, but not necessarily in respect of every single academic who has succeeded in satisfying the hitherto less than onerous demands of a three-year period of probation. There *are* economic, managerial and educational reasons for wanting changes in the system of tenure, but these are rightly opposed when, as is sometimes the case, they merely disguise political prejudice.

It is to be hoped that recognition of the entrenched nature of views on the future of tenure will encourage moves towards some kind of compromise. This might offer existing kinds of open-ended contracts only to more established and productive academics, and be coupled to the introduction of extensive periods of probation and the division of the existing lecturer-senior lecturer/reader scale into three or four steps, spanning, for example, scale points 1 - 6, 4 - 13, 10 - 20 and 18 - 23, plus a professorial range. The effect would be to introduce a greater measure of hierarchy into the structure of the university profession, bringing it closer to public sector higher education, to the civil service and other kinds of public employment.

The practicability of 'buying the rule book' in this way turns on the possibility of introducing early retirement and redundancy terms a good deal more generous than those of the existing PRCS, and perhaps not dissimilar to the 'Crombie' arrangements which applied to staff of the former colleges of education.

Changes in the structure of the academic profession such as those discussed in previous paragraphs have important consequences for institutions. But even without them, institutions will be affected by current trends.

Even with the lubrication that a generous early retirement scheme might provide, the average age of staff will go on rising at a time when maximum flexibility of response in the face of changing external conditions will be damanded. Quite apart from such incommensurable factors as the relation of innovativeness to age, this will make it more difficult for institutions to cover new development in many subject fields and to keep abreast of research.

The sharper clashes of interest that go with diminishing resources will call for more sophisticated political management, and for accounting techniques that enable competing claims to be adjudicated on the basis of arthmetic rather than committee clout. The last few years have seen a spate of publications concerning the calculation of staff/student ratios and workloads. Internal and external concern with such matters are both likely to increase.

If these and other consequences will be felt within institutions, there are others which have to do with the relations between the two sides of binary. Despite the post-Houghton equalization, and the attempts of policy makers to assert the realities of 'parity of esteem' between the sectors, there are very great differences in the average levels of qualification of staff in universities and polytechnics, such as to make it unlikely that we shall see a move towards a unified academic profession.

Halsey (1981) has shown that whilst in terms of social class mix, educational origins and schooling there are few crucial differences between university and polytechnic teachers, the former contain a much higher proportion of first-class Honours (42.9 per cent against 18.9 per cent) and that whilst a quarter of university teachers have published twenty papers or more, half the polytechnic teachers have published nothing at all. Yet there is a sense in which university and polytechnic teachers constitute two strata in a single hierarchy. Asked to name the best departments in their subjects, both university and polytechnic staff chose university departments, with Oxford, Cambridge, Imperial, LSE, UCL, Manchester and Edinburgh strongly to the fore. Given the chance of a job in a university at the same salary, three-quarters of the polytechnic staff would take it. Half of the university teachers would not go to a polytechnic even with increased pay. On many matters affecting conditions of service, such as common salary scales, staff/student ratios and support services, university staff disagree sharply with their polytechnic counterparts.

Halsey found that the contrasts in the proportion of first-class Honours graduates recruited to the two kinds of institution after 1970 were still very marked. Competition for students in those subjects and professional specialisms taught in both universities and polytechnics might leave some of the latter with less able groups and fewer postgraduates, diminishing the attractiveness of polytechnic teaching. It seems likely, however, that a shortage of opportunities for academic employment may enable non-university institutions to recruit larger numbers of well qualified staff from among recent postgraduates. Anecdotal evidence suggests that such a trend has become marked over the past three or four years.

Institutional change in the eighties and nineties will thus inevitably be affected by the kinds of people who hold academic appointments during this period, by the structure of the academic profession of which they are members, and by the patterns of salary and reward, incentive and sanction, freedom and constraint to which they feel themselves to be subject.

SUMMARY AND CONCLUSION

I have argued in this paper against identifying institutional change, or lack of it, with change in curriculum, pedagogy and assessment, and for the importance for giving due weight to process and content. I have suggested that during periods of growth adaptation and change take place largely within systems rather than within institutions, but that contraction demands a response from individual universities, polytechnics and colleges.

Institutional change demands the availability of large volumes of information. Much of this is generated within the more or less 'spontaneous orders' of the political, administrative, managerial, employee, professional and academic networks by means of which those involved in higher education interact. Disciplinary and professional networks are transbinary in ways that the others are not, and generate the judgements needed as a basis for informed political, administrative and managerial decisions. Present arrangements, however, do not give sufficient emphasis to such academic and professional considerations and values.

There are few signs of the once hoped for weakening of the binary distinctions that characterize the institutional framework of higher education. In certain respects gaps between the sectors are widening. An aspect of this is the division of academic and resource control in the public sector, which none of the proposals so far made for the establishment of a national body will remedy. A possible way forward might be to restructure the CNAA in ways that place course approval and academic validation in a more fruitful relationship.

An important area of institutional change concerns the structure of the academic profession. There are dangers in confusing a defence of tenure based on academic freedom with the retention of kinds of job protection beyond those offered by employment legislation. Given the lack of flexibility and skewed age distribution consequent upon rapid growth followed by stagnation in recruitment, there are good reasons for looking again at scales and contracts. In the present context, however, any such re-examination, whatever its motive, is likely to be interpreted in relation to cuts and job security.

Scant justice has been done in the preceding paragraphs to the range of problems that institutions will face in responding to rapid technical and social change in a climate of contraction and financial restraint. Much might have been said about the implications of new technologies on both employment and higher education delivery systems. The Open University and 'open tech' do not exhaust the present and likely future possibilities of distance education. Nor has attention been given to the implications for that substantial number of institutions who will undertake initial and in-service teacher training of devising new patterns of professional preparation involving greater co-operation with teachers and schools over longer periods than at present, such as have recently been under consideration by ACSET and others. I hope that these, and the many other aspects of institutional change that might have featured in this chapter, will be covered in other volumes in this series.

REFERENCES

Crosland, A. (1974) Pluralism in higher education. In *Socialism Now* London: Cape

Halsey, A.H. (1981) *Higher Education in Britain — a study of university and polytechnic teachers* Report to the SSRC (mimeo)

Hayek, F.A. von (1976) *Law, Legislation and Liberty* Volume 2 *The Mirage of Social Justice* London: Routledge and Kegan Paul

Pedley, R. (1969) *The Comprehensive University* Exeter: University Press

Taylor, W. (1980) Managing contraction. In Farquar, R. and Housego, I. (Editors) *Canadian and Comparative Educational Administration* Vancouver BC: University of British Columbia

Taylor, W. (1981) *Organisational Culture and Administrative Leadership in Universities* Paper for Conference on Administrative Leadership, University of Illinois, July 1981 (mimeo)

Taylor, W. and Simon, B. (Editors) *Education in the 80s: the central issues* London: Batsford

Venables, P. (1973) *Dissolving the Walls between the Worlds of Education and Work* Paper for the Anglo-American Conference, Ditchley, Park, September 1973 (mimeo)

6

THE CONTRIBUTION OF THE PUBLIC SECTOR

by Brian Cane

THE PUBLIC SECTOR

The traditional full-time university Honours undergraduate is by no means the typical student at initial course level in higher education today. The public sector has about as many full-time students as the university sector; additionally, the public sector has a substantial number of part-time students whereas the university sector has very few, apart from those at the Open University.

FIGURE 6.1
England and Wales: all students on advanced courses in 1977/78 [1] (excluding postgraduate)

	Full-time	Part-time	Total
Universities	194,359	3,140	197,499
Public sector	192,751	118,501	311,252
Both sectors	387,110	121,641	508,751
Open University	–	49,062	49,062
Total	387,110	170,703	557,813

The varied range of provision in the public sector is summarized in official tables under the heading 'Advanced Courses'. This term covers a range which includes degrees, higher diplomas and professional qualifications varying in course length from two to four years full time and in standard from Pass to Honours degree or the equivalent. At first, this variety may seem a disadvantage in comparison with the predominance of the three-year Honours degree in the English universities. But it may be argued that the strength of the public sector is its variety, and that the public sector institutions offer the best chance this country has for the adaptation and development which is required.

A significant change in recent years in the public sector has been the successful diversification of former colleges of education and, in some cases, their amalgamation with colleges of technology. A special aspect of these colleges and institutes of higher education (which number some sixty or seventy) is that one-third have voluntary status. Number of students have increased considerably.

FIGURE 6.2
England and Wales: students on advanced courses in the public sector 1977/78 [2] (excluding postgraduate)

	Full-time	Part-time	Total
Degree courses	79,373	6,785	86,158
HND/HNC/TEC/BEC higher	24,712	39,307	64,019
Initial teacher training	57,076	1,352	58,428
Professional qualifications	17,759	59,979	77,738
Additional advanced courses	11,875	11,013	22,888
DipHE	1,956	65	2,021
Total	192,751	118,501	311,252

FIGURE 6.3
Colleges and institutes of higher education: students on advanced courses 1979/80 [3]

Degree courses	29,331
Other advanced courses	20,586
Total full-time	49,917
Part-time advanced courses	72,383
Total full and part-time	122,300

These institutions are uniquely placed to play a useful role in any future developments. Quite a number share with the polytechnics validation by the CNAA and familiarity with technical awards. Many others are validated by universities. They thus bridge the binary line. They also encompass both a strong collegiate tradition and the seamless robe of further education.

SCHOOL-LEAVER PARTICIPATION
The recent Select Committee on Higher Education received evidence on the participation of school-leavers in higher education. After allowing for mature students, this showed that the United Kingdom, with 13.9 per cent participation of young people in 1975, was near the bottom of a league of industrial competitors which included the United States at 29.4 per cent, Japan at 26.0 per cent and France at 19.8 per cent.[4] The figures quoted suggested that the rate for Britain might have declined to 12.4 per cent by 1978 and might drop below 12 per cent in the early eighties.

There may have been some underestimate of the British position in that part-time degree students were excluded from British figures but were included for most others. The United Kingdom participation rate is 'improved' by 1.5 to 2.0 per cent when these are taken into account. And a further 'improvement' of 3 to 4 per cent might be claimed against those in the age group who delay entry to higher education until their early twenties. The corrected participation rate therefore appears to be about 17 to 18 per cent for 1978, which still leaves much to be desired by comparison with competitors.

What happened to the talented 10 per cent or so of the age group who might have reached higher education as did their American or Japanese counterparts but failed to do so? There were about seventy thousand of them in England in 1977, so they are worth worrying about![5] About one-third or more continued with their education having already achieved 'A' levels or good 'O' levels: some of these complete ONC courses in a further education college but go no further, and others take a vocational qualification at sub-degree level (secretarial, catering, nursing, etc.) but discontinue education subsequently. The remainder — again with 'A' or good 'O' levels — go straight into employment at sixteen or eighteen years of age.

Many of the boys and girls in both groups are matriculated. But if they all went on to higher education, the age participation rate might not reach 20 per cent. To achieve this kind of figure, we would have to consider whether what is provided in higher education meets the needs of these young people. But it is unrealistic to expect *all* those who matriculate to enter higher education, so there has to be a review of matriculation requirements as well as a reconsideration of what is offered in higher education.

Matriculation
Access is perceived as well as achieved. Those who have to deal with recruitment and admissions know that awareness of admission requirements in relation to course possibilities is often minimal. The confusion of information and the extent of misunderstanding is certainly a barrier to access. The school/college advisers and careers officers do a magnificent job, but the problem remains.

Most degree courses at English universities require Honours standard from entry, and the usual expectation for admission is an 'A' level score of nine (say three C grades). This requirement would exclude more than half of those young people who matriculate. If we add to a high 'A' level score a requirement that certain subject combinations must be satisfied, access is further limited. The impression given to the average sixth-former is that he is inadequate or has failed if he obtains low 'A' level grades, or a low grade in one or more subjects he imagines as essential to entry.

It is no accident that — in general — the 'A' level scores of entrants to degree courses in the public sector are lower than those in the universities. It is not that universities may 'cream off' the high performers from the sixth form, but rather that the expectation and understanding of sixth-formers is largely in terms of the traditional university Honours degree. Knowledge of other routes to success is limited.

A matriculation review must go further than provide better information about alternatives. It should question whether an 'A' level system developed for the fifties and sixties is adequate for the eighties and nineties. The question is usually raised at the school end. What is needed is a study from the higher education perspective. This discussion would run parallel with further developments in course structure.

COURSE STRUCTURES AND INSTITUTIONAL MANAGEMENT

Orientation

British higher education has a considerable orientation towards the workplace already, much more than is often believed. Taking university and CNAA first degrees awarded in 1977 as illustrative, together with the Higher National Diplomas and Certificates, 52.4 per cent offered a direct vocational preparation and a further 19.6 per cent were in the sciences.[6] Thus, a total of 72 per cent of awards was made purely in science, engineering, technology, business and professional subjects. This left only 28 per cent in the arts, languages and social studies areas.

Although we may have an absolute shortage of young people aiming for awards in strictly vocational areas, we have a *sufficient proportion* of those entering higher education doing so. The problem might be that our system encourages too large a proportion of young people to decide to opt for specific vocational preparation when they are sixteen years of age and too immature to make such a decision. For they may become dillusioned in their choice by the time they are eighteen years of age, and opt out of higher education into employment, wrongly assuming perhaps that they are unqualified to continue except by the specific route they have rejected.

There is a strong case for a broader first stage to the degree (including matriculation) which would delay the choice of vocation but allow specialist training when the choice is made. This is the trend of some of the reports on professional education.[7] Many industrialists and businessmen, whilst requiring specific knowledge for particular posts, do not insist on vocational training for all undergraduates. Nearly half the jobs available to graduates are for graduates in any discipline, with training given after appointment. The emphasis is on adaptability and personal qualities, and a sympathy for the business as distinct from the academic environment.

Improving the First Stage of Degree Courses and Advanced FE Awards
The impetus for improvement is the need to encourage recruitment into higher education of many eighteen-year-olds — average sixth-formers or ONC candidates — who are as yet undecided about a career. The following conditions may determine progress:

    i   that there should be more opportunities in all institutions for students to qualify for specialist study after entry, not at entry;
    ii   that a form of unclassified degree should be available in most institutions roughly comparable to the TEC/BEC Higher Diploma;
    iii that institutions should provide more opportunities to study first-year courses and subject combinations which do not require specific matriculation requirements;
    iv that alternative methods of matriculation should be introduced.

At least the first year of study, and possibly the second year, might be designed so as not to commence specialist study, but to select those students who are capable of following specialist study at the second stage. Students will thus have a second chance to prove their abilities whilst at college.

A characteristic of public sector institutions has been their willingness to develop subjects in higher education which do not often find a place in universities. Examples include performance arts (music and drama), physical education, industrial archaeology, the handicapped individual, and design studies. Such subjects can fit well into a broader first stage to a higher education programme.

The Art Foundation course is an exception for those talented in art or design. In a sense, the Royal Schools of Music provide another alternative in that Grade 8 passes are acceptable as an equivalent to 'A' level by some universities. What is needed in schools and FE colleges is a development of subject combinations which provides foundation courses in practical areas such as art, music, drama, physical education, craft and design studies. The latter is particularly important for prospective teachers. Sixth-form courses are also needed in areas such as psychology, sports science, and environmental science, to name a few. General studies is more acceptable for matriculation than is often acknowledged in schools.

I would go further and suggest institutions and feeder schools/colleges might have special relationships based on trust and knowledge of each other such that specific sixth-form courses could be validated for matriculation by the higher education institutions. In the USA this process is known as accreditation. It is more acceptable perhaps when matriculation is not sought for direct entry to a traditional Honours degree course.

To achieve a broader degree programme, the public sector will need to loosen some of the established restrictions. There is a tendency to block initiatives which do not fit comfortably into established norms. Nowhere is this more evident than in the field of business studies. More than half the students in higher education should be given some understanding of the industrial and business world as part of their general education. Yet attempts to do this by including industrial orientation studies in a general degree programme are seen as a threat to business studies specialist degrees. The arrangements in advanced further education must allow aspects of specialist studies to be used in general programmes.

At the same time, it has to be recognized that many practical disciplines require a great deal of course time to achieve required standards. The mixing of classroom with practical subjects may be to the advantage of the first and the disadvantage of the second. Where a student is taking three subjects together, it is probably wise to allow two of these subjects to cover different aspects of one practical discipline, which then becomes a central interest for the student. This consideration applies to performance arts, design studies and physical education.

An Alternative for Degree Courses
The above suggestions for broadening the first part of a degree course can be applied to existing degree structures. The three-year Honours degree dominates full-time provision. A three-subject pattern in the first year, with qualification for Honours at the end of that year, permits some flexibility. Likewise, it might be possible to introduce new patterns for the TEC/BEC Certificates to provide for less specialization in the early stages.

Neither of these modifications would be entirely satisfactory since they merely tinker with traditional courses that are essentially specialist. What is missing is the chance for our average sixth-formers to take a more general two-year qualification which would allow students to:
  i   redeem previous failures, or compensate for incomplete teaching provision in schools or colleges;
  ii delay the choice of specialism for the first two years of higher education;
  iii provide more young people with at least a minimum period of higher education;
  iv provide a prestigious award at the end of two years which would be valuable in its own right but allow access to additional higher education later.

The DipHE has proved a failure in providing a general solution, although the Open University Pass degree might be said to go some way to meet the part-time requirement of mature students. Another structure has been championed, however: namely the solution advocated by Pippard, Caine, Robbins and others.[8] This proposes that alongside the present provision there should be a full-time two-year Bachelor degree course. I would see this alternative degree as distinct from the three-year Honours or Ordinary degrees, and awarded unclassified but with a profile of grades on the degree certificate. There would be a chance to reconsider matriculation requirements allowing access with 'alternative matriculation'. The two-year degree might involve study of three subject areas in each year, with a chance of changing at least one subject from one year to the next. All combinations of science, arts and technological subjects might be considered.

This new degree would fit nicely with the local college provision envisaged by Charles Carter recently.[9] Colleges of higher education would find the suggestion a natural development within their diversified curricula. Polytechnics would have a problem bringing together teaching provision in subjects drawn from different faculties and departments, but the possibility exists. Both in polytechnics and large FE colleges, the new degree would provide a chance further to enhance the educational quality of the TEC/BEC Higher Certificates by effectively introducing a generalized programme alongside the specialized certificates.

The award of a degree after two years' study is known in the English tradition. Thirty or so years ago, many London University graduates were awarded a degree after two years' study following an Intermediate BA/BSc examination from which exemption was obtainable on the basis of the sixth-form Higher Schools Certificate examination. In the past, it was not uncommon for a BA Ordinary degree to be awarded to candidates in the Part I Tripos examination at Cambridge following two years of study in which a standard lower than Honours was achieved. These historic precedents from two English universities suggest there is no statutory bar to a degree awarded after two years' study in higher education. Moreover, contemporary Open University practice supports this viewpoint: an Open University Pass degree is awarded after completion of six credits part-time, say two each year; this part-time provision might be equated with two years' full-time.

It is most important that the best two-year graduates should be able to proceed to a more advanced stage if they do well enough. Therefore, it is essential for an alternative route to include a new type of two-year taught Masters degree to follow directly after the two-year Bachelors degree. The selection for entry would be such as to make the standard of this Masters degree no less than an Honours degree but I would envisage an unclassified Masters degree with a distinction for outstanding candidates. This Masters degree would have the following aims:

i   to permit a *proportion* of the alternative Bachelors degree graduates to qualify for a more specialized award at a good standard;
ii to allow the development of new patterns of vocational preparation, including combinations of specialized study of traditional disciplines with industrial orientation courses;
iii to encourage transfer across institutions, as well as between the university and public sectors;
iv to link part-time and full-time provision more effectively.

An alternative Masters degree of this kind offers versatility in that it fits the circumstances of most existing higher education institutions. It could be a very specialized subject-orientated degree in a university department; in a polytechnic it might have a strong vocational bias; in a liberal arts-type institution it might offer a high quality performance arts experience, or it might combine English literature with a business orientation course. The sandwich mode, or a work attachment scheme, would be relevant to some of these schemes.

Some institutions might wish to go further and entirely replace their BA Honours degree scheme with the alternative pattern of a two-year BA followed by a two-year MA. The alternative MA degree would incorporate not only specialized option studies from the BA Honours course, but also some specialized postgraduate work. In the case of preparation for school teaching, the alternative MA would embrace the Graduate Certificate in Education.

The Masters degree stage would carry the less economic options and smaller tutorial groups, and entry would be restricted, say, to 50 per cent of those finishing the two-year Bachelors degree. The use of more standard programmes with core subjects, together with less favourable staffing ratios, might enable entry to the alternative Bachelors degree to be 20-30 per cent greater than usual for Bachelors degree courses without an overall increase in cost.

Figure 6.4 summarizes the possibilities.

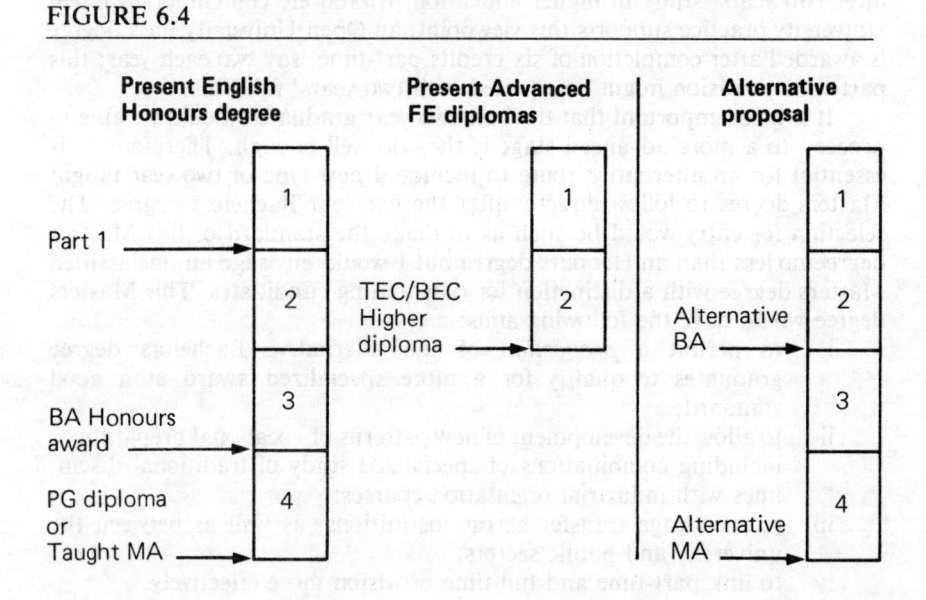

FIGURE 6.4

Present English Honours degree	Present Advanced FE diplomas	Alternative proposal
Part 1 → 1, 2	1 → TEC/BEC Higher diploma → 2	1 → Alternative BA → 2
BA Honours award → 3		3
PG diploma or Taught MA → 4		Alternative MA → 4

Two-Year Courses in the Public Sector
Those university academics who have pleaded for a two-year higher education degree have not seen a clear way forward. The public sector has already shown the way. Higher Diplomas (full-time) and Higher Certificates (part-time) are essentially two-year Pass degree awards for entrants matriculated with Ordinary National qualifications. Admittedly these are specialist in content, but so are many first degrees in higher education. The TEC/BEC Higher Diploma replaces the Higher National awards, but retains the principle of a two-year period of study. Many other advanced courses for professional preparation in the public sector are similar. Professional and governmental bodies have effectively equated two-year Higher National Diploma and other similar awards with Pass degrees for recognition of professional status and salary scales. This existing model also includes a modified matriculation requirement since one 'A' level pass together with three good 'O' levels are acceptable in place of the Ordinary National qualification.

The development of my design would provide less specialized, alternative two-year courses — combinations of humanities, social sciences and performance arts, as well as sciences, not only combined with each other, but also combined with technological or professional course units. We would then have a choice of very technical, general liberal arts, or mixtures of these two. Many colleges and institutes of higher education can provide them now.

The proposal would fail if there were not a second stage for promising students to aim at. In the public sector, this possibility exists when — for instance — a good TEC Higher Diploma engineering student transfers to a BSc Honours engineering degree taking four years in all. My suggested 'alternative MA degree scheme' discussed on page 119 presents a further solution which perhaps the public sector is best placed to pioneer.

Part-Time Attendance
The part-time mode is the crown of the public sector in Britain. It is not sufficiently recognized and acknowledged that it represents a major support for industry and commerce, an opportunity for late developers unable to take up full-time degrees at universities, and most significant of all, probably the most cost-effective approach in higher education. Surely there should be considerable discussion of the possibilities for developing this approach further.

Three proposals facilitating the development of part-time courses are suggested for consideration. First, validating bodies should relax matriculation requirements for mature students, as is already done by the Open University and in some advanced courses in the public sector. Secondly, priority should be given to the support of certain part-time students rather than other categories of full-time students. Thirdly, maintaining authorities should be more flexible in their approval of part-time courses in colleges and institutes of higher education, and the DES should provide encouragement in this respect.

It is often not appreciated that many part-time students are largely self-financing. Industry supports many — perhaps more than half — but there remains a significant proportion who not only do not ask for or get student maintenance grants, but who also pay a major share of academic expenses. Such a cost-effective operation must surely deserve support!

For the special category of unemployed part-time students, there is a rule that supplementary benefits will be paid to such students not involved in more than twenty hours instruction per week during a period of not more than three days each week. Perhaps there is a way forward here for some young people willing to pursue higher education on a part-time basis: unfortunately, the necessary range of courses is not at present available.

Productivity
We are expecting more students to complete courses of higher education without a significant increase of staff or facilities, and hoping that we can arrange for them to do this without reducing the standards of existing courses. This cannot be done without change, both within and across institutions. Ten years ago, Halsey and Trow reckoned that in no society could élite institutions such as British universities provide for 20 per cent participation or more and remain the same institutions.[10] They saw the need not only for the different academic styles and values now evident in the binary system, but also for a plurality of employment for academics across institutions.

Major improvements in productivity are needed now not just as a reaction to cut-backs resulting from government economic policy, but, more importantly in the long term, to ensure that fundamental changes and developments occur in British higher education. Under the clouds of gloom and complaints arising from government cuts in both the university and public sectors, there is little attention given to the second reason. Perhaps this may result from the absence of a general overall view of the system: the binary line is not quite a Berlin wall, but even in the DES the administrative divisions mitigate against coherence. What chance is there for radical reform when academics live in one camp or the other, and must necessarily confine themselves to polite acknowledgement that there is something useful happening over the wall!

A major expense in higher education is research activity, which may constitute 25 per cent or more of costs where medicine and sciences are involved. The role of research in higher education needs to be more carefully considered and made more explicit. It is often quoted as justification for the high costs in universities. But by no means all university staff are researchers. Halsey and Trow found that nearly half the university staff in arts, social sciences and technology regarded their orientation as 'primarily teaching' and, except in medicine, 70-80 per cent of staff reported that they undertook 'little' research during term-time or 'almost none'.[11] Moreover, during their entire career, many dons had either published no papers at all or up to four papers only. The proportions of staff with this rather small publication record were arts 37 per cent, social sciences 37 per cent, technology 41 per cent, science 20 per cent, and medicine 9 per cent. Obviously we should not read too much into these reports, but they suggest that the 'research load' is not universally applied. Some rationalization might be reasonable therefore.

It is impossible, of course, to make rigid distinctions between the teaching, research and ancillary advisory/administrative roles of academics. But some further analysis is needed in the interest of providing more opportunities for young people without increasing the load on the taxpayer. In allocating monies to university departments, it must be clear which research activity has formal support, just as in the public sector. I am not suggesting that there should be any restriction on voluntary research by staff, but there must be accountability for the amount of staff time 'officially' devoted to research.

The teaching function in higher education covers first degree courses, taught postgraduate Masters and Diploma courses, and the supervision of research degrees. I am not convinced that the formulae used to allocate staff teaching resource always matches the need. I know that the cry of 'standards at risk' will go up, but the question must be asked: would not a more realistic approach allow some reallocation of teaching time to ensure greater productivity? Likewise, in the public sector there should be discussion about, and accountability for, the time not committed to teaching on the timetable. It is not good enough to say that this approach will destroy the goodwill of conscientious staff: there must be decisions about priority and in most cases those decisions have been made by individual members of staff in an ad hoc way. Any system of higher education which intends to be reasonable and cost-effective ought to have a consistent approach to the use of staff time.

Co-operation between Institutions
Universities and public sector institutions receive their funds for teaching purposes almost entirely from the public purse. Each institution is a 'branch' of the same national enterprise. Yet each tends to operate as an autonomous entity, jealously guarding its resources for its own institutional requirements and seldom planning to share them with other institutions, although supported by identical paymasters.

The impediments to co-operation between neighbouring institutions are formidable but not insurmountable. Successful co-operation is established already — and could be further developed — in respect of resources for which there is no direct or obvious competition and where little inconvenience arises from sharing. Resources such as libraries and computer services are examples. The employment of visiting staff on a fee, secondment or exchange basis for short periods is well known but again is a tradition that could be extended. A major sharing of staff expertise has occurred during the validation of degree courses by the CNAA or by a university. In the latter case, the university has assisted a college in successful academic developments, and the assistance rendered has usually been much greater than that measured by the validation fees!

There is a limit, however, to 'convenient' co-operation on the small scale. For instance, it is seldom that joint appointments are satisfactory: a lecturer must be seen to be employed by one institution. Often major items of equipment cannot sensibly be shared on a regular, day-to-day basis, although the layman might think so. The more significant problems in co-operation are those relating to the organization of major academic developments, the operation of joint teaching programmes, and the sharing of resources over a long period. Solutions to these problems would generate large gains in productivity.

The hopeful mandarin sitting in Elizabeth House — or the councillor intent on tidy administrative policies — may consider that the quick and obvious way out is to amalgamate institutions. The ultimate logic of this objective is to amalgamate all higher education institutions in a region! Clearly, amalgamations do not necessarily achieve the educational benefits and economies of scale that are claimed. Some of the reorganizations resulting from the reduction in teacher training numbers have demonstrated that. This is because the problems of multi-site operation remain after amalgamation, degree structures may be curtailed or restricted, and the amalgamated institution may limit the initiatives, pride and effectiveness of component institutions without producing compensating gains. It is therefore sensible to explore the benefits which might arise from closer co-operation between associated colleges without going so far as amalgamation.

Often, academic plans include the introduction or removal of a subject area to or from the programme of an institution. Such a change may follow a national or local policy. The present dilemma is that policy decisions of this kind are not co-ordinated across the binary line, or sometimes not even between institutions in the same sector. Decisions are seldom informed by a total perspective, and are often limited by a narrowly interpreted definition of an institutional role. They are insufficiently related to resource management at all levels. Mistakes of this kind can be made within an amalgamated institution as well as across separate institutions.

I do not think that the proper way to solve this dilemma is to have directives from the DES, or the UGC, or from maintaining authorities. Rather the central bodies might encourage co-operation. What matters is that institutions must be involved in policy decisions of this kind with all the facts at their disposal, and given the opportunity to make decisions collectively and responsibly within financial and other constraints.

It is rare nowadays for an institution to be invited to initiate a major course, yet minor developments within an established programme may still be relevant. The enthusiasm for such proposals comes from an institution. How can such goodwill be harvested? Quality in education requires imagination and dedication as well as academic excellence. The problem is that a particular initiative can arouse resentment when alleged overlap appears to threaten another institution in an era of contracting recruitment.

The crux of the matter is how to constitute an effective body of liaison between institutions which is neither too large and formal for good communication nor too weak in its power base to produce results. One answer may lie in avoiding generalized liaison and focusing it instead within single subject areas where the staff report proposed solutions to governing bodies. Another answer is to set up a liaison committee between two or three neighbouring institutions, including key figures from the lay governors, the academics and the maintaining authority where appropriate, without making the group too large. There are important areas — for instance, computer education, in-service training, industrial orientation — where such liaison is critical. But it is surely crucial in helping all institutions to make better use of staffing and major resources.

Other matters are relevant too, particularly attempts to organize alternative degree programmes, broader foundation courses and a good range of postgraduate provision. Within a small group of institutions, it would seem possible to make more progress with accreditation across institutions by seeking correlation of courses. The confidence arising from discussion and association might catalyse the process, with a resulting increase in the numbers of students moving from one institution to the other at different stages of their programmes.

Each of two neighbouring institutions may have resources which are only partially used. They exist whether used or not. It makes sense for the two institutions to share resources in some way, so that not only is extra cost avoided but more is achieved with the same expenditure. An exchange of staff time on a pro rata basis is easy to administrate but involves an agreement to compensate across the two institutions. A course which is available in both institutions might be staffed by both institutions according to an agreed formula, although this requires some flexibility in timetabling. The nub of the problem is the agreed formula, and this becomes still more difficult to determine when the chances of compensation by exchange or sharing of staff are few. One possibility is to credit the donating institution with the appropriate full-time equivalent of students taught in the other institution. Another is to establish a national credit clearing house organized by the DES on agreed criteria. Certainly, the DES should be investigating mechanisms of this kind to promote better use of funds which have already been distributed.

NOTES
1   (a) Statistics of Education *1977 Vol. 6 Universities* University Grants Committee, pp.2 and 30. London: HMSO.
    (b) Statistics of Education *1977 Vol. 3 Further Education* England and Wales, pp.16, 27, 29. London: HMSO (Note: In-service Training is

counted as postgraduate work and excluded.)
 (c) Central Statistical Office *Regional Statistics 1980* London: HMSO. (Note: This volume included Open University students for 1977 — I assume these were chiefly undergraduates.)
2. Statistics of Education *1977 Vol. 3 Further Education* England and Wales, pp.27-29. London: HMSO.
3. Statistics issued by the Standing Conference of Principals and Directors of Colleges and Institutes of Higher Education (1981).
4. House of Commons, Fifth Report from the Education, Science and Arts Committee, Session 1979-80 *The Funding and Organisation of Courses in Higher Education* Vol. 1, Report, September 1980, Annex 6, p.1xvi. London: HMSO. (Note: The figures quoted have been reduced by 30 per cent as suggested by Dr L. Cerych in the Annex, to arrive at rates which exclude older students.)
5. Statistics of Education *1978 Vol. 2 School Leavers CSE and GCE* England, p.13. London: HMSO.
6. (a) Statistics of Education *1977 Vol. 6 Universities* University Grants Committee, p.44. London; HMSO.
 (b) Statistics of Education *1977 Vol. 3 Further Education* pp.52, 54-56. London: HMSO.
7. For example:
 (a) (1968) *Royal Commission on Medical Education 1965-68* Report (Chairman Lord Todd). London: HMSO.
 (b) DES (1972) *Teacher Education and Training* Report of the Committee of Inquiry under the Chairmanship of Lord James. London: HMSO.
8. (a) Pippard, A.B. (1972) The structure of a morally committed university. In Lawlor, John (Editor) (1972) *Higher Education — Patterns of Change in the 1970s* pp.69-87. Routledge and Kegan Paul.
 (b) Caine, Sir Sydney (1969) *British Universities — Purpose and Prospects* pp.258-266. The Bodley Head.
 (c) Robbins, Lord (1980) *Higher Education Revisited* pp.12-30 and 106-107. The Macmillan Press.
9. Carter, Sir Charles (1980) *Higher Education for the Future* pp.45-56. Basil Blackwell.
10. Halsey, A.H. and Trow, M.A. (1971) *The British Academics* p.464. Faber and Faber.
11. Op. cit. Halsey and Trow, p.295-297.

7

THE POLITICS OF SECTORAL CHANGE

by Maurice Kogan and Christopher Boys

THEMES

This chapter explores the political and organizational processes of change within higher education as a whole. It concerns an area of social activity which displays quite exceptional characteristics. The politics, government and organization of higher education involve tension between the needs of society as largely identified and acted upon by central political agencies, and the desire to sponsor freedom and excellence within the academic enterprise itself. Hitherto, the British system has sought to achieve a balance between respect for the inner life of higher education and the need to control its scope and purposes in the interests of the economy, of resource control and other social ends. These tensions of value and of function have been reflected in the politics of change in the higher education sector and we seek now to demonstrate the different ways in which the many levels of decision making and action relate to each other and to their political and social environments.

We first describe the administrative and governing structures of the higher education system and propose some models by which it can be summarized and typified. We also briefly enumerate models of change that are relevant to this sector. Secondly we produce some of the themes that emerge from the recent history of different sectors of higher education. The conclusion is drawn that a particular model of government and politics, namely a centralist managerial model, has assumed greater prominence than other models. Finally we move on to analyse the characteristics and consequences of the four models of government and politics, namely, the centralist-managerial, the political, the market and the free-oligarchic models. On the basis of this analysis, we propose some conclusions for policy that might be drawn.

THE PATTERN OF GOVERNMENT AND POLITICS

Mapping the System of Government and Administration

Figure 7.1 is a simplifed version of an exceedingly complex and changing system of government and administration, authority and power. It displays the different entities that have, since 1945, emerged on the higher education scene and indicates some of the linkages between them.

In order to make sense of so complex a system, we classify the entities and modes of linkages between them in the following terms. First, we distinguish between *authorities*, which have the legitimated right to allocate

128   IMPLEMENTATION

FIGURE 7.1
Main entities in the higher education system

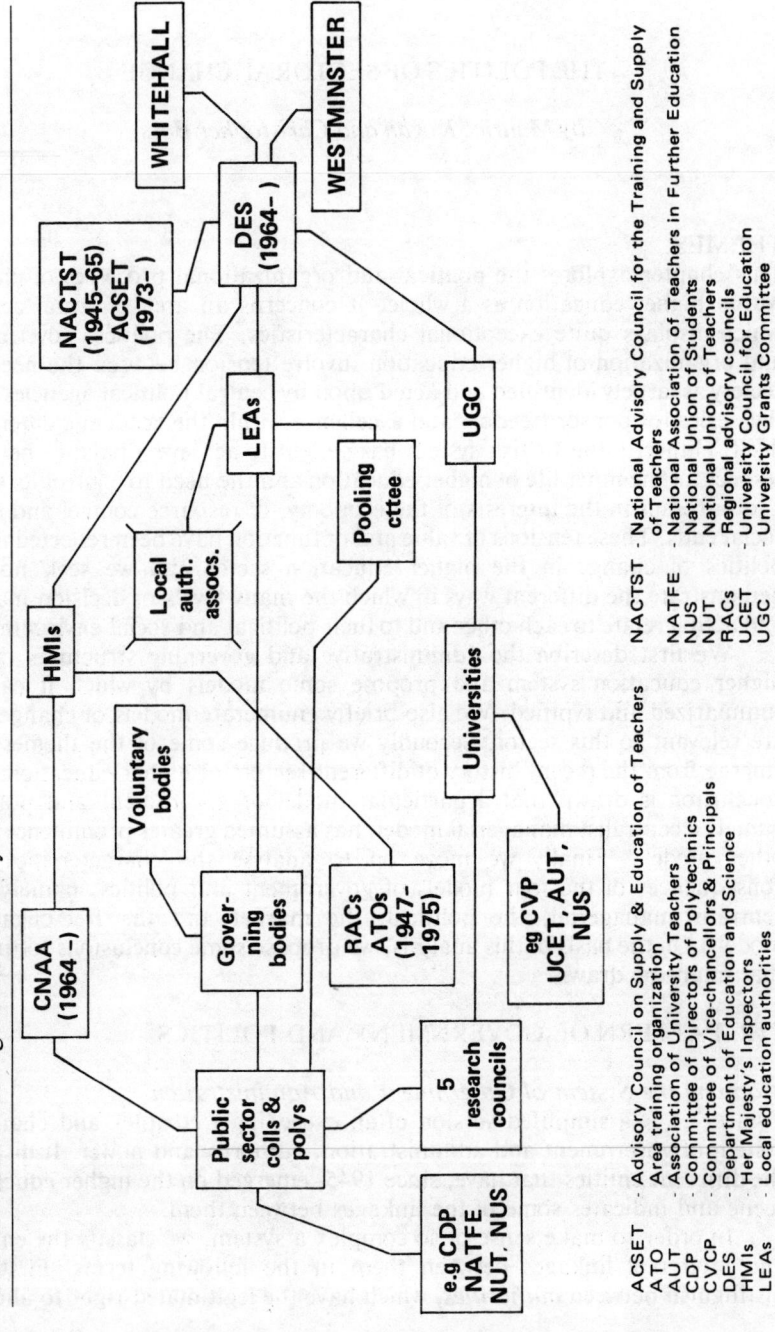

ACSET - Advisory Council on Supply & Education of Teachers
ATO   - Area training organization
AUT   - Association of University Teachers
CDP   - Committee of Directors of Polytechnics
CVCP   - Committee of Vice-chancellors & Principals
DES   - Department of Education and Science
HMIs   - Her Majesty's Inspectors
LEAs   - Local education authorities

NACTST - National Advisory Council for the Training and Supply of Teachers
NATFE - National Association of Teachers in Further Education
NUS   - National Union of Students
NUT   - National Union of Teachers
RACs   - Regional advisory councils
UCET   - University Council for Education
UGC   - University Grants Committee

resources, establish or disestablish institutions, and prescribe activities; *intermediate authorities* which act on behalf of authorities in such specialized functions as the allocation of monies or validations of academic awards on behalf of the authorities (for example, the UGC and the CNAA); *interest groups* which divide between those which are accommodated in the official processes of decision making and those with a less clearly legitimated part in decision making; the *social, political and market environments* within which the system moves and to which, in differing degrees, it responds; and, finally, the *institutional structure* itself of central authorities, higher education institutions, units within institutions, and individual teachers, researchers and students.

The relationships between these five entities vary from those of authority (where, for example, the DES or a local authority allocates resources) to less clear relationships of power and influence or the exchange of information.

The Entities in Slightly More Detail

The Authorities The legal authorities in higher education are the Secretary of State for Education and Science (and his Scottish and Welsh equivalents) operating through the Department of Education and Science (DES); the local education authorities, for public sector institutions; the governing bodies, namely the councils and senates of universities and the governing bodies of public sector institutions.

The DES, acting on powers conferred through legislation and with funds voted by parliament, has authority to determine the overall size of the whole of the higher education sector, both private (universities) and public (polytechnics, colleges and institutions of higher education). It exercises this authority by determining the number of students to be allowed in each sector, the amount of money to be sought in parliamentary estimates for grants made through the University Grants Committee, and those amounts allowed by central government for public sector institutions through the finance made available to local authorities. It determines the balances to be struck between the different types of courses, and certain categories of skilled manpower are controlled by the places made available in distinct specialities at universities, polytechnics and colleges. It approves advanced courses in further and higher education (other than in the universities) on such criteria as the demand for places in given subjects throughout the country. It is responsible for the setting up and appointment of intermediary authorities that are concerned more directly with academic judgements. The most obvious examples are the establishment, through the award of a Royal Charter, of the Council for National Academic Awards (CNAA) which approves all degree courses in public institutions, and the appointment of the University Grants Committee which, on the basis of demands by the DES for the encouragement of certain emphases within the universities, makes the academic judgements from which allocations to individual institutions flow.

The DES also maintains the boundaries between education and the other concerns of government as represented by the economic policies laid down by the Treasury, and the specialist manpower needs represented by such departments as the Department of Health and Social Security (DHSS).

In undertaking its functions the DES works through the language of operational decisions such as the amount of money that may be spent, the number of student places that can be sanctioned, the broad economic justifications for national investment in different kinds of academic activity. It eschews direct and overt judgements on educational matters. Its public style is that of rationalistic planning in which it detects the needs of the nation for skilled manpower or for higher education policies denoting different types of distributive policy.

Central Intermediary Authorities Burton R. Clark (1975) has noted how even the most centralized higher education systems (for example in Sweden or France) co-opt 'The Guild of Professors' into academic decision making. The Secretary of State makes grants to universities but on advice from the University Grants Committee which is almost wholly, with its sub-committees, composed of academics. The DES delegates to the CNAA the task of ensuring that the public sector institutions' degrees are of an appropriate standard. In the case both of universities and of public sector institutions, the DES assumes that academics will themselves, through such devices as the appointment of external examiners, validate their own standards.

It is a characteristic of the relationship between British government and all of the main professions (for example, medicine, law and nursing) that content and standards will be validated through the use of intermediary authorities composed of members of the occupations being assessed. The University Grants Committee is a particularly important example of how government's financial allocations are converted into academic judgements on individual institutions by members of the academic profession.

Similarly, the Secretary of State has the duty to award the status of qualified teachers. But he has always delegated that authority to area training organizations (until 1975) or, more recently, regional organizations.

Interest Groups The interest groups concerned with higher education do not possess authority, except inasmuch as some members of them might, as individuals, also be members of central intermediate authorities. They have instead differing degrees of rights to be consulted about and bring influence to bear on decisions made by the authorities.

It is possible to classify interest groups in terms of their degrees of acceptance, or legitimation, by the central authorities. The Committee of Vice-Chancellors and Principals (CVCP) and the Committee of Directors of Polytechnics (CDP) are consulted on major changes in the structure of higher education and on the conditions under which it must work, although this generalization must be modified in the light of recent drastic changes made in, for example, the level of funding of universities. Both they and the representatives of the main teacher associations (the Association of University Teachers, the National Association of Teachers in Further and Higher Education (NATFHE), are members of the standing machinery by which higher education salaries are negotiated. The National Union of Students is now consulted on matters beyond student grants, a subject upon which they have had a longstanding conventional right to be consulted. The local authority associations are party to discussions about salaries and conditions of work in public institutions and about general local authority finance which determine the amount of resources that will reach public higher education.

The legitimated groups may be contrasted with those that remain outside, in the general political and social enrironment, without a voice in decision making. The DES senses the market for higher education through its analysis of the numbers of pupils staying at school or going to further education in order to gain 'A' level passes and of the pressure on institutions for the award of places. There is no clear way, however, in which parental and potential pupil interest are expressed. The Confederation of British Industries (CBI) and Trades Union Congress (TUC) may make representations about the size of higher education, about access to it and about its structure and orientations but they have no clear locus within the system for making their voices heard on particular issues. It is fair to say that the legitimated interest groups who have a direct and continuing place in the consultative system are those who either work in higher education, or are beneficiaries of it, as students or teachers, or who maintain the system, as local authorites or vice-chancellors or directors. The larger client groups in society are not easily brought together into distinct interest groups. Nor do they constitute the type of constituency visible in, for example, American higher education. (We return to this point later.)

At the national level parliament has the role of 'aggregating and articulating' the feelings and needs of these wider constituents. It has been a commonplace of British politics that, hitherto, parliament has lacked the power to directly affect educational policy making (Kogan 1975). More recently, however, the establishment of the specialist committee on education has, it is generally accepted, made it possible for MPs to inquire more closely and persistently into the ways in which higher education policies are formulated and to bring together the opinions of wider groups for airing in the public forum of debate. The impact of these arrangements has yet to be assessed.

The Social, Political and Market Environment Higher education has proved itself to be susceptible to changing assumptions about what is expected of it in the wider political, social and market environments. Government has responded to those expectations in reaching its framework decisions about the shape and size of higher education. For example, because more people pressed upon the system, the government felt it necessary to establish the Robbins Committee and to accept its recommendations that all who were qualified to benefit from it should receive higher education. It may also be inferred that the present government has picked up a degree of disillusionment with higher education from the general political environment. This may have contributed to the decision to reduce the number of places available in higher education. Responsiveness to environment is also a fact of life within institutions. The range and orientation of individual courses have changed greatly in the last thirty years and departments within institutions are sensitive to 'market' preferences.

The Institutional Structure We have already referred to one of the levels of the institutional structure, namely the central authority and the intermediary authorities. In Britain it is fair to say that all higher education sectors have a relationship either for resources or for validation with central authorities, as is not the case with, for example, the American private universities and colleges. It will be seen later that the main levels are those of: the central authorities; the institution; the basic unit within the institution; and the individual. In the case of the public sector institutions, however, the local authority is a further entity between the central authority and the institution. Questions might be raised whether the local authority is a 'true level' for higher education if that is defined as a point of entry for distinctive values and for the exercise of authority in the making of key decisions.

Linkages The linkages between the entities considered above are those of authority, power and communication of information. By authority we mean the sanctioned right to affect behaviour through the allocation of resources, institutional legitimacy and so on. By power we mean the ability to influence behaviour through persuasion, or exertion of psychological and political pressure. The relationship between the centre and the institutions is that of authority. But power operates both ways; the central authorities depend upon political and psychological support from those over whom they may have authority, and the central authorities may choose to move through persuasion or influence rather than through direct decision making. The relationship between interest groups and the authoritative structure of the system is that of power and influence. Communication and information are a feature of all of the relationships between entities. The knowledge that the DES may possess, for example, can give it power in its relationship with parliament, or with the institutions, or with the central intermediary authorities. In acting as a 'gate keeper' for information, the central authorities are able to modulate the pressures, or power and influence, that are felt within the system. The media and their control over the dissemination of information and, to some extent, its generation as well, exercise power that causes assumptions to be changed and with it the propensity of different groups to use their authority in different ways.

Models of Structure and Interaction In this conclusion to our first section we draw attention to two forms of models that will become directly relevant to our analysis of present and future higher education policies. The first set concerns the analysis of different structural levels of the decision-making process. The second set of models concerns the range of choices open to the central authorities as to how they might work together with the other levels, particularly when change is thought desirable.

Models of Structure Figure 7.2 shows a model of a higher education structure (taken from Becher and Kogan 1980). It is concerned to display two dimensions of analysis. First, it identifies four principal levels, namely, that of the central authority, the institution, the basic unit (a department or other main unit of work) and the individual teacher, student or researcher. The second distinction is between the normative mode which is concerned with feelings, values (norms) and the operational mode concerned with their translation into actions (operations or behaviour). This does not imply that in practice we can easily separate them. Such an analytical device may allow us to begin to locate the problem of behaviour in the education system. It leads us to consider, for example, the possible conflict or compatibility between an individual's values and the tasks he is required to carry out — that is between a 'normative' and 'operational' mode. These two modes may be associated with either individuals or groups. Further, we suggest that there is a tendency to bring into equilibrium these two modes, a tendency to integrate the task with the affective or normative state. Yet the notion of equilibrium is complex. As Festinger has observed (1957), there may be a tendency to adjust the image of an action to the constraints of the situation rather than to adjust the action itself.

Structural Levels The definition and enumeration of levels of higher education vary. Whilst Green (1980) conflates the structural components with those characteristics of the different levels that might be discovered empirically, the model employed in this paper attempts to define levels in a way which will enable it to be used against varying characteristics. At each level there are distinctive values which justify a 'function' and a sufficient quantum of authority and discretion for those values or norms to affect operations. If we superimpose the operational and normative modes on to the four levels we obtain a model as in Figure 7.2, with its vertical and horizontal relationships.

The central level involves authorities which are responsible for overall planning, and resource allocation, and monitoring the component parts of the system in terms of the 'public interest'. Theoretically the 'public interest' composed of, among other things, consumers, producers and sponsors (tax payers), may transcend the needs and wants of any one part. In practice, the

FIGURE 7.2
The structure of higher education

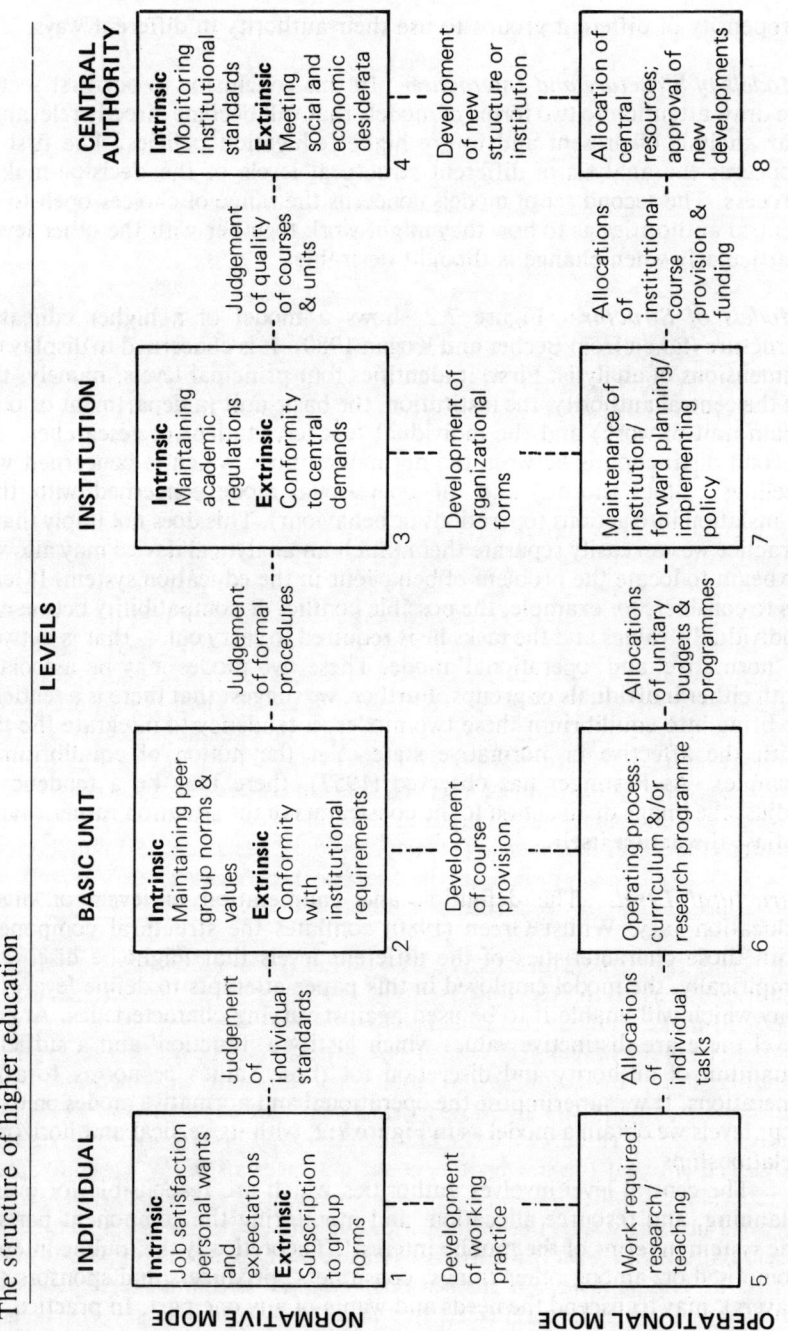

	INDIVIDUAL	BASIC UNIT	INSTITUTION	CENTRAL AUTHORITY
NORMATIVE MODE	**Intrinsic** Job satisfaction personal wants and expectations **Extrinsic** Subscription to group norms **1**	**Intrinsic** Maintaining peer group norms & values **Extrinsic** Conformity with institutional requirements **2**	**Intrinsic** Maintaining academic regulations **Extrinsic** Conformity to central demands **3**	**Intrinsic** Monitoring institutional standards **Extrinsic** Meeting social and economic desiderata **4**
	Judgement of individual standards	Judgement of formal procedures	Judgement of quality of courses & units	
	Development of working practice	Development of course provision	Development of organizational forms	Development of new structure or institution
OPERATIONAL MODE	Work required research/teaching **5**	Operating process: curriculum &/or research programme **6**	Maintenance of institution/ forward planning/ implementing policy **7**	Allocation of central resources; approval of new developments **8**
	Allocations of individual tasks	Allocations of unitary budgets & programmes	Allocations of institutional course provision & funding	

LEVELS

ways in which the 'public interest' is expressed depends upon the distribution of power, the nature of the task performed, and the interaction between the various groups.

The institution has a legalistic and corporate identity: for example, a university, a polytechnic, or a college. 'Its primary task is to maintain and develop a collective character, style and reputation, incorporating but reaching beyond those of its constitutent basic units. . . .'

The 'basic unit' is the smallest component which has a corporate life of its own (such as a department or research unit). It is a level with a distinctive value set and may, but need not be based upon a boundaried discipline. Finally, there is the level of the individual teacher or student or researcher with distinctive values and specific tasks.

This model shares the assumptions of many authorities (for example, Clark 1981) about the importance and resilience of the 'basic unit'. It also assumes that the relationship between the central level and the other levels is 'negotiative' rather than 'managerial' or 'consensual'. But a negotiative mode does not of itself denote the nature of the underlying relationship. It is, in fact, a different order of category from 'managerial' or 'consensual'. It implies that there will be a particular style which will be employed within relationships that can themselves vary. The dominant underlying assumption of higher education until recent years in Britain has been that there will be an *exchange* relationship, conveyed through a negotiative style, between the central authorities and higher education institutions. The concept has wide application in social theory in its development by Blau (1964) and others. The argument is that universities, polytechnics and colleges of higher education have something to offer society. Their staff will be trusted to use independence and control over their own resources to undertake the research, scholarship, teaching and other services which society needs. In return, the state, representing society, will give resources. Similar exchange theories are being applied to the relationship between central and local government (Rhodes 1980; Ranson 1980).

Applying the Structural Model The model (Figure 7.2) helps to place the entities discussed in preceding sections. It assumes that the central authority (Box 8) makes judgements about the social and economic objectives which should be met by the higher education institutions with which it has authority relationships. In doing so, it monitors, through intermediary central authorities, institutional standards. Thus, the operational decision to allocate central resources to the newly designated polytechnics was based on a judgement that the universities could not meet all of the needs for higher education, or in the right way. There is thus a direct relationship between the central authority working in its normative and in its operational modes. It has relationships with institutions by virtue of the judgements that it makes, often at one remove, on institutions, courses and units and it is these judgements which are reflected in the allocation of course provision and funding (Boxes 4 and 8).

If we then take as another example the statements contained in the model about the basic unit, we must ask, first, what are the values or norms which underlie its work or operations. It is concerned with maintaining peer group norms and values but, simultaneously, conforming with such institutional requirements as those of due process in assessing students, in the appointment of staff, and in meeting external validating procedures. The intrinsic norms are concerned with what the peer group thinks to be appropriate academic behaviour and performance. These underlie its operational mode in creating a curriculum, in providing a base upon which research might be undertaken.

The relationship between operational and normative modes at each level is thus one form of analysis. The relationships between levels are, however, also to be thought of as containing both the normative and operational modes. One level makes a judgement of another in terms of the quality of what it provides, of the way in which it keeps to academic due process and judges standards. On those normative judgements or evaluations are based operational actions concerned primarily with allocations. It is argued that an important source of change within the system is appreciation that normative and operational modes are no longer consistent with each other.

Examples of these generalizations are not difficult to find. A central authority does indeed make a judgement of the quality of the courses and units that an institution maintains. On the basis of these judgements the UGC makes allocations and the CNAA decides to approve courses. Similarly, an institution makes judgements about the procedures adopted by the basic units in their maintenance of group norms and values and in conforming with institutional requirements. It determines its allocations on the basis of these normative judgements and its evaluation of how a basic unit performs contributes towards its forward planning for the institution.

The normative-operational equilibrium can also be demonstrated from recent events. It must have been as a result of DES ministers' beliefs that the higher education system for which they were responsible was not meeting government's social and economic objectives and the wishes of other groups in the external environment that so drastic a set of decisions was made on the allocation of resources. The normative-operational imbalance led to a determination to make drastic changes.

The same analysis can be applied to discussion of the role of local authorities in the public sector of higher education. Our criteria are: is there a distinctive 'local' values input and, if so, are there commensurate authority and power to back value judgements made at the local level? We need not reach a conclusion on this matter here but simply state some of the considerations. First, higher education is normally thought to meet national rather than local needs. The basic units respond to academic norms set up by national and international criteria. Against these considerations, however, is the belief that higher education institutions ought to participate strongly in the development, maintenance and enrichment of their local and regional areas. It is therefore argued that local authorites have a place in helping to determine what the institutions offer. At the same time, however, it is assumed that funding will be national, through the 'pool'. The tension between these different normative assumptions is reflected in the patterns of control that were established in the mid 1960s, and which are now under scrutiny (DES 1981).

Models of Interaction and Change It is thus assumed in our model that basic units will sponsor the creative individuality of peer groups and of the people working within them. The power and resilience of the basic unit reflect the notion that academic disciplines have their own culture, language, and expertise which are capable of being judged by external peer groups within the same discipline but not too easily by those who allocate resources from the institutions or from the central authority. Clark has pointed out that academic organization derives primarily from the overwhelming need to differentiate between specializations and to create new amalgams which themselves become differentiated specializations. There is thus a functional justification for the strength of the basic unit. At the same time, however, both the costs of higher education to the public purse and its importance in the furtherence of national social and economic policy make inevitable the evaluative and allocative strengths of the central authority. Tension between these two strong entities underlies all models of interaction and change.

Four Models of Interaction We here deploy four models of interaction: the centralist and rationalist; the market; the political; and the oligarchic and freedom models. We emphasize that in virtually all systems of higher education, except those of totalitarian states, ingredients of each are to be found. The different models provide a range of choices from which policy makers can select.

Model A — The Centralist: Rationalistic Model In describing the centralist model we will conveniently take up the main components that will apply to the other three and which will not be repeated in detail as we come to them separately. First, there are ways in which policy issues are identified. The centralist-rationalistic model rests on the assumption that the political authorities are authorized and competent to read off the needs of society and to translate them into plans for the creation and maintenance of institutions, for the type and number of students that will enter them, and for the general orientation of the courses to be provided. In our view, this has been the way in which issues have been presented in teacher education policy, although serious attempts to strengthen the authority and discretion of the basic units were made for a limited period during the time of college expansion. The central authorities identify issues, convert them into allocative procedures and decisions and either convert them into academic norms or cause them to be so converted by intermediary authorities.

The second element of the centralist model concerns the political process. In brief, the assumptions are those of traditional ballot box politics which assume that government is sanctioned to govern, that it may take counsel of those directly affected but that it is capable of perceiving the impact of its own decisions once they are taken and that it does not need to compete with other, perhaps inchohate and unformed constituencies within the political environment. Indeed, the concept of the political environment is somewhat weakly represented in the centralist-rationalistic model of decision making.

The third component of the centralist-rationalist model concerns the authority and discretion allocated to the different levels. The authority maintained at the centre is plain. But what about, for example, the basic units? We should emphasize that considerable authority and discretion in the basic units are not logically incompatible with the centralist-rationalistic model. The centre can make framework decisions on access to higher education and the balance between subjects and yet leave the basic units to determine curriculum. Thus it is clear that the DES did not seek to interfere in detail with the content of teacher education curriculum although it maintains exceedingly strict controls over all of the other framework determinants of the size and nature of teacher education.

The fourth aspect to be considered of our different models is their relative outcomes. Here we can do no more than suggest some of the criteria that might be applied. A centralist-rationalistic model would imply an ability to determine social outcomes, such as the production of trained manpower. A second outcome of centralist planning might be changes in academic quality. We know no research evidence, however, of changes in content or quality caused by changes in the governing systems. A third outcome might be responsive to the needs of those with a stake in higher education. Recent statements about educational planning (OECD 1979) refer to the need to reduce the power of the centre which should be willing to listen to the different groups, to consult them and to modify its actions in response to the needs and demands and wants of new groups. So far, no good model of the more responsive centralist planning is available from empirical evidence.

Model B — The Market Model There are potentially two kinds of market models for higher education. The first is that of the economic market, in which sellers find buyers and exchange money for education goods. In all of the modern history of higher education, with the exception of some of the private institutions in the USA, this has not been a dominant model. Instead, we deploy a *social market* model, in which clients and needs are identified, and resources are allocated to meet their demands, but the market is regulated and financed by public authorities.

The interaction between the basic unit and the client is at the centre of the market and the powers at which the demands are assessed are multiple. Instead of attempting to determine the social aims of higher education on its own criteria alone the government would take account of the wishes of the many groups outside itself and sanction resources accordingly. It is itself thus a part of the market negotiation. The institutions and the basic units then respond to demands placed upon them by external groups and make their own demands accordingly. Negotiations take place between the resource givers and the resource users on their understanding of demands.

The political process employed in the market model is that of open politics. Within them central government would not keep its own counsel on the assumption that the electoral process is sufficient to provide it with inputs from the society at large. Instead, central government and the other levels would maintain conditions under which others could bargain for support for higher education. The central government identifies clients and facilitates the satisfaction of their demands. It thus defines the market. And it must play an essentially political game in manipulating or determining how the market will behave.

The role of central government in a market model is paradoxical. Its primary function is to facilitate or manage or affect markets to be enjoyed by clients and by institutions. At the same time, however, it pursues its own interests, including the control of resources, by determinant decisions. In the market model, as in all the others, the central authorities evaluate and allocate. The issue is not whether they possess authority but the extent to which that authority is modified by the demands and expertise of other levels and groups concerned with higher education. The client groups will strongly condition allocative decisions.

What might be the outcomes of a market model? Social demands will be met. It may be, however, that other major objectives such as greater equality or positive discrimination in access, or decisive changes in economic performance, are less likely to be achieved.

Academic quality will, on the American experience, which is nearest that of the free market, be far more varied because academics will be compelled to respond to external forces rather than maintain themselves through oligarchies of free academics. The responsiveness of the system, however, will obviously be considerable.

Model C — Political Model A political model of governance is not far different from a market model. It has been described by Baldridge et al. (1978) in these terms:

> '... any specific decision process resembles a political struggle: interest groups are formed, influence tactics are used against decision makers, coalitions are constructed, legislative bodies are pressured, viable compromises are negotiated. But, over time, these individual decisions create power structures, the various groups gaining long range power and control until changing events undermine their position.'

Baldridge is concerned primarily with intra-institutional politics and has not applied the model to relationships between different levels of a national system. But some of the characteristics can be projected to the British case. In such a model different groups compete with each other. The assumption underlying the political model is, however, that even central authorities, let alone institutions and the other levels, must negotiate their positions if they are to remain in power and to make their policies stick.

In Britain, we can observe that the political model is weak. There are no active and strong political constituencies with an interest in higher education, and with power to challenge the centre. This is evident from the story of the closure of many teacher training colleges. It is also obvious that at the time of the first great retrenchment of the university system, most of those protesting against it have been directly associated with higher education as beneficiaries of one kind or another. There are no external constituencies to whom appeal can be made and who are capable of applying electoral or other punishments to those who reduce the resources and the standing of higher education.

Within a political model, authority remains at different levels as in the centralist or in the market models but that authority fluctuates more obviously in response to negotiation and power games. Thus at one time an institution may be exceedingly strong against its constituent departments. At another, the basic units may be able to retrieve great discretion through their abilities to come into coalitions in senate or in the appointment of a new vice-chancellor or polytechnic director. These interactions are relatively modestly performed in British higher education.

What would be the outcomes of a political model? If the power game is conducted mainly among the professionals the criterion of social demand is likely to be observed only in fragmentary fashion. Demands will not be presented systematically to the system, which must pursue them. The result will be a failure to achieve either central authority approval or the approval of the market forces. It depends how open the political model is to groups outside those with established authority. It is likely to be responsive more to a particular demand of groups than to the society in aggregate.

Model D — The Free Oligarchic Model The free oligarchic model is that traditional to universities in Western Europe and the USA. It assumes that strong professoriats on lifelong tenure are allowed to regulate both resources and academic developments and judgements through collegial means. The external society, including sponsors of all sorts, allow the maximum of discretion on the basis of terms of reference that might have been drawn up centuries ago through acts of gift and of trust. Self-governing institutions, such as the Oxbridge colleges, are thus able to assume the use of their own resources for ends maintained through the norms set by the collegium rather than by external sponsoring and funding and controlling bodies.

There is now hardly any entirely free oligarchy in higher education.

Institutions are dependent on the state for funds for their students through awards. Collegial finances do not cover the whole of the costs of teaching and research; they are met from the University Grants Committee, research councils and private sponsorship.

Moreover, as Clark has observed, the freestanding academic did not prove inconsistent, in Germany, Sweden and France, with centralist-rationalistic planning. It was possible for the state to lay down the law of higher education, governing access to it and the way in which universities conducted themselves, whilst co-opting academics who would help them determine what chairs there should be and who should get them.

Within the oligarchic system there need be, in principle, no identification of issues for conversion into social norms. Academic norms are generated from academe itself. The pursuit of knowledge through teaching, scholarship and research is the process by which academic policies and practices are created. It follows that the political processes are essentially internal. Academics negotiate with other academics for shares of resources, for status and for the allocation of academic boundaries. The academics respond to the criticism and judgements of peers within their own discipline, within the institution and within the larger national and international systems.

The outcomes in terms of our criteria are equally obvious. The premium is more on academic quality than on responsiveness to social desiderata.

Models of Change There are no adequate predictive models of change and those which seek to generalize the process from historical example are none too successful either. 'Social systems provide many sources of change. To attempt to reduce them to a single factor is to believe that social change is a very specific phenomenon which must have very specific causes' (Cohen 1968).

Despite this warning, we can usefully consider the likely outcome of the different models of structure and of interaction, in terms of change, discussed above (pp.137-141). Clark's 'forms of order' produce different propensities for change. The *political* form allows for co-ordination to facilitate change by means of interest group struggle and domination by party and state officials. Alternatively, the interest groups may exercise their power to resist changes which threaten their established positions and practices.

The *oligarchic* form relies on personal initiative and small groups who must secure consensus to create change. Such groups, who rely upon the guild model of academic organization as particularly exemplified by the traditional professorial chair, resist change from the outside.

The *rational and bureaucratic* form relies on planning to facilitate change. But planning then takes on the characteristics of any carefully worked out technology and itself becomes resistant to change. There are internal struggles for resources and the guarding of the planners' own areas.

The *market* form relies on competition and 'loose couplings' that allow enterprises and sectors to move disjointedly in various directions. Consumer demand is in the saddle. But, as Clark remarks, under some conditions market co-ordination can be stagnant and heavily retarding. Enterprises might voluntarily imitate the established type.

Clark makes a particularly telling point about market arrangements, that 'institutions can settle down in mutually acceptable divisions of labour, enjoying the comforts of protective niches.' The market's ability to cause change depends upon the balance between incentives for institutions to adapt or to accept a 'niche already won'.

Our own model shares Clark's assumption, that the basic unit within the institution is exceedingly retentive of its authority and power and that only wholesale demolition or recreation can affect this fact. He refers to the forces that act on the educational system: consumer demands becoming more varied with a widening of the range of students entering higher education; increased diversity in the labour market; and the splintering of subjects within higher education itself. Whilst the first two are external to the higher educational system, it is nonetheless the system and its institutions which must make decisions on how, and to what extent, to respond to them. The third element, of fragmentation of subjects, is intrinsic to the evolution of the system. It involves 'the development and reforming of the self-interest and of individuals and groups around differentiated specialities and organisational parts that support and carry them'. Academic differentiation might be a way in which the group protects itself. New disciplines in institutions or even new sectors may arise because established groups resist their incorporation into existing structures. And new groups may seek new pastures in order to escape the control of established groups. The reverse procedure, Clark's 'de-differentiation' may result from new groups seeking incorporation into existing and prestigious subjects, institutions and sectors.

A further classification derives from the Becher and Kogan model described above. As will be recalled, it is argued that change is caused when there is disequilibrium between work in the normative and operational modes. Whilst it may be a truism that discontent, and hence change, may result from an appreciation, at any level of the system, that work being done is not in accordance with feelings about what ought to be done, the point is capable of broader application. When central authorities attempt to cause deep-seated change in academic behaviour the changes are generally stated in terms of operational issues: number of students, sizes and shapes of institutions, and so on. The normative aspects of such changes are not well disclosed, let alone negotiated. It is not easy for central authorities to penetrate the normative and inner lives of academics but nothing less than that would be necessary for central planning to make an impact on the way in which basic units and individuals eventually work. Having said that, however, academics are responsive to changes in their markets, their status systems and, indeed, their individual prospects and security. So issues stated as operational may indeed begin to affect the normative frames within which the academic enterprise works.

We now turn to illustrate some of these theoretical points by attending to recent changes in higher education in Britain.

CHANGES IN POSTWAR BRITISH HIGHER EDUCATION

British higher education, as that of other countries, has undergone massive changes since 1945. The proportion of age groups entering courses conferring degrees increased from under 3 per cent to 13 per cent. The teacher training system expanded from 24,000 to 120,000 before being reduced again to 40,000 places. Single purpose teacher colleges were first expanded and then either closed or combined with other multi-purpose units. The public sector was developed to include 30 polytechnics and nearly 400 other institutions offering higher education courses.

Our concern in briefly referring to historical cases is again to seek answers to our central question. How, in the course of these changes, was the function of the central authorities to interpret social needs and provide for them reconciled, if at all, with the maintenance and development of the norms of academic self-identity and control within the institutions and basic units? What were the interactions between the different groups involved: central government, the professionals within the institutional system, and other external constituencies and client groups?

There is not space in this chapter to give more than brief glimpses for illustrative purposes. We have therefore selected the cases of teacher training and of the universities because they lie at two ends of the spectrum of relative independence of central control. As we shall see, teacher education has been strongly controlled by government. The universities enjoyed a period of considerable expansion and freedom before also coming under increasing control from the centre.

Throughout our period, central government held firm control of the teacher training system. Why should this be so? First, teacher training has to produce manpower for a major public service. The supply of teachers is strongly conditioned by demography and by the demands created by such educational policies as decisions on the length of the school life. It follows that the central authority, the DES, will take on a managerial role and will determine most of the structural issues facing the colleges. Secondly, teacher training has persistently suffered from low status and weak professional autonomy because historically it has been associated with low status clients. Evidence from ATCDE to the McNair Committee referred to 'the "historical stigma" attached to the establishments in which are segregated the teachers of the children of the poor' (Brown 1979). Moreover, teacher education is a derivative from academic disciplines outside itself and a form of 'brokerage' between them and the clients (primarily schools). It thus always has to justify itself by extrinsic criteria. This accounts for the relative weakness of the basic units and institutions, compared with those of other forms of higher education.

The weaknesses of the teacher training institutions and strengths of the central authorities account for some of the difficulties experienced by the National Advisory Council for the Supply and Training of Teachers (1949-65). Although it saw itself as a negotiating body, throughout its history it was largely a sounding board against which the central authority could test policies which it wished to see implemented. When the three-year course was introduced, there were attempts to enhance the status of teacher education through the broadening of the curriculum to include a wider contribution from general education. Had the colleges been able to establish such a dual tradition it is possible that the basic units could have become stronger, but this opportunity was never tested.

The authority of the centre thus seemed a natural feature of teacher education. The central authority itself often seemed driven by inexorable pressures of an operational kind. One DES official, for example, once retorted to the Treasury that affecting the birthrate was entirely beyond his department's control. Often, too, decisions must be made on such logistical grounds as the location of existing buildings. But there was no issue resulting in operational decisions that did not have its normative frame. The size of the system was determined not only by natural demography but also by the demography induced by educational policies. The location and development of colleges were tied up with thinking about whether institutions should be multi-purpose and co-educational, and whether places should be allocated to denominational or local authority colleges. The strong emphasis on central planning was not simply a concern that resources should be used sparingly but also had the normative justification that producing teachers was a national concern if all the nation's schools were to get the teachers that they needed.

In terms of our models of government and change the DES were centralist and rationalistic. In the view of the House of Commons Sub-Committee of the Expenditure Committee (Fookes 1976), they did consult the interest groups but on an ad hoc basis. The National Advisory Council for the Supply and Training of Teachers was, from the beginning, the recipient of DES planning documents and recommendations but because it attempted to act politically by taking on the role of a general policy-making body, it failed to achieve a consensus over policy issues (Hicks 1972). the NACTST drifted towards being a negotiative body, representing the disparate interest groups involved in teacher training. This was not in accord with its role as perceived by the DES. In setting up the council the department did not follow the recommendations in the McNair Report for a central council with planning as well as advisory functions. This resistance to giving planning powers to national bodies of professional and other interest groups has been a consistent feature of DES policy. In the view of the OECD Examiners (1976):

'The feeling exists strongly within the Department that . . . informal methods, utilised by sensitive and fair-minded government surveys are superior to highly structured formal procedures which invite half baked and politically sectarian opinions, and encourage demogogy, confrontation and publicity battles, leading to a lot of waste of time.'

What of the market, the political system and other ingredients of higher education patterns? There was certainly a market for the products of teacher education. But there was no market model. Institutions were not allowed to seek their clientele and fashion their offerings accordingly. The market was, in fact, strongly controlled by the authorities. There was also political activity, on salaries by the teacher and college authorities as size and responsibilities increased, and by the denominations to ensure that they got their share of the expanded system. But the decisions that were ultimately taken were more the result of central government determinations than of the conflict between different groups and different constituencies. Even less was there the freedom associated with the academic oligarchies of the traditional universities.

1972 was a watershed in the history of teacher education in Britain. For the first time the government made it clear, in the White Paper of that year, that teacher education must begin to be reduced, and this at a time when modest expansion of higher education generally was still contemplated. The colleges which had expanded and had been allowed to develop a more strongly individual character through their plans for three-year courses were soon to be absorbed into other institutions or to be transformed into multi-purpose colleges and institutions.

The events of this period illustrate two of our themes. First, the operational decisions were taken on the basis of 'hard' data about the size of the population and about the amount that could be spent on higher education in general. These framework issues were dominant and the more intractable normative implications somewhat overlooked. Thus the centre responded to the prescriptions of the Treasury and the population data from the Registrar General's office. But the educational effects of drastically reducing and amalgamating institutions, which might be both necessary and meritorious in their own rights, were not a significant part of the public discussion. And questions of qualitative change, as taken up in the James Report on Teacher Education (1972), with its proposal for three cycles of teacher education, never fully engaged the minds of the central decision makers.

Centralist and rationalistic decision making is affected by politics. The DES failed to reduce the expansion of the teacher training system until quite late because the whole educational system was conditioned to believe there would always be a shortage of teachers. It was difficult for ministers to summon sufficient political will to arrest the process of expansion. Issues such as teachers' pay, in any case, absorbed much of the DES's energies (Harding 1978). So a planning paper published in 1970 still assumed that yet more places would be needed, although the birthrate had begun to decline as early as 1964.

With what politics did the planner have to contend? The different groups concerned with the decisions taken did not negotiate or compete on equal terms. The DES had control over the institutions and over resources. It consulted but did not bargain. Parties other than the DES did not have access to all the information available to government, particularly after the demise of the National Advisory Council for the Supply and Training of Teachers. It has, in fact, been assumed that the DES, because it had to make painful decisions affecting individual institutions and teachers, preferred to act in secrecy (Hencke 1978).

The limited nature of the politics involved can be illustrated by the way in which the Association of Teachers in Colleges and Departments of Education responded to the challenge. It was not able to resist government policy, and for several reasons. The DES was acting legitimately in the face of overwhelming demographic and economic factors. The ATCDE had to weigh the futures of disparately placed members. The small colleges were the first to go and their fate was to be entirely different from some of the larger, which in some cases actually benefited from the changes. The DES managed the changes piece by piece so that the total strategy was not easy to grasp or to oppose. The ATCDE had its own mixed constituency but found it virtually impossible to enter into alliance with other interests who had other objectives to pursue. And it had nothing upon which it could appeal to the more general public or wider political constituencies.

On the face of it, the universities present a different case of the politics of change. In terms of our models of interaction, they seem to represent a combination of the free oligarchy of academics pursuing their own aims and of the market model in which different forms of sponsorship are won by responding to different market demands. In practice, however, following the 1939-45 war, once universities began to receive the bulk of their income from the central government, rationalistic planning increasingly took over.

Throughout our period the resilience of the basic unit has been evident. Change in curriculum and academic organization has been an internal process. Individuals have felt that the rewards and sanctions of the academic life will be made on the judgement of their peers in their own disciplines. At the same time, however, the basic units have responded to two main external frameworks. The first has been that of consumer demand. Hence, the development of 'new' subjects such as business studies or environmental studies. Attempts have been made to cross disciplinary boundaries in order to provide students with combinations of subjects which might attract them. Secondly, the framework of allocation by the government has helped determine the way in which the basic units might develop. The balance between arts and science students, undergraduate and postgraduate, research and teaching activities are framework decisions made by the DES and mediated through the University Grants Committee which then decides how to allocate monies on the basis of academic judgements.

In terms, therefore, of our schema, the following points might be made. The needs of society as interpreted by the central authorities have been fitted into a rationalistic planning system in which the DES made resources available through the UGC. In deciding the level of funding, the government first accepted the Robbins principle of social demand as the imperative. But the objective if not the techniques of manpower planning were never far away and now can be divined as a principle somewhat unsystematically applied in the 1981 UGC allocation letters.

The political process of change has been not far different from that affecting teacher education. In the past, vice-chancellors and chairmen of councils might have had an influence on the leaders of political parties. In recent years, and certainly from 1967, government has made up its own mind in response to what it felt was needed. Whilst government believed that expansion or at least a 'steady state' in the universities was appropriate, no serious issue arose. But now that the hardest case of all is presented, namely, the 'need' for an absolute reduction in places and monies for the universities, the frugality of the political system in higher education becomes evident. There is no constituency to which the universities can appeal. They have no power in the political system, as have their equivalents in the USA, the alumni of powerful universities, and they are not organized to bring pressure upon political representatives. The only hope for our universities is in the action of parliamentary select committees,[1] but they have no particular purchase on MPs in the way that university leaders in the USA might have on state senators and representatives.

Political interplay, if somewhat internalized, can also be found out within the University Grants Committee. Subject committees push hard for their sub-sector within the total calculations of the UGC. The UGC has to balance these subject demands against the pressures put on it by the government for particular 'tilts' in subject areas. The institutions put what pressure they can upon the University Grants Committee for better allocations. But the criteria by which an institution is judged are not public and neither is the process. Indeed, in times of expansion universities have not objected to the process being internal and discreet.

We thus come to a break point in the history of higher education and in the ways in which changes occur. Social expectations of expansion and the consequences of it were internalised and became the accepted norms of most institutions and basic units. Shifts of attitude gave rise to large-scale increases in student numbers. The size and nature of the student clientele pressed upon the normative modes of working of the basic units. As the virtual monopoly of the university was broken by the creation of the binary system, so the role of the state was strengthened. Changing values in the larger environment affected the beliefs and actions of the central authorities. Thus they promoted the expansion of higher education for both social and economic reasons: to increase access to larger groups in the society and to enhance the economy. Until recently, structural relationships continued largely unchanged because norm setting in the basic unit was allowed to remain a dominant feature of the system. The tension between the centre and the basic units continued until contraction entirely changed the rules of the game.

We thus now have a system in which the resilience of the basic units within universities has become more questionable. We cannot predict how far the behaviour of teachers and their departments will change in response to far more sharp demands for changes in balance in the kind of higher education being provided. It may be that basic units will react to the changes in external constraint in different ways. Some might become more permeable to the norms of their neighbouring departments, and combinations of both units and of subject matters might become more prevalent. In some institutions collegiality might give way to intense competition between departments for a place in a shrinking universe. The alternative to internal conflict might be, however, that universities will be forced willy nilly into a market pattern where they seek to escape the managerialism of the centre by earning funds, sponsorship and political support through the deliberate creation of other and less 'social' markets.

The most recent changes in the policies of the centre will, therefore, almost certainly change the political framework within which the universities move. Unlike teacher education their functions are assumed to be primary and demanding autonomy if they are to perform their tasks adequately. This is not consistent with wholesale managerialism from the centre, and relationships different from those of the entirely subservient teacher education system can be expected to develop.

CONCLUSIONS AND POSSIBLE POLICIES

Our main conclusions can be put to work in discussing future policies for British higher education. Our concern is to make proposals that will enhance the possibility of beneficial change in higher education through improvements in its political and administrative arrangements.

Before turning to definite proposals, we analyse the issues in terms of values underlying higher education, its structure, and the different modes of relationship.

Values

The recent history of British higher education, as depicted here, displays attempts to reconcile conflicting values and objectives. British higher education has, usually at one and the same time, tried to meet the social and economic objectives, including the production of manpower and the development of individual freedom, identified by central government; to promote academic excellence in teaching, scholarship and research through the encouragement of discretion in the basic units; to meet local and regional needs through the mechanisms lodged with local authorities in the public sector institutions; to encourage more democratic control of higher education, again through the place allocated to the local authorities; and to meet demands placed on higher education by changing groups and their expectations.

At any one time these values might conflict and the constant debate and more recent searches for different structural forms and relationships between different levels reflect the tensions experienced within this range of objectives.

Structure
As we have described this structure, it has implied that, first, there will be an allowed and acceptable tension between central authorities and basic units which will enable several of the objectives to be met simultaneously. At the same time, public sector institutions are required to pay more attention to central planning and local needs.

Modes of Relationship
The structure and its different levels can be operated through the four different modes of relationship, namely, the centralist-rationalistic; the political; the social market; and the free-oligarchic. For the most part, universities have been allowed, but in changing degrees, to operate in a free-oligarchic mode but within increasingly centralist planning frameworks. A range of relationships is visible within the public sector. Teacher training has been governed on managerial and centralist lines whilst the polytechnics have been in a somewhat intermediate position between the universities and the teacher training institutions. Our views on the principles that should be applied to structures and modes of relationship are as follows. The dominant feature of the higher education system is that those who provide teaching and research need freedom to develop their skills and knowledge which can then be placed in a market relationship with the consumers and clients of higher education. We do not, therefore, argue for a traditional, free, oligarchic system but for an essential component of it, namely, the continuing discretion of a basic unit. These should find their place within the social market where central planning will help furnish the conditions under which negotiation, reconciling the conflicting needs of the different groups, can take place.

This does not diminish the role of the centre. Central authorities would remain accountable for ensuring that the higher education system meets the social and economic needs of the country. But they would do this through a system which eschews the cruder forms of centralist and rationalist planning and management. The tension between the central and other levels in the system can be used positively as well as negatively. The central role of the centre would be that of facilitating the market and, where necessary, manipulating it, on behalf of what it sees as national needs.

But structure and relationships apply not only to the formal levels of the higher education system but also to the encouragement of its politics.

Interests surface within the existing political arena. New groups may emerge while existing groups may realign. But we have been concerned at the extent to which higher education has lacked broader constituencies. Some may emerge in reaction to recent drastic policies as, for example, the formation of 'Campus' by a group of industrialists and employers in support of the University of Salford. In general, however, institutions lack such constituencies and any change in the governing relationships should take account not only of the formal political system, embodying traditional ballot box procedures, and the representation of the more obvious interest groups, but ways of bringing in those whose support and criticism of higher education are now lacking.

This brings us to two current sets of issues: namely, the possible establishment of a national body for the public sector and the place of local government in the governing of public sector higher education.

At the national level we have argued that there is certainly a place for framework decision making by central government. We share the view of the select committee that central planning should be subjected to the critique of a national body, at a minimum. At the same time, however, it should have a role well beyond that of the technocratic and should be able to put up the counter analysis that might be derived from representing a wide range of groups in the whole political system. We find it difficult to be clear on the relationship between the government and such a national body. If external constituencies are to become interested in and committed to higher education development, the national body will have to have powers beyond those of merely giving advice to the all-powerful DES. It could, therefore, take on planning functions, given an adequate staff, and a wide representation beyond those groups with an existing commitment to higher education. There might then be creative tension between the department, retaining the ultimate authority over resources and major framework decisions, and a national planning body whose advice it is bound to consider and respond to, if it is capable of saying something worth hearing.

The role of local government in this structure has been explicitly taken up in the recent DES Green Paper (DES 1981). The case for local government's role in higher education is that local democratic control and consumer interests should have a voice in higher education development. There is also the negative argument that strong local government interests in higher education will offset the power of the centre.

We feel that too easy an analogy has been made between higher education and the other levels of education. Local authorities have had control of public sector education but it is by no means clear that local consumer interests and democratic control have been asserted successfully in relationship to strong basic units. Local authorities could only have performed the functions allocated to them by denying the inherent characteristics of higher education. Its market is national, as much as local. Its educational norms are international and national rather than local. Yet the importance of all higher education institutions responding to the needs of their localities needs to be more fully recognized. For those reasons it could be argued that local government should continue to have a very large number of places on the governing bodies of public sector institutions and on universities as well. Indeed, it may well be that once they are relieved of the burden of management and of resource constraint in public sector institutions, they will be able more fully to contribute the local democratic and consumer voice to the development of the polytechnics and other public institutions.

Whatever structures and relationships are adopted, they will have to take account of the need to balance conflicting interests and to allow conflict to come out into the open for resolution rather than assume that politics are a bad thing in education. The alternative to open politics has proved to be a long period of assumed consensus, and tolerance of the tension between the centre and the institutions, which is now being shattered by a drastic display of decision making at the centre.

NOTES

1 Recent decisions might cause this to change. See the recent campaign ('Campus') launched in defence of the University of Salford (advertisements in the national press, 23 July 1981).

REFERENCES

Baldridge, J.V., Curtis, D.V., Ecker, G., and Riley, G.L. (1978) *Policy Making and Effective Leadership* Jossey-Bass

Becher, T., and Kogan, M. (1980) *Process and Structure in Higher Education* Heinemann

Blau, Peter, M. (1964) *Exchange and Power in Social Life* John Wiley & Sons

Brown, J. (1979) *Teachers of Teachers: A History of the Association of Teachers in Colleges and Departments of Education* Hodder and Stoughton

Clark, Burton R. (Forthcoming) *The Higher Education System: Academic Organisation in Cross-National Perspective*

Clarke, Burton R. (1978) *Academic Coordination* Yale Higher Education Research Group, Working Paper

Cohen, P.S. (1968) *Modern Social Theory* Heinemann

Education and Science, Secretary of State for (1981) *Higher Education outside the Universities (Policy, Funding and Management)* A consultative document

Festinger, L. (1957) *A Theory of Cognitive Dissonance* Stanford University Press

Fookes Committee (1976) *Tenth Report of the Expenditure Committee, Sub-Committee on Education, Arts and Home Office*

Green, T.F. (1980) *Predicting the Behaviour of the Educational System* Syracuse University Press

Harding, H. (1978) Harding replies to Hencke over college closures *Education* 29 December 1978

Hencke, D. (1978) *Colleges in Crisis* Penguin

Hicks, D. (1972) *A Study of the National Avisory Council on the Training and Supply of Teachers* MA Dissertation, London

James Committee (1972) *Teacher Education and Training* HMSO

Kogan, M. (1971) *The Politics of Education* Penguin

Kogan, M. (1975) *Educational Policy Making* Allen & Unwin

Lynch, J. (1979) *The Reform of Teacher Education in the United Kingdom* Guildford: Society for Research into Higher Education

McNair Committee (1944) *Teachers and Youth Leaders*

OECD (1974) *Educational Development Strategy in England and Wales* Paris

OECD (1979) *Educational Policies in Perspective: An Appraisal*

Plowden Committee (1967) *Children and their Primary Schools* Report of the Central Advisory Council for Education in England

Ranson, S. (1980) Changing relations between centre and locality in education *Local Government Studies* 6 (6) Nov-Dec

Rhodes, R.A.W. (1979) *Research into Central Local Elections in Britain: A Framework of Analysis* Appendix II of *Central Local Relations* SSRC

Robbins Committee (1963) *Report of the Committee on Higher Education*

Willey Committee (1969) *Report of the Select Committee on Education and Science*

8

THE POLITICS OF INSTITUTIONAL CHANGE

by John L. Davies and Anthony W. Morgan

INTRODUCTION

Given the likely long-term effects of demographic downturn, and the contemporary traumas affecting universities and polytechnics as a consequence of government economic policy, it is almost inevitable that a study of the politics of institutional change in British higher education should have as its primary focus the management of change under conditions of contraction (or expected contraction) and related conditions of uncertainty.

Much of the substantial British literature on the planning and management of higher education has different foci. An excellent study by Fielden and Lockwood (1973) is biased towards good administrative process, practice and structure in times of relative plenty, and another by Moodie and Eustace (1974) of governance, structures and roles is similarly located in time. Burgess and Pratt (1974) provide most salutary reminders of the gulf between policy intent and actual implementation, but their prime purpose is not the micro-politics of institutions, neither is the Becher and Kogan (1980) framework for the analysis of institutional adaptation to change. The various works of Sizer (1980, 1981) and Birch, Calvert and Sizer (1977) have focused on a rationalist view of institutional management, which is highly necessary, of course, but when considered in isolation has limitations.

The purpose of this chapter is to build on various issues raised in the above literature, by identifying a series of political and behavioural questions in the development of institutional responses to contraction and uncertainty. There are three main sections. The first reviews models of higher education institutions as organizations.

The second section examines various aspects of the institutional response to contraction and uncertainty. It considers the consequences of the different perceptions and expectations of participants and some of the constraints on decision making. An analysis is made of the political nature of change in institutions and the varying degrees of resistance offered by departments to the threat of contraction. The interplay between rational and political criteria of decision making is examined, and alternative strategies of policy formation are investigated. The motivation to develop consensus in institutions is assessed in terms of the methods used, and the implications of this on the centralization/decentralization question are noted.

The third and concluding section reviews the significance of external stimuli, and traces the ramification of all three sections on leadership priorities and leadership roles.

As the bulk of the literature on contraction and instability is based on North American studies, we draw heavily on this source, since contraction has been a part of the US scene for several years. As hard and systematic published research on the politics of contraction does not exist in the UK in any quantity, we have undertaken a case study type of analysis of a number of British universities and polytechnics as a means of assessing the current situation and of generating perspectives and hypotheses therefrom. Evidence from these cases is incorporated.

Finally, we recognize at the outset that some institutions are still marginally growing and that others have reached a quite stable equilibrium; we also recognize that even within apparent stability there is a constant flow of internal changes at the departmental level.

Also, we do not mean in any way to imply that the higher education sector will or should undergo further resource contraction; our focus for research purposes has simply been on this particular phenomenon, as a matter of pressing concern.

INSTITUTIONS AS ORGANIZATIONS

There appear to be four main organizational models of the higher education institution.

The Bureaucratic model assumes the institution comprises a formal organizational structure, with specified roles, clear hierarchies and chains of command, and predetermined procedures and regulations. It is assumed that people behave and the organization works according to the formal structure (Weber 1947). Richman and Farmer (1974) and Becher and Kogan (1980) observe that institutions are much less predictable than this prescription, because of the many social, psychological and self-actualization needs unfulfilled in the model; the increasing number of issues which have no precedent and venture solution; and the fact that the head does not exercise unequivocal managerial authority.

The Collegial model (Millett 1962) assumes a fraternity of scholars seeking individual and collective fulfilment, through full participation in decision making. In this model consensus decision making by academics does not admit of an influential administrative role. The model does tend to ignore the existence of academic hierarchy and academic ritual, and assumes, often wrongly, a genuine spirit of co-operation, deep commitment to the institution, similar shared values, and abundant resources.

The Political model (Baldridge 1971a, 1971b) takes conflict as the natural state of academic affairs, and focuses on the issues created by interest groups with different goals, values, styles of operation, and methods of generating and pursuing policy preferences. Participation is fluid, decisions are normally negotiated compromises, achieved informally and processed through legitimate decision-making arenas which translate pressures into policy. Whilst a helpful explanation of current phenomena, it clearly does not apply to all institutional conditions.

The Organized Anarchy model (Cohen and March 1974; Olsen and March 1974) posed the problem of the institution being caught in an 'Anarchy trap' as a result of ambiguous goals; ambiguous means-ends relationships; ambiguous systems of rewards and sanctions; high autonomy of subordinates with strong extra-institutional affiliations; and weak market feedback mechanisms. Decentralization is necessary because leaders and administrators are not sufficiently knowledgeable in all disciplines to be able to make informal decisions (Parsons and Platt 1973; Beyer and Lodahl 1976; Corson 1973). Cohen and March believe that decision processes in institutions are not so much mechanisms for solving problems but for participants to air grievances and pose preferences which may have but passing relevance to the issue ostensibly under discussion. Their conclusion is that the institution head needs to develop tactical responses in order to influence decisions. Unlike Enderud (1977), March and Cohen are not so much interested in strategic policy generation — a significant limitation — and somewhat underplay the extent to which institutions can be managed.

None of these types, of course, are pure forms. Becher and Kogan (1980) indicate the linkages which occur because of the functioning of individual managers such as vice-chancellors, directors, registrars, deans and heads of department. They operate within both the hierarchy and the collegium, through executive offices, committees, and informal political arenas. Richman and Farmer (1974) develop a more comprehensive, open systems approach, with a view to prescription and prediction, coupled with a strong contingency element. Enderud (1977), as we shall see later, locates the four models above in a phased evolution of policy decisions, where each has a role to play at a particular time in the delivery of effective policy. However, the incidence of contraction inevitably generates more insecurity and thus more conflict and politicization than in times of plenty or even in steady state. In general therefore, the Political and Organized Anarchy models seem to have more affinity with the current situation in higher education.

The contemporary external pressures for institutions to develop corporate policies for the internal management of programmes, personnel, finance and space are clearly very considerable. We therefore have widespread plans for senior management to develop rational and imaginative policies which are academically sound, financially viable, and politically acceptable, internally and externally. In this case, many highly intelligent institutional heads would tend to adopt systematic approaches to the generation of policy incorporating: a definition of desired outcomes; the identification and weighing of alternative solutions and options; the attribution of costs and benefits; a decision based on a mix of appropriate options; and a systematic evaluation of the efficiency and effectiveness of adopted policy mixes. As Davies (1980) demonstrates, each of these activities is impregnated with potential conflict and disagreement, which clearly hinders satisfactory progress. We observed the following tendencies in the institutional case studies we studied.

Joint policy decisions are slow and problematic to make.

Ones which are carried through are usually partial, short-range and based on compromise.

Policy decisions and criteria have to be attacked over and over again before a conventional wisdom gets established.

More institutional bureaucracy is created, in the sense of more participant involvement, more requests for information to executives, more referrals of decision for subcommittee consideration, etc.

The academic finds himself in several concurrent dilemmas — he doesn't like meetings yet he must generate or attend them to preserve his interests and influence, the direction and substance of his plans; he does not wish to spend too much time himself on planning matters, yet he is reluctant to trust others, including administrators; he wishes to plan in the sense of having a stable framework in which to operate, yet he resents being constrained by a substantive plan; he wants a power fixer on whom he can rely to sort out difficult issues, yet he resents the growth of power centres which are beyond the effective control of himself and his colleagues.

Policy decisions, given the economic realities, environmental uncertainties and political context, may increasingly be concerned with the marginal decision consistent with a very broad loose framework rather than the grand fixed strategy of a development plan. Points of specificity in planning may only be possible on particular issues, but this in itself does not remove the anarchy trap.

Difficulties with planning and policy making originate with questions of the reluctance and inability of participants to plan, ie to imagine the future of the institution as a whole; the role of the rector or central planner would thus seem to be as much concerned with creating an appropriate psychological climate for participants to be creative, as with the more conventional technical aspects of information collection and analysis. To this point we shall also return.

In this context, yearnings for corporate rationality may be illusory.

It becomes quite vital, therefore, for institutional leaders charged with the development of policy to have a very precise understanding of how their institutions behave or are likely to behave. If they assume collegiality where none exists and push decisions accordingly, they will very likely be disappointed. Both the policy-making process they develop, and the roles in policy formation which they play used to be carefully attuned to the variables of the particular situation.

PERCEPTIONS, EXPECTATIONS AND CONSTRAINTS
Are personnel redundancies really necessary or are there alternative cost savings or income-maximizing strategies which might be employed to avert

such drastic action? What will be the duration and extent of financial and/or enrolment pressures? Should an institution attempt to make difficult programme and personnel cuts now or wait until more is known about the probable extent and duration of current trends? Will postponement of the initiation of more radical, long-term actions until more is known in fact preclude the viability of such actions? Will present legal and contractual stipulations permit any significant programme rationalization schemes under contraction? These and related questions, labelled here as 'perception, expectations and constraints', pose some of the serious impediments to effecting institutional change and adaptation in an era of potential and real contraction.

Roles and Differing Perceptions
Institutional administrators, particularly those operating at a high policy level, perform an interface function: ie they interact with key governmental bodies and other influential publics external to the institution (Thompson 1967; Pfeffner and Salancik 1978). In performing this role, administrators must interpret the direction and level of intensity of external pressures. Interpretation is of course judgemental and subject to error. Overreaction to transitory issues and pressures is therefore a charge often levied by faculty against administrators. The Association of University Teachers' recent response to the interim report of the Swinnerton-Dyer Committee illustrates this phenomenon: 'the committee . . . has taken the worst possible set of assumptions and then assumed that will inevitably happen. To project present trends for a period of nearly ten years, as the committee has done, seems to us completely unrealistic' (Times Higher Education Supplement, May 1981).

Faculty, on the other hand, are in most cases marvellously insulated from pressures imposed by external sources — an insulation by design in large part. Insulation does, however, create a barrier for the emergence of a common set of expectations. Mayhew's (1979) chronicling of presidential decisions and faculty perceptions at Boston University offers a good example of the problems caused by disbelief and lack of trust in administrators. Faculty tend to believe, at least during the initial stages of contraction, that budgetary cuts can be handled through centrally held funds, economies in non-academic and non-personnel categories of expenditures, or that new funding will be forthcoming. This last expectation illustrates a very common response — one that Levine (1978) has termed the 'Tooth Fairy Syndrome'.

Perceptions in Different Stages of Contraction
Prior to or in the initial stages of contraction, most individuals in any particular organization most commonly believe that contraction will occur elsewhere. In a national survey of US college and university administrators, Glenny (1976) found that although most administrators felt enrolments in higher education were likely to decline in the future, the vast majority of

them did not expect a decline at their institution. As modest financial decline comes, most people in an organization will initially believe that personnel cutbacks, other than a freeze on vacant posts, are not necessary (Behn 1980). Administrative action beyond these expectations are commonly met with a high degree of distrust and suspicion reflected in charges of a 'hypothetical deficit' being used to 'rush through major academic changes' (language used in an internal document circulated among faculty at a British polytechnic).

As contraction becomes more of an organizational reality, usually through widely publicized press coverage and visible signs of resource cuts in a person's work environment, differences in perceptions become more pronounced and are substantially influenced by actions being taken at other institutions. The accentuation of differences in perceptions is illustrated in the case of a British polytechnic where the governors and the directorate, who are close to the financial pressures from government and local authorities, took the view that compulsory redundancies were necessary to deal effectively with short and longer-term financial conditions. The faculty union, on the other hand, opted for further non-personnel savings and a voluntary redundancy scheme. The union's case was bolstered by its reference to actions being taken at other institutions: ie, '. . . other polytechnics . . . have managed to deal with similar financial circumstances in much less draconian ways'. Delay in a decision to proceed with compulsory redundancies provided sufficient time to identify a substantial number of voluntary redundancies and other savings which appeared to meet immediate financial deficit targets. The 'comparative standard' or 'what are other institutions doing' proves to be a powerful psychological force shaping perceptions. The fact that many institutions have absorbed substantial budget cuts without dismissing tenured faculty forms a basis for suspicion of 'bad management' or the probable continuing existence of 'slack' (Johnson and Mortimer 1977).

Uncertainty and Perceptions
A substantial level of uncertainty surrounding the sources, duration and extent of financial pressures complicates the task of developing a common set of expectations upon which to build intermediate-range policies and plans within institutions. The primary causes and duration of current downward fiscal pressures in Britain are most commonly perceived by faculty to be linked to the term of the present government. Even within the time frame outlined in the government's 1981 White Paper on expenditures, there is the possibility of an easing of financial pressures on higher education. An HMI staff inspector for higher education recently stated that the government's plan for cutting higher education is short term (one to two years) and that beyond that higher education will probably receive stable financial support (Times Higher Education Supplement, 10 April 1981).

United States institutions have been living with a considerable degree of uncertainty surrounding future enrolments and finances for nearly a decade now and the level of uncertainty does not seem to be subsiding. On enrolments, for example, opinions and forecasts vary widely depending upon assumptions made as to traditional and non-traditional student participation rates, college retention rates and the effects of the job market on these rates. One widely circulated analysis demonstrates how slight increases in the participation rates of a dozen target populations could not only offset a projected enrolment decline of 9.2 per cent by 1990 but also progressively effect an enrolment increase in the range of 25 per cent (Frances 1980). Such optimistic possibilities are counterbalanced by projections predicting a 40 per cent contraction in degree credit enrolment between 1980 and 1990 and a 33 per cent contraction between 1980 and 2000 (Dresch 1975). With this range of variability in projections, it is not surprising that administrators have difficulty in developing consensus within their institutions as to a probable future equilibrium level.

Constraints upon a Planned Response to Contraction
As the discussion above indicates, differing perceptions as to the causes, duration, and extent of contraction constitute a major constraint upon any planned, orderly response to contraction. Two other principal constraints are worth mentioning here: time and legal obligations.

Bowen and Glenny's case studies (Bowen and Glenny 1980) in five American states clearly demonstrate that time available to make budget cuts is the most pervasive constraint on institutional options. Selective programmatic cuts require substantial lead time for programme evaluation, consensus building, and planning (Dougherty 1978).

If an institution attempts to buy its own lead time, ie by anticipating and targeting a certain level of contraction one or two years in advance, it may well be opening itself to a self-fulfilling prophecy. The City University of New York (CUNY) offers a case in point. Faced with a 13 per cent budget cut from 1975 to 1976, CUNYs board of higher education and its chancellor decided upon a 'stonewalling' political strategy — an all-out opposition to any cuts. A complementary strategy was to concentrate efforts on this external siege rather than divide the university from within through specific, contingency reduction plans. Offering further rationale for this strategy, Chancellor Kibbee said, 'knowledge of the fact that the University has developed a plan for dealing with reduced budget levels can serve to guarantee the reductions' (AAUP 1977). The result was that CUNY, at least on most of its eighteen campuses, did not develop anticipatory contraction plans and consequently had to give 30-day termination notices to approximately 1,000 teaching and non-teaching staff when massive cuts did come.

Time as a constraint upon institutional change and adaptation is a two-edged sword. Lead time is needed to develop plans and internal political support for selective programmatic cuts. Such plans can, however, serve notice on external bodies that such cuts can be made and in fact are anticipated being made. Moreover, the types of severe financial contractions which produce a widely perceived need for institutional contraction tend to come about without much advance notice. If notice were given, and not widely believed, serious plans for pruning would be unlikely to emerge internally.

A second and equally important type of constraint on an institution's rational planning of contraction is the myriad of statutes, employment agreements, tenure provisions and other legal restrictions that play a central role in personnel dismissals. Edmond Volpe, President of Staten Island College of the CUNY system during the massive retrenchment of 1976, cites the underlying importance of legal restrictions and how the legally based retrenchment guidelines issued by CUNY overshadowed any programmatic considerations (Volpe 1977). Widespread agreement as to the existence of a financial emergency necessitating dismissal of personnel has also been a key legal issue in the US, where claimants have questioned whether such dismissals were based upon the existence of a bona fide financial exigency or upon arbitrary or at least unjustified administrative action (AAHE 1978). In the British context universities and polytechnics have been reluctant to initiate a policy of compulsory redundancies because it would entail groundbreaking legal work in determining the level of redundandancy payments to be made in testing the strength of individual contracts. University and polytechnic administrators confirmed this view during interviews conducted for this chapter. However, this may well change as the universities hardest hit by the recent round of UGC allocations run out of alternatives.

THE POLITICAL NATURE OF CHANGE IN INSTITUTIONS OF HIGHER EDUCATION

All kinds of power problems are implied in the discussion so far. Decision making and change processes are basically reflective of the underlying power structure and the environmental context of institutions (Clark 1978). Institutions of higher education are built around a strong core of professionals who exercise considerable autonomy and influence over central institutional processes. Decision making and change processes are therefore characterized by a substantial degree of bargaining, persuasion and manoeuvering, hence 'gamesmanship' or politics, among peers. Were educational and research outputs and 'production functions' more clearly understood and quantifiable, the degree of gamesmanship would be reduced, although certainly not eliminated. But because decision making in institutions of higher education is characterized by widely distributed power among numerous, semi-independent entities and by what has been described as the 'complexity of joint action' (Pressman and Wildavsky 1973), any constructive change moving through the organization is subject to such 'political' forces as (Bardach 1978):

    a   The players involved
    b   What they regard as the stakes
    c   Their strategies and tactics

d   Their resources for playing
e   The rules of play (which stipulate the conditions for winning)
f   The rules of 'fair' play (boundaries of acceptable play)
g   The nature of communications among players
h   The degree of uncertainty surrounding the outcomes

Institutional leaders have always had to contend with such forces, but the prevailing consensus or collegial norms, coupled with a certain respect for the authority of legitimate office holders, was usually sufficient to sort out behavioural aberrations without too much fuss. Under conditions of expansion, the conflicting interests of organizational sub-groups could most often be accommodated by giving partial funding now and policy commitments for future funds. As long as powerful individuals and groups received what they perceived to be reasonable shares of expanding resources, the core organizational coalitions were maintained in relative harmony (Cyert and March 1963). Those not receiving their fair share and who had marketability elsewhere often exercised that ultimate market sanction against deterioration in organizational performance — 'exit' (Hirshman 1970).

The politics of institutional change under conditions of instability or contraction are different from those most commonly characteristic of expanding organizations in that they are more intense and 'defensive'. As resources to meet the policy commitments and funding demands of competing organizational groups have diminished, institutional administrators have experienced an increased level of conflict, particularly as options to exit the organization have diminished (except for that select group of highly mobile research and consulting 'stars'), leaving what Hirshman (1970) terms 'voice' or the political response as the only viable option for members of the organization. In their study of forty-two US institutions of higher education, Cohen and March (1974) confirm that financial adversity did result in a precipitous rise in conflict and in the time required to arrive at decisions. Richman and Farmer (1974) and Baldridge (1971a) observe that in many cases none of the formal or informal ordinary mechanisms of power can cope. Non-compliance and the limited effect of traditional sanctions leads to increasing reliance on regulations, due process and sterile legalism.

Interest Group Politics and Coalition Politics
Bacharach and Lawler (1980) discuss four sources of authority and power — office, personal, expertise and opportunity, and argue that only the first is a prerogative of official institutional leaders. Other leaders of informal sub-groups may wield much more effective authority or influence deriving from personality, expertise and control of information related to a particular issue, and the ability to create and exploit opportunities. Cohen and March (1974) illustrate the illusions in the role of the president by attempting to demonstrate that his formal powers over recruitment, planning and the budget are only operative at the margin, and in any case he is reactive to

initiatives made elsewhere.

In our case studies we have witnessed the interplay of interest groups as a manifestation of the apparent divisiveness which contraction or expected contraction induces. For example, high cost faculties are set against low cost faculties; high SSR faculties against low SSR faculties; younger faculty members against older faculty members; academic purists against those who are more market oriented; departments against the centre; unions against management. These tendencies are greatly exacerbated as a result of contraction, and intensified territorial defence is the result.

In each issue which comes to the institutional agenda, interest groups must decide whether to pursue the 'live and let live' mode of operational typical of expansion, or to join a coalition of interest groups in pursuit of a common goal. A distinction may thus be drawn between institutions dominated either by interest group politics or by coalition politics. Coalition politics involve more than transient, issue by issue relationships and much hard bargaining between groups on the content and price of areas of common agreement. Bacharach and Lawler (1980) suggest that conditions either facilitate the emergence of coalitions or reinforce the maintenance of interest group politics. These include a range of hypotheses indicated in Figure 8.1, and a summary is indicated in Figure 8.2. As yet, British higher education institutions do not display strong tendencies towards lasting coalitions of interest groups, but more towards interest-specific groups. The universities in our case studies appeared to be less coalition prone than the polytechnics, possibly because of the severity of the financial contraction in the latter at the time of the study. In one university, a suggested structural rationalization based on a large comprehensive faculty of social science was successfully resisted by an interest-specific grouping of lawyers and educationalists, on the grounds that the 'special' needs of professional schools would be lost in such a rationalization. A polytechnic example was of two faculties of business and management, who had differed on most issues since their inception, suddenly finding unity against a proposal to merge them! One could not imagine such grouping developing any permanency.

There are many implications in the above for institutional leaders. If, as Bardach says (1978), implementation of change is an 'assembly process', ie inducing or in some other way securing the assent or contributions of influential individuals or groups within the organization; it becomes critically important for the leader to develop a system of 'political mapping' of the institution. There are several means which may be used to do this (Bardach 1978; Brosan 1978; Davies 1980), but all rest on the assumption that the leader needs to know the nature of the political jungle, to develop appropriate tactics for stimulating alliances in favour of policies, to create incentives to secure the non-opposition of other groups, and to use the most relevant arenas. The style and tactics which the head of an institution needs to adopt differ considerably depending on whether interest-group politics or coalition politics is the dominant mode. The former does permit a certain degree of informal 'dividing and ruling', using the tactics recommended by Cohen and March (1974). The latter may be much more difficult to contend with, since the tactical sophistication developed by the coalition may be much higher — as was the case in one polytechnic we studied.

FIGURE 8.1
Some hypotheses on the development of coalitions in institutions

1 The greater the resource scarcity within the organization, the greater the likelihood that interest groups will coalesce with others.
2 The greater the proportion of total organizational resources controlled by an interest group, the lower the likelihood it will join a coalition.
3 The greater the proportion of total organizational resources controlled by a prospective coalition, the greater the likelihood that other interest groups will join (because of its potential influence on decision making).
4 The greater the potential conflict of interest, the less viable the coalition option.
5 The more general the issue, the greater the likelihood that groups with divergent interests will engage in interest group politics rather than coalition politics.
6 The shorter the time period between the emergence of an issue and the point at which final action is necessary, the greater the likelihood of interest-group politics rather than coalition politics.
7 The lower the number of communication lines between different interest groups, and the lower the frequency of communication, the greater the difficulty of coalition mobilization.
8 In the face of potential retaliation, longer-term interest groups with co-operative agreements with mutual defence will be more likely to form than more limited coalitions.

Bacharach and Lawler (1980)

FIGURE 8.2
Relationship of ideology and functional goals to institutional politics

IDEOLOGY	FUNCTIONAL GOALS	
	CONVERGENT	NON-CONVERGENT
CONVERGENT	1 Coalition politics	2 Issue-specific outcomes
NON-CONVERGENT	3 Issue-specific outcomes	4 Interest-group politics

Bacharach and Lawler (1980)

RESISTANCE OF ORGANIZATIONAL SUB-UNITS TO THE THREAT OF CONTRACTION

Several recent studies of relative influence within universities indicate that academic units representing disciplines with a high degree of theoretical or 'paradigm' consensus, eg physics or engineering, and attracting outside research funding, command a disproportionate share of influence and resources with the institution (Pfeffner and Salancik 1974a and 1974b; Hills and Mahony 1978; Beyer and Lodahl 1976; Pfeffner and Moore 1980). This experience seems to be paralleled in the recent UGC allocations to British universities. A separate but related stream of research suggests that the influence of organizational sub-units is dependent upon the degree to which they can mitigate organizational uncertainty, ie in a highly unstable environment the sub-unit(s) that copes best with uncertainty and provides the larger organization an added measure of stability is likely to emerge as a powerful and influential group (Thompson 1967; Hickson et al. 1971).

Such research findings suggest that during a period of instability and contraction those sub-units which continue to attract outside research funding or student enrolments, and/or reduce uncertainty in other ways such as possession of information or external political influence, become even more influential. Our interviews with faculty in various departments confirm that those who felt most secure were basing such expectations upon either research or other external funding resilience, externally and internally recognized reputations including widely recognized signs of high quality programmes, and/or buoyant student demand. Those expressing the highest degree of confidence were those strong in all three areas. Almost all units were actively soliciting student applications as a strategy for enhancing their security. In polytechnics and other non-university institutions, student demand as reflected in applications and actual enrolment levels constituted a far more important factor than it did in the university sector.

Departmental size also proved to be used as a criteria by those considering selective as opposed to across-the-board cuts. Small departments or research-service units, often relatively new and not fully developed, whose potential for fiscal savings could be added to one or two other small units were most often considered in programme closure discussions. To close these types of units, as opposed to large, well-established departments, was considered easier both in terms of rationale and politics. As one pro-vice chancellor indicated, it is easier 'to cut than weed'. Cutting selected small units is usually justified on the basis of partial development and little prospect for future full development. Selection of personnel to be terminated is made easier by discontinuing the whole programme or 'cutting'. Politically, such small developing units have often not had time to build up important symbols of an academic reputation or a large and influential clientele advocating their cause.

Cutting into large and influential departments poses a more difficult change strategy for the administrator. Selective personnel 'weeding' requires a well established and well documented evaluation system in order to make a reasonable and legally defensible case. Across-the-board cuts, often decried as an irrational institutional response, can therefore be used to force large departments into 'weeding'. The danger, expressed by many of those interviewed, is that the department will not weed within any systematic context of programme need, but instead will tend to be governed by factors such as tenure or eligibility for premature or early retirement schemes.

Another important factor is clearly the political strength of the department within the university community. Mediger (1978) identifies its elements in Canadian universities as membership of key committees, access to information, and chairmanships, as well as a range of more informal positions of influence.

The factors discussed pose another range of political problems and constraints for the leader in his attempts to find solutions which are rationally sound yet politically acceptable.

DECISION CRITERIA

In the formulation of policy to cope with contraction, the political 'crunch' issue is how to decide which departments grow; which remain in steady state; which contract, and which are to be immediately cut, or progressively phased out. At some point in the argument, the search for appropriate decision criteria becomes a matter of considerable interest.

The balance between 'political' and 'rational' or universalistic decision criteria does, as the above discussion suggests, shift towards the political under resource scarcity. Hills and Mahony's empirical study (1978) of the University of Minnesota confirms this thesis in finding that (1) rational decision criteria were a significant influence only during times of abundant resources, and (2) the relative political power of organizational sub-units was more significant under resource scarcity.

There was evidence in the cases examined that several institutions did strive to develop 'rational' decision critera. Those used by Lancaster University included the numbers of undergraduate applications, taking account of competition; postgraduate taught causes; research students; studentships; percentage of completions; staff-student ratio; research grants; publications; general contributions to the higher education system internally or externally. On this basis, several departments were recommended for closure, but the recommendatins were rejected by senate. Sizer, in Chapter 2 of this volume, outlines a highly systematic means of balancing internal and external criteria in a decision matrix. In the polytechnic sector, one organizational unit within North East London Polytechnic, for example, was initially earmarked for a loss of some twelve academic staff positions on one calculation of workload. The director recommended no loss of positions and the governors compromised on three. We also found an increased level of interest among all academic sub-units in the methods of calculating workload with the participants in the debate well aware of funding and bargaining implications. It is clearly not just a technical question what constitutes a full-time equivalent student, in other words whether a polytechnic should use pooling committee norms or its own versions for internal evaluation and resource allocation or disallocation. Technical questions become political totems, or what Edelman (1964) calls 'condensation symbols'. The debate is not really about whether .5 for a part-time MSc really represents the true resource consumption or the academic status of an MSc vis-à-vis a BEd: it is about teachers' jobs.

We did not find that 'educational' criteria were missing in the debates on contraction. The University of Lancaster, for example, decided to protect an innovative independent study programme even though workload and cost criteria would have targeted it for probable elimination. Similarly Aberdeen University's controversial decision to fill a chair in classics on the basis of a minimum core of faculty needed in that subject area was criticized by those departments with high workloads. The latter example demonstrates how differing perceptions of what constitutes 'educational' criteria can easily form the basis of a political or coalition form of decision making.

However, senates and academic boards find it difficult to grapple with a systematic array of indicators and criteria which encompass input, process, response and impact considerations. The absence of absolute standards enhances the ambiguity already referred to, and thus opens the door to political power play. This in itself is provoking, in the institutions studied, acute tensions between traditional departments who advance conventional academic criteria of performance, and those departments with a considerable market orientation (eg business/management) who advocate criteria related to market penetration, income generation, etc., and moreover, many demand the operational independence to be entrepreneurial.

GENERATING EFFECTIVE POLICY

Alternative Views of Policy Formation

So far it has been argued that there are many mutually reinforcing factors within and without the contemporary higher education institution, which place severe limits on the extent to which it can be managed with any degree of certainty. Furthermore, the environments in which institutions exist vary widely in terms of the degree of hostility, time permitted for decision making, and the degree of both control and competitiveness. It is these latter factors, fuelled as they are by contraction (or the threat of it) which really pose problems for the managers of institutions. The situation imperatives are invariably for clear, firm guidelines as soon as possible to allay fears and solve problems. The ambiguity in the organization itself does not usually lend itself to such precise conviction. So what avenues are open to senior management to develop effective policies to cope with contraction and its attendant issues? At a conceptual level, Enderud (1977) postulates three possible courses of action:

1. To straighten out the anarchy, by reducing the ambiguities and increasing the degree of rationality and structure in decision making. This may involve:
   a. Increasing the degree of structure and formality in organizational charts, regulations and procedures related to planning (highly unlikely to succeed, since non-compliance, informal bypassing of formal structures is likely to increase; as a result, information overload will create reactions against more clarification).
   b. Increasing coercion by the hierarchy (unlikely to succeeed, given the increasing democratization of institutions and the shortage of sanctions to enforce the coercion).
   c. Applying radical shocks to the system, through controlling key elements which influence academics' job satisfaction — validation, monitoring and evaluation of research; control of monies; manipulating balance of teaching, research and administration time (possible, but requires the existence of steady state or contraction, and a stable coalition of appropriately strong institutional interest groups, to make it last).
   d. Actively seeking to manipulate and control all the variables which go to create the anarchy. If these factors are responsible for creating the bulk of our planning difficulties in the first place, it would appear to be logical to try to remove them, if they are hindrances to the effectiveness of the institution. (This would seem to be well beyond the reasonable capabilities of institutional administrations.)
2. To accept the ambiguities of the anarchy trap as inevitable, and use a 'muddling through' style of planning process — non-interventionist and procedural.
   If this course is followed, it may rest on the assumption that it is highly desirable to maintain the anarchy in order consciously to limit the influence of macro-policy matters, and to protect the essential characteristics of academic autonomy. It is a matter of judgement whether external agencies would enable this stance to be taken, what the costs to the institution would be, and whether the problems associated with the contraction would ever be resolved.
3. To evolve a policy/planning process which recognizes the existence of ambiguities at certain points, but uses them positively and consciously in the delivery of workable decisions.
   This would seem to require a fusion of the explicit elements of Lindblom's Theory of Muddling Through, and Enderud's Four Phase Model (1977).
   The assumptions would seem to be that:
   a. Any planning system which attempts to create a massive and fundamental re-think and re-casting of the nature of the institution and a considerable switching of resources across the board over a

short time scale is most unlikely to succeed. A planning system which encourages and facilitates shifts at the margin on a continuing and incremental basis is likely to succeed.
b   The opportunity must be seized within the planning process to ensure that relatively small-scale changes have maximum pay-off in psychological impact and practical effect, particularly to undermine historical relics.
c   Each relatively small-scale change should be approached via a decision-making process which uses the ambiguity rather than is used by it. The administrator must therefore be highly effective in the management of these small-scale planning changes since they create a pattern for the future of the institution.
d   Such successful planning decisions will need to create internal commitment to the means of achieving an end, without necessarily having widespread agreement to the end itself, which is likely to be the subject of value differences.
e   Successful planning decisions may be more opportunist than cyclical in their timing and incidence. They may not necessarily coincide with particular stages in the budget process, but do not have to be ad hoc or unco-ordinated in intent as a result of this.
f   Such a planning process may call for more political/behavioural skills than technical skills (and we do not imply Machiavellianism, or a Nixonian dirty-tricks department; but rather enhanced sensitivities to the realities of others' beliefs, 'references and modes of action').
g   A firm and stable coalition needs to exist over the period of the genesis and implementation of the decision, consisting of key groups who, to collaborate, need incentives, which may be provided by the administration. Furthermore, they must be determined to use the formal structure to effect their desired changes, but in ways best suited to their particular purpose.

A Model of Policy Formation for Conditions of Politicization and Ambiguity
Figure 8.3 is an extension by Davies (1980) of Enderud's Four Phase Model of policy formation. Policy here is concerened with the non-routine, non-programmed decisions of high visibility and potential conflict. The essence of the model lies in the following.
1   The sequence is based on a gradual evolution of the planning decision, to ensure that there is a proper allowance for an essentially high ambiguous period (Phase 1); a political period (Phase 2); a collegial period (Phase 3); and an implementation/executive period (Phase 4). These reflect hitherto alternative views of the institution as an organization. To miss any phase, or to allow insufficient time for it, is to invite problems subsequently, since one may find that, for example, the wrong participants have been coupled (Phase 1); or that one comes to

IMPLEMENTATION 169

FIGURE 8.3
A four-phase political systems model of policy formation

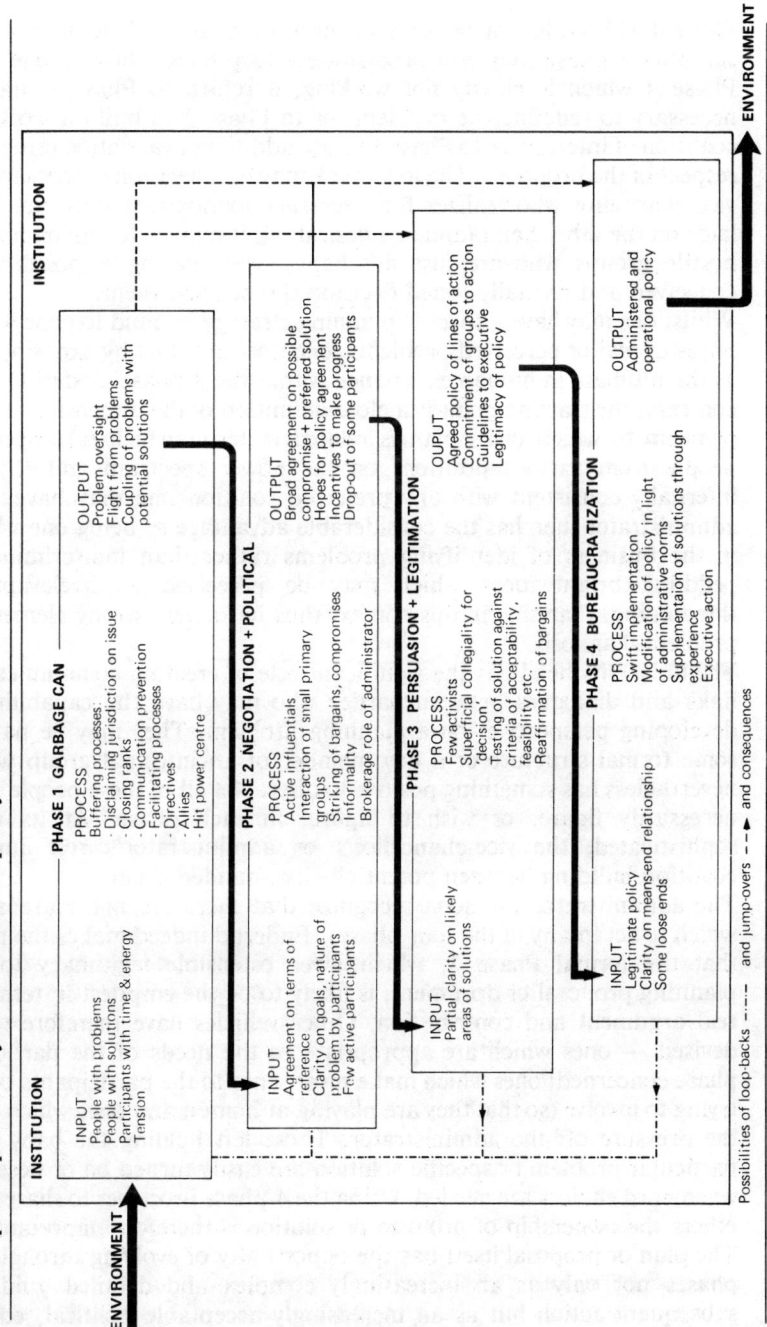

INSTITUTION

PHASE 1 GARBAGE CAN

INPUT
- People with problems
- People with solutions
- Participants with time & energy
- Tension

PROCESS
- Buffering processes:
  - Disclaiming jurisdiction on issue
  - Closing ranks
  - Communication prevention
  - Facilitating processes
- Directives
- Allies
- Hit power centre

OUTPUT
- Problem oversight
- Flight from problems
- Coupling of problems with potential solutions

PHASE 2 NEGOTIATION + POLITICAL

INPUT
- Agreement on terms of reference
- Clarity on goals, nature of problem by participants
- Few active participants

PROCESS
- Active influentials
- Interaction of small primary groups
- Striking of bargains, compromises
- Informality
- Brokerage role of administrator

OUTPUT
- Broad agreement on possible compromise + preferred solution
- Hopes for policy agreement
- Incentives to make progress
- Drop-out of some participants

PHASE 3 PERSUASION + LEGITIMATION

INPUT
- Partial clarity on likely areas of solutions

PROCESS
- Few activists
- Superficial collegiality for 'decision'
- Testing of solution against criteria of acceptability, feasibility etc.
- Reaffirmation of bargains

OUTPUT
- Agreed policy of lines of action
- Commitment of groups to action
- Guidelines to executive
- Legitimacy of policy

PHASE 4 BUREAUCRATIZATION

INPUT
- Legitimate policy
- Clarity on means-end relationship
- Some loose ends

PROCESS
- Swift implementation
- Modification of policy in light of administrative norms
- Supplementation of solutions through experience
- Executive action

OUTPUT
- Administered and operational policy

Possibilities of loop-backs ----- and jump-overs ---▶ and consequences

ENVIRONMENT

Derived from H.G. Enderud (1977)

Phase 4 without having tested a key group's support of the proposition. Jumping a phase may well necessitate a loop-back: thus, if one is in Phase 4 which is clearly not working, a return to Phase 1 may be necessary to redefine the problem, or to Phase 2 to build a workable coalition of interests or to Phase 3 to use additional validation criteria in respect of the proposed. The loop-back may be a decision of the sensitive vice-chancellor who realizes the necessary foundations have not been laid: on the other hand (and less desirably!) it may be forced on him by hostile groups who are just not happy with having a possibly ill-conceived and partially tested decision thrust upon them.

2 Whilst one may have a specific planning strategy in mind to cope with a series of real or perceived problems, one does not start by exposing this as the ultimate in human experience within the 4-phase model! On the contrary, the starting point is a close definition of the dimensions of the problem to which one's plan is related in terms which (a) appeal to people from various positions on the power spectrum and (b) are internally consistent with any preferred solution one may have. The administrator then has the considerable advantage of being one who is in the business of identifying problems rather than indiscriminately peddling bright ideas which may be perceived as irrelevant or threatening. Planning in this context thus has a very strong element of problem diagnosis.

3 The university head has the significant role of creating communication links and dialogues between parties who may have the capability of developing perspectives on a planning problem. They may be part of some formal structure or a key member of an informal group which nevertheless has something positive to offer. Not all of these people need necessarily figure, or wish to figure, in each phase. At its most sophisticated, the vice-chancellor's or administrator's role involve coalition building between potentially like-minded groups.

4 The administrator will soon recognize that there are many arenas in which to act in any of the four phases. Enderud indeed makes the point that the formal Phase 3, which gives ostensible legitimacy to the planning proposal or document, is likely to be the emptiest in terms of real argument and contribution. Other vehicles have therefore to be devised — ones which are appropriate to the needs of the particular phase concerned; ones which make most sense to the participants one is trying to involve (so that they are playing at home); and ones which take the pressure off the administrator. Those left holding the baby of a particular problem or specific solution are easily turned on or deserted when hard choices are needed. Using the 4-phase processes to share with others the ownership of problem or solution is therefore important.

5 The plan or proposal itself has the opportunity of evolving through the phases not only as an increasingly complex and detailed guide to subsequent action but as an increasingly acceptable political, educa-

tional and resource package. Consequently, the model is one which facilitates close attention to task and process concurrently — one of the perpetual problems of organizational theorists, and practitioners (Blake et al. 1981).

Applications of the Model
When this model is applied to the British cases studied by the authors, some very interesting perspectives begin to emerge. The tentative conclusions (at the time of writing) are thus:

1 There are few cases where agreed policy requiring contraction has been delivered at the end of Phase III in order to be implemented at Phase IV. Senates or academic boards have normally referred back or flung out executive proposals for departmental rationalization encompassed in a 'Grand Strategy' type of document, thus creating a loop-back usually to Phase I, for a redefinition of the problem.
2 The reasons why proposals have foundered eventually at Phase III are normally to be found in the neglect or failure of critical processes in the preceding Phases I and II, eg:
   a Failure to appreciate the magnitude and dynamics of political feeling generated by proposals.
   b Neglect of informal action by senior administrators (especially Phases I and II) and an undue reliance on the ability of senates to process controversial proposals.
   c Reluctance of top management to get involved in bargains and incentives to develop support for policy packages (Phases II and III).
   d Unwillingness of top management to play a brokerage part between interest groups, particularly in the passage of vital information (Phase I and II).
   e Neglect of the vital function of building alliances in support of proposals, even when potential opposition groups had not yet crystalized their joint preferences, and were still disorganized.
3 In all cases, the head of the institution stated his personal reputation as chairman of a steering committee/working party/development committee; to produce strategies for contraction thus jeopardizing his subsequent freedom of manoeuvre, especially in full senate meetings.
4 The working party concept, whilst a time-honoured device of collegial contemplation has tended to act as a closed system collecting 'objective' information and presenting it cold to senates without prior political preparation.
5 Grand Strategy documents give the distinct impression of being ultimate statements, rather than snapshots on the way to an evolving solution. Consequently, in full senate debates, they tend to polarize positions into 'winners' and 'losers': in general, not a good strategy for managing change.

6 The Grand Strategy mode of operation is clearly very vulnerable, especially when all the critical information on the performance of departments underlying such analyses is not made publicly available. This is usually for admirable gentlemanly reasons of not wishing to expose too cruelly the weakness of colleagues' departmental leadership. Senates have interesting ways of reacting to disturbing tidings, not the least being the almost intuitive formation of negative coalitions; the collegium defending itself against the bureaucracy!

7 It may well be that one abortive attempt to push through such proposals is needed to test the process! Certainly, in the authors' view, some institutions who have undergone the harrowing experience of having policies rejected have learned a great deal about the process of managing change and there is considerable evidence that some of the tactics used once will not be used again — or will be substantially modified.

BUILDING CONSENSUS

Consensus building is seen here as the development of commonly held values and beliefs which can be used subsequently to deliver a range of policies which stand a chance of being implemented by general consent and goodwill. In Enderud's terms, it would be a means of recognizing and working with the ambiguities. It has very much to do with organizational climate, and can be seen to be an essential element in effective corporate strategy, and in reducing conflict levels and ambiguity. However, consensus building, like other key change processes, is permeated and substantially influenced by the general characteristics of periods of contraction already described: eg a high degree of environmental uncertainty and consequent differences in perceptions as to the duration and extent of enrolment and budgetary contraction. Consensus building, by its very definition, is highly dependent upon a reasonable degree of commonly-held expectations as to future conditions. In the cases reviewed, those institutions exhibiting a relatively high degree of consensus under conditions I classify as Category I (slowed growth) and II (moderate contraction) types of environments were those which had: (1) anticipated a period of instability or contraction and initiated a serious 'programme review' or 'corporate strategy' exercise while normal levels of trust and confidence existed within the institution; (2) built over time a widely-held consensus as to what constitutes the institutional 'core'; or (3) chosen to present a strong, if temporary, stand ('stonewalling') against any threatened or possible external constraints.

Programme Review

The first approach, that of anticipatory rethinking as a basis for corporate strategy normally requires considerable lead time in institutions of higher education because of the existence of strong norms for widespread consultation and peer review. The case of the State University of New York

(SUNY) at Albany illustrates the time and extent of consultation required in using this approach (Shirley and Volkwein 1978). In 1970 SUNY-Albany initiated a series of academic programme reviews which included all-graduate programmes on the campus. Ninety-eight separate teams of external consultants as well as internal bodies were employed in building up a wealth of information in the determination of campus priorities. Based upon these evaluations, which included programme quality as well as need and cost criteria, programmes were clustered in six categories: (1) to be continued at the present level of activity; (2) to be continued but at a reduced level of activity and resources; (3) to be continued but at an increased level of activity and resources; (4) to be singled out for further development as areas of excellence; (5) to be phased out; and (6) new programmes to be developed. When SUNY—Albany sustained major financial reductions in 1975-6 and 1976-7, a presidentially appointed Select Committee on Academic Programmes and Priorities relied heavily upon these programme reviews undertaken since 1970 and recommended selective programme cuts in such areas as an experimental four-year degree programme, an art history programme, astronomy and space science, comparative and world literature, history and systematics of science, speech pathology and audiology, the school of nursing, and the secondary education training school. The existence of peer reviews in these and other programmes, confirmed by the judgements of two select committees on overall priorities, provided a fairly widely accepted and legitimate base upon which to shed some programmes.

Lead time may not be sufficient to initiate this type of comprehensive, consultative, peer-review-based, programme-review, mode of consensus building. Given a shorter time frame and a more politicized environment, many institutions have used the small, carefully chosen committee appointed to examine institutional priorities as a mechanism to compensate for lack of time and consultation. Lancaster, Southampton, and Sussex Universities, as well as the highly publicized Swinnerton-Dyer Committee at London University, illustrate this mode. Consensus is more difficult to achieve under these circumstances. In the cases of Lancaster, Southampton and Sussex, the initial faculty reaction to reports issued was an accusation of premature and precipitate action on the part of the administration and therefore a rejection of recommendations. In each case, however, the committee's report has served an educative function by raising the level of awareness as to the problems facing the university and serving as a powerful agenda-setting mechanism for further discussions. In fact within less than a year after reporting, most of the recommendations contained in each of these three institutional reports have either been implemented or are in the process of negotiation.

The select committee mode of consensus building relies heavily upon the credibility and legitimacy of its membership, the importance of being able to initiate and set the agenda, and the rationale used in recommending major changes. The rationale used in the British cases cited above was not necessarily detailed nor specific to individuals affected but generally did coincide with widely perceived reputations or notions of the viable size of the unit concerned: eg the Swinnerton-Dyer Committee's interim report placing the London School of Economics and Imperial College on the top of its 'untouchables' list of preserving areas of highest quality (The Guardian, 2 June 1981).

The case of North East London Polytechnic (NELP) illustrates how the failure to build on membership credibility and a rationale coinciding with widely perceived reputations of quality can work against the select committee method of consensus generation. In February 1980 a small group of governors and administration proposed programme closures in sociology, applied economics, humanities and mathematics as well as substantial reductions in many administrative support areas. The initial report was very brief and appeared to rely primarily upon loosely constructed references to national manpower needs as a rationale. Several of the academic units identified for elimination responded vigorously and cited relatively high student demand, high student-staff ratio, reputations of quality, and their tendency to be identified with unpopular political activity as a rationale for defence. The response of NELP's academic board, joined by an increasingly strong union, was a broad-based coalition opposing the proposed cuts and eventually turning back the proposals altogether.

We found that attempting to build consensus on academic programme priorities through a carefully developed programme review mechanism encounters increasing difficulty as the amount of lead time diminishes and as the magnitude of the contraction increases. Faculty interviewed in the NELP case, for example, unanimously confirmed that any programme review efforts mounted at this stage in the contraction, whether initiated by the governors, director or even the academic board, would be highly suspect for hidden agendas. Behn (1980) also cautions against the use of the 'study panel' technique in that 'the committee might recommend cuts which conflict with the manager's corporate strategy'.

Conducting evaluations and reviews in a highly charged political environment gives rise to both offensive and defensive evaluation strategies and tactics (Davies 1980). The former may include shrewd appointments of key evaluators, control of circulation of reports, and sophisticated use of media relations. Those on the defensive may challenge the validity of the concepualizations, methodologies and statistics in a review in an attempt to discredit it. The concept of the Self Evaluating Organisation (Wildavsky 1977) is a very difficult one to operationalize in troublesome times.

'Core' Values and Programmes
Some institutions may not need the SUNY-Albany type of formal programme review process for arriving at a consensus on institutional priorities. Clark's research suggests that some institutions have developed a relatively cohesive set of publicly expressed beliefs and values, rooted in the institution's history

and its unique accomplishments, which provides a means of organizational unity around which priorities form (Clark 1972). The University of California at Berkeley provides a case in point. Having sustained substantial specific budget cuts in its instructional and research budgets in 1966 and 1971, the Berkeley campus set out a plan for the 'steady state' in 1972, with the most recent revision of that plan last year. Essentially Berkeley's budgetary strategy has been to preserve intact its core academic programmes as a first priority, necessary services on which these programmes depend as a second priority (eg admissions, registrar, accounting, some student services, etc.) and other programmes that 'supplement and enrich the academic programme' (eg some business functions, some physical plant and student services, some administrative functions, logistical services, experimental academic programmes, public service and cultural activities, etc.) as a third priority (Berkeley 1980). While the stated plan envisions preserving all established colleges and schools as 'core', priorities within the core were developed by influential faculty and senior academic administrators during closely held contingency planning exercises undertaken in anticipation of a possible 25 per cent budget cut. (A voter initiative on the California ballot in 1980 would have cut state income tax by 50 per cent.) This relatively informal and confidential contingency plan reportedly would have eliminated two professional schools, thereby preserving the core of academic tradition and strength in the sciences, humanities, and social sciences. Incidentally, Michigan State University's recently proposed cutbacks offer another case. Budget cuts gave priority to (1) the traditional undergraduate and graduate curricula, (2) the university's land grant mission, and (3) the professional areas of high student interest.

As Clark (1972) points out, however, a crisis period does offer an opportune time for a major change in the organizational saga. In a survival atmosphere, an organization may

'relinquish the leadership to one promising a plan that promises revival and later stength . . . Deep crisis in the established organization thus creates some of the conditions of a new organization. It suspends past practice, forces some bordering groups to stand back or even to turn their backs on failure of the organization, and it tends to catch the attention of the reformer looking for an opportunity.'

Faced with varying degrees of fiscal and enrolment crises, many institutions are ripe for the type of non-incremental change Clark describes. Many emergent institutions, including new universities and polytechnics have been caught at a stage of partial institutional development. Contraction or steady state has come at an awkward time in the institution's history, preventing in many cases the development of a 'proper' balance among disciplines, and forcing a re-evaluation of previously planned evolutionary development.

The organizational saga is therefore a highly variable but often important factor in building consensus about the direction of change. In some highly diversified and entrepreneurial institutions, such as North East London Polytechnic, a clear and reasonably cohesive organizational saga did not appear to be an important element in consensus building.

Cases reviewed also suggest that a weakly held organizational saga quickly disintegrates as the contracting environment moves from Category I through Category II. Strongly held organizational sagas, on the other hand, appear in other cases to be one of the most important variables in determining institutional response, particularly in Category I and II types of environments. We have still to see what the recent UGC decisions will uncover in terms of the resilience of organizational sagas in universities.

The Use of Incentives
Consensus building cannot be viewed solely as the generation of common views about a series of phenomena in institution: it is also very much about whether people subsequently behave as if there were common views. In the task, therefore, of trying to generate some sort of basic agreement about the shape of an institution and its academic and other policies, the role which incentives play at present, or could play in the future, is likely to be significant.

Why would faculty, in particular, change their behaviour and performance just because a document encompasses a desired institutional change? Such a comment may be regarded as distasteful by custodians of public accountability (who would argue a legal basis for compliance); by proponents of rational planning processes (who may not admit the possibility!); and by the professional academic community (who would argue that the concept of a collegium embraces dedication, professional standards and doing the right thing in the interests of the institution).

However, because of the manifestations of organized anarchy, because of the rapidly increasing visibility of collective bargaining schemes and because of the onset of steady state, it cannot be denied that certain types of reward and incentives may (a) contribute to a complex set of motivations; and (b) be necessary in the future.

In our case studies of British universities, we did not find much evidence that senior administrators were admitting to thinking about explicit incentives as a means of delivering policy agreement. (This was less so in the polytechnics we visited.) It may be because such an admission would be perceived as somehow unprofessional. Yet, if institutions are trying to become increasingly explicit about policies, this in itself may necessitate more formal incentive structures to translate these goals into work expectations and faculty behaviour. Three immediate examples of such corporate policies frequently mentioned in the context of the next five years are:

    a   The movement towards recurrent/community/non-traditional education, given the declining birthrate in many countries.

    b   The attempt to get more faculty to engage in research in some UK polytechnics; to be more immediately competitive with universities in the battles to come.

c The attempt to encourage many research-oriented faculty in universities to improve their teaching performance or become involved in new teaching programmes, to be in a better position to cope with polytechnic challenges.

Let us conjecture what incentive structure would be needed by an institution to move its members in these directions. It can certainly be said that such movement depends on:

a The degree to which institutional goals are well formed and articulated.

b The degree to which faculty behaviour in support of organizational goals is evaluated and rewarded.

If one looks at some of the examples quoted, it is clear that the incentive structures in some institutions are stacked against implementations of such policies. In the case of movements to recurrent/community education, for instance, the necessity of creating highly flexible programme structures, modes of study, and attendance patterns may be thwarted by strong disincentives consisting of the bother of inventing new fee structures; low, full-time equivalent weightings for part-time students; absence of time-off in lieu for working unsociable hours; and the low academic status often accorded to such work in most institutions. If, in the case of the UK polytechnics, few faculty choose to participate in further research programmes, it is because research-related policies do not coincide with teaching-related incentive structures. In the third case above, if the production of extensive publications and the acquisition of research money do not result in any career advancement because promotions are based on administrative roles, this policy will find it hard to survive in fact.

The literature on the use of incentives in higher education policy formation and actual implementation is somewhat sparse. Fenker (1977) describes one process for eliciting the nature of the relationship between policies and incentives. He suggests that one should (Figure 8.4):

a Define the variety of work-related behaviour that faculty or others are expected to perform, specifically and unambiguously.

b Develop a system for weighting the behaviour according to their importance in determining overall performance — based on faculty perceptions, administrative expectations or a combination of each.

c Identify the incentives operating within the institutional environment, and rank them according to their relative importance. This will yield institutional norms, capable of classification into those externally or internally generated. (See Figure 8.5)

d Determine the relationship between the performance of job behaviours and the incentives — actual, ideal and perceived. This may be done via a matrix.

e Analyse the data and suggest the changes needed to restore the equilibrium between policies and incentive structures. Such an analysis throws up questions regarding the (relative) importance of incentives to faculty; the importance of different incentives in different rank positions; the relationship between the institution's operational structures and processes and the faculty's perceptions of incentives; the preferences displayed for monetary vis-à-vis professional incentives by faculty.

FIGURE 8.4
The nine faculty behaviours used in the incentive analysis

Behaviour
1 If I were to moderately revise or improve a course I am presently teaching . . .
2 If I were to make substantial, creative changes or improvements in a course that I am presently teaching . . .
3 If I were to design, develop, and teach an entirely new course for my department . . .
4 If I were able to make demonstrable improvements in my teaching performance during the year and document it with the faculty evaluation questionnaire . . .
5 If I were to teach a one-course overload because of departmental need or student interest . . .
6 If I were to engage in an educational activity (attending a school on teaching or seminar on use of media or taking lessons in public speaking, etc.) designed specifically to improve my teaching ability . . .
7 If I were to present the results of my research or creative activity at a public meeting (such as a convention, conference or recital) . . .
8 If I were to publish an article in a professional journal . . .
9 If I were to submit a grant proposal to an agency outside of the university and have it funded . . .

It may well be that incentives will play a more prominent and explicit part in the process of bargaining within the institutions in the future.

It is a feature which does not rest happily within bureaucratic or collegial modes of institutions, but has far more affinity with political models and the behaviour associated with them. However, there is little hard-researched evidence of the effect on the ethos of the organizations had by incentives to operate consensus, particularly in times of contraction. One suspects from the polytechnics visited that consensus thus generated would tend to be relatively shortlived — but this may be because of the particular politics of the institution rather than the inherent characteristics of incentives themselves.

Although most heads of institutions we visited were of the view that consensus was a quality to be sought and nurtured, they fully recognized (1) the tendencies to divisiveness in the contemporary scene, (2) that swift executive action as a response to urgent problems might be increasingly necessary. The interrelationship of these factors could have serious effects on their success in building consensus.

FIGURE 8.5
Incentives identified by faculty
---

1   One-year sabbatical
2   Promotion in rank
3   One-semester merit leave of absence
4   Tenure
5   Five per cent salary increase
6   Recognition of outstanding teaching
7   Travel funds for one conference
8   One-course load reduction
9   University research grant
10 Faculty development grant
11 Recognition for outstanding research
12 Teaching award
13 Student assistant for 15 hours/week
14 Two-week leave for professional development
15 Research award
16 University activities package
17 Free reserved parking place

CENTRALIZATION AND PARTICIPATION
An increased degree of centralization is a commonly observed tendency in decision making under periods of organizational stress and contraction (Trow 1975). Our review of published cases and cases undertaken for purposes of this chapter confirms, at least in some general respects, the validity of the assumption, particularly when moderate and substantial financial contraction occurs suddenly. Governing bodies, by virtue of their legal responsibilities alone, are necessarily more involved in personnel policies and actions and in most cases take a much more active and directive role in financial decisions. Central administrators too have a more active role in conditions of decline for similar reasons and by virtue of the fact that they are normally in the position of proposing policies for response by governing bodies and internal constituents. Since financial criteria tend to dominate policy formulation under contraction, those in possession of financial information and controls, the administration and governing body, naturally become more proactive. This logical chain of events and distribution of formal responsibilities can be misleading, however, in the simplicity of its

conclusion. Indeed some argue that the organizational conditions created by contraction necessitate not only centralized decision making but abandoning the traditional, unobstrusive style of organizational change in favour of a highly directive and 'intrusive' style (Behn 1980).

The thesis of centralized decision making requires qualification when applied to institutions of higher education. Our review of cases suggests that a strong, top-down, corporate strategy approach to contraction decisions results in substantial political conflict within the institution and an erosion of trust and confidence between top administrative personnel and affected faculty and staff. How serious or permanent the erosion is depends upon the style used and the level of the existing stock of trust and confidence. In the case of North East London Polytechnic, the erosion was widely perceived as serious and was cited by the director in his letter of resignation. The University of Lancaster's plan, although similarly voted down by the faculty senate, was developed in a more consultative and representative style and the administration generally enjoyed a higher level of trust and confidence among faculty. In the cases reviewed, then, central administrative initiative was not as much at issue as the manner and style in which it was carried out.

In 'normal' times organizational members tend to be 'fluid' participants in the decision-making process, ie an individual may be actively involved for a short time on a particular issue but in general is not highly active across many issues. We found that this characteristic of 'fluid participation' generally held for slowed growth environments and that as institutions encountered contraction only moderate increases in participation levels were experienced. Faculty were more generally aware of circumstances and policies and were found to be more active in seeking up-to-date information, eg THES was actively read and departmental heads and administrators were expected to keep faculty informed. Active participation in decision making or in lobbying decision makers was still left, by and large, to those representing faculty interests, eg union officials, department heads, etc. Regular attendance at union meetings, with the exception of a 'crisis' issue meeting, has not appreciably changed, although union membership at our case study institutions has.

The absence of a dramatic change from decision making characterized by fluid participation could be interpreted as contributing to if not asking for more centralized decision making. Our interviews do not substantiate this conclusion. Despite continuing levels of relatively low direct participation, faculty expectations for involvement in decision making were higher than they were before slow growth or moderate contraction affected the institution. Expected modes of involvement most commonly mentioned were early consultation with respect to changes in the environment and alternative policy responses. High levels of environmental uncertainty induce considerable stress among organizational members, who may not actively seek direct participatory roles but who have a heightened sense of a 'need to know' and preferably not by reading about it in the newspaper. The four phase model analysed above (pp.168-172) makes it clear that 'participation' is by no means to be equated with 'representation' or 'committees'. There are many arenas, formal and informal, where participation, access, consultation and information can take place, and if senior administrators are to cope successfully with ambiguity, the implications for their roles are clear.

CONCLUSION

Significance of External Stimuli

The evidence and findings presented here on change under conditions of instability and contraction can be read either negatively or positively. On the negative side, institutions of higher education could be viewed as extremely conservative organizations generating little change in and of themselves and exhibiting a highly defensive and traditional posture. On the positive side, the conditions created by instability and contraction could be viewed as critical yet ideal periods for effecting programmatic and institutional mission changes that would prove difficult under other circumstances. From our review of cases we believe that fiscal uncertainty and stress can be a creative force for change, particularly programmatic reformulations, within institutions of higher education. One of the lessons to be learned from the Great Depression is that of opportunities lost. The American Association of University Professors report evaluating the impact of the depression on higher education concludes that 'expediency', rather than rationally planned reorganization, was the determining factor in achieving budgetary reductions (Willey 1977).

Organizations, particularly public ones, seem to have a reputation for resistance to change. While there is certainly evidence to substantiate that reputation, there is often more change occurring than meets the eye of the casual observer. For example, a research study (Natchez and Bupp 1973) on changes in budgetary allocations within the US Atomic Energy Commission revealed that over a 15-year period very significant shifts occurred within an overall budget that changed only incrementally. The realignment of priorities within the agency was clearly not revealed in the image of stability portrayed in the totals. In a very fundamental sense, change goes against the nature of an organization. Hence evaluation and change efforts within institutions often run headlong into such pillars of organizational conservatism as benefits, careers, and clientele. Given the natural tendency of organizations to resist change, many theorists as well as politicians view a heavy dose of external inducements and directives as necessary to effect any significant change (Pfeffer and Salancik 1978). We acknowledge that external proddings are often needed to stimulate internal changes — indeed that a general pattern of environmental stimulus and organizational response is characteristic of all organizations. Overly concentrating on external prodding of change can, however, divert attention from another fundamental element in the nature of organizations with relevance for change, ie organizations need sources of support that encourage stability as well as change (Wildavsky 1979).

Constructive and socially useful changes within institutions of higher education are very difficult to achieve in a perpetually turbulent and highly uncertain environment. US case studies cited confirm that such environmental conditions encourage delays in decision making (a state of perpetual remaking of decisions in many cases) and render long-range planning virtually impossible (Rubin 1980; Bowen and Glenny 1980).

Reformulation of an institution's role or mission or even more marginal changes such as programme 'rationalization' require time and some idea of what new level of fiscal equilibrium might be expected. Governments caught in recessionary times and the attendant difficulties of predicting revenues may well have difficulty in providing assurances of new equilibrium levels. Governments committed to inducing new equilibrium levels as a matter of policy, on the other hand, may misjudge the viability of the levels set and/or the time required to achieve those levels with an acceptable level of rationality.

One of the key tasks of both government and higher education leaders is therefore to develop mutual understanding as to probable financial equilibrium levels over a period of time. Once reasonably stable parameters have been established and assuming that they provide both pressures for change and sources of stability, educational leaders in concert with their faculties can proceed to develop long-range plans.

Leadership Priorities

The difficulty of achieving this type of mutual understanding between government and higher education leaders is twofold. The first is that the British and American political systems do not necessarily lend themselves to stability of policy, ie short-term, election-relevant actions tend to be pursued. Government leaders may therefore find it 'politically irrational' to give higher education a greater measure of support and stability than they enjoy themselves or in fact can provide.

The second difficulty emerges from the fact that institutional leaders are, by the very nature of their roles, advocates for their particular institution, genuinely believing in the need for and value of programmes offered by their institutions. They are naturally reluctant to agree to any 'equilibrium' that might undermine the viability of these programmes. Yet without some reasonable estimate of resources available it is difficult to engage in positive planning efforts, ie goals are dependent upon resources.

Another set of major tasks for institutional leadership in conditions of instability and contraction concerns maintaining a positive climate in which to work. The first element here seems to us to be a sense of institutional initiative or 'master of our own destiny' feeling within the institution. This may take the form of institutionally initiated 'programme rationalization' or pruning, or a united stance against contraction pressures. Whatever the particular response, the general psychological benefit is one of a proactive attitude. Another key element, closely related to the first, is to avert a paralysis of action by the institution. One of the well recognized deficiencies of widely distributed patterns of influence, such as those found in institutions of higher education, is a tendency to paralyse action altogether (Banfield 1961). Carefully formulated initiatives guided through the thickets of academic environment by leadership sensitive to genuine consultation and to political gamesmanship were a rare phenomena to observe in our review of cases.

In formulating such initiatives, institutional leaders need to balance political feasibility with educationally sound strategies. There are, for example, strong pressures for uniformity of treatment both in the context of institutions vis-à-vis the government and sub-units within the insitution. This tendency toward uniformity derives from (1) political pressures of equity, and (2) the uncertainty of doing otherwise. Krier and Ursin (1977) identify the political forces operative within the US Congress which lead to uniform standards for air pollution legislation. They also identify the high degree of technical uncertainty surrounding the establishment of anything other than uniform standards.

Davies (1979), discussing the evolution of policy appropriate to contraction in school systems in the USA, uses the term 'Policy Portfolio' to describe the range of necessary policies. Strategic policies are concerned with the desired shape and size of the institution. Substantive (or 'bread and butter') policies are concerned with precise plans for curriculum and research development, personnel, space allocation, cost effectiveness, student services, etc. Climatic policies are concerned with creating a collaborative mood in the organization where people are prepared to be open and confront problems. They include, for instance, openness of information (for staff), secondment and staff development personalities, rewards and incentives. Interest groups are rarely mobilized by lofty strategic thoughts, but they are activated by the substantive policies which affect them directly. It is desirable that climatic policies be operational before leaders start pushing strategic and substantive policies through, otherwise the loop-backs described earlier (pp.170-171) will surely occur, and it is much more difficult to resurrect a good climate once it has disappeared.

Leadership Roles
We have tended to talk of the vice-chancellor or institutional head as the 'change-agent'. Yet it emerges from the cases that it is not a good thing for him to be the 'front man', leading his troops into battle on a white charger. Defeats (and there will be some) weaken his position. It appears to be far more effective to develop a strong senior leadership team to share the load. In this case functional specialisms may develop within the team. Collectively they stand a greater chance of participating across the whole range of discussions and meetings throughout the institution to assist in problem

clarification, information dissemination, the sowing of seeds and the proposal of solutions. This view is strongly confirmed by Mayhew (1979) and Enderud (1977) in the various phases of his Four Phase Model. However, this needs to be balanced and supported by a broad-based alliance of people in different parts and in different levels of the organization. Davies (1979) also refers to the role of central planning and service organs as agents of change, rather than as hatchet men. In this sense, they would need to consider colleagues in the departments as clients needing specific assistance to overcome problems associated with contraction. With the exception of certain curriculum and educational technology units, we did not get the impression that those in central units saw themselves as providing help or giving a service; they were in the business of maintenance and control rather than organizational development. If contraction is about institutional change, then it follows that those in key staff positions need to develop capabilities in this area to supplement their technical expertise, and personally act in a low-key, informal, influencing role. Kipnis, Schmidt and Wilkinson (1980) have observed what techniques administrators have used in a variety of organizations to influence superiors, subordinates and peers. Their conclusions make interesting reading. It appears that there are quite different tactics used by administrators depending on the benefit sought from the target person; the power and amount of resistance shown by the target person; the size of the work unit; the presence or otherwise of unions; and the administrator's own level in the organization. This field of influencing tactics is one about which we found administrators in our cases reluctant to be too specific, perhaps understandably! Yet, in some ways, it is one of the most crucial aspects of the whole exercise. When Sizer, in Chapter 2 of this volume, speaks of managers of change, it is surely the considerations represented in this paper which represent the qualities he has in mind, both in terms of executive leadership and staff roles.

The other level of leadership is that of middle management, which seems to us to be in a most difficult position, if the evidence of the cases is anything to go by. The role of dean is ambiguous, and usually part-time for a limited period (Buggins' turn). It is not a position which in universities gives appreciable financial reward, intense job satisfaction or great career prospects. The amount of autonomy and authority a dean has will be determined by the degree of centralization in the university, the latitude allowed him by heads of departments in the faculty, and his own style and personality. In polytechnics, there is a growing tendency to appoint full-time, permanent deans, and in some larger institutions they may also double up as assistant directors with a functional responsibility across the institution. If the phenomenon of contraction necessitates middle management which can anticipate cutbacks through meaningful contingency planning; establish priorities in a calm rather than crisis setting; develop faculty wide consensus; enhance the external fund-raising capability of the faculty and deal with the considerable number of personnel problems likely to emerge, it is not at all clear at present what type of deanery is likely to be the most effective. One is not searching for administrative skills, nor scholarship alone, but a rare combination of expertise.

Finally, it has been suggested to us that institutions and their leaders lack the political will to make the decisions associated with contraction, because of the personal unpleasantness involved, the ethical questions raised by butchering one's colleagues, or the shortage of rational or political skills. It has been widely noted that a much more proactive UGC role in specifying precisely what should go or stay in individual institutions would meet with some sighs of relief from vice-chancellors. The evidence collected in our cases does not confirm this view. We saw, even when early attempts had been unsuccessful, a determination to get things right but in ways which made sense in the historical development and character of the institution. Considerable learning and adaptation has taken place in a relatively short period. Nonetheless we come back to the point of viewing problems as opportunities — a trite phase in many ways, yet one which ought to encapsulate a managerial philosophy for the 1980s in higher education.

REFERENCES

Association of American University Professors (1977a) The State University of New York *AAUP Bulletin* August 1977 pp.237-260

Association of American University Professors (1977b) City University of New York: mass dismissals under financial exigency *AAUP Bulletin* April 1977 pp.60-81

Bacharach, S.B. and Lawler, E.J. (1980) *Power and Politics in Organizations* San Francisco: Jossey-Bass

Baldridge, J.V. (1971a) *Power and Conflict in the University* New York: Wiley

Baldridge, J.V. (1971b) *Academic Governance*. Berkeley, California: McCutchan

Banfield, E.C. (1961) *Political Influence* New York: The Free Press

Bardach, E. (1978) *The Implementation Game* Cambridge, Mass.

Becher, T. and Kogan, M. (1980) *Process and Structure in Higher Education* Heinemann

Benn, R.D. (1980a) Leadership for cut-back management *Public Administration Review* November/December pp.613-620

Beyer, J.M. and Lodahl, T.M. (1976) A comparative study of patterns of influence in US and English universities *Administrative Science Quarterly* pp.104-129

Birch, D.W., Calvert, J.R. and Sizer, J. (1977) A case study of some performance indicators in higher education in the UK *International Journal of Management in Higher Eucation* 1 (2)

Blake, R., Mouton, J.S. and Williams, M.S. (1981) *The Academic Administrator Grid* San Francisco: Jossey-Bass

Bowen, F.M. and Glenny, L.A. (1980) *The University in Public Higher Education: Response to Stress at Ten Californian Colleges and Universities* Sacramento, Calif: The California Post Secondary Education Commission

Brosan, G.S. (1978) *Models of Management in Education* Paper presented to Second European Higher Education Management Programme. London: Anglian Regional Management Centre

Burgess, T. and Pratt, J. (1974) *Polytechnics: a Report* Pitman

Carnegie Foundation for the Advancement of Teaching (1980) *Three Thousand Futures* San Francisco: Jossey-Bass

Clark, B.R. (1972) The organisational saga in higher education *Administrative Science Quarterly* June pp.178-184

Clark, B.R. (1978) Academic power: concepts, modes and perspectives. In Van de Graaff, J.H. et al. (Editors) *Academic Power* New York: Praeger Publishers

Cohen, M. and March, J.G. (1974) *Leadership and Ambiguity* New York: McGraw Hill

Corson, J.J. (1973) Perspectives on the university compared with other organizations. In Perkins, J.A. (Editor) *The University as an Organisation* New York: McGraw Hill

Cyert, R.M. and March, J.G. (1963) *A Behavioural Theory of the Firm* Englewood Cliffs, N.J: Prentice Hall

Davies, J.L. (1967) *Organisations in Action* New York: McGraw Hill

Davies, J.L. (1979) *Declining Enrolments, Conflict and Ambiguity: the search for an appropriate policy formation process* Paper presented to British Education Management and Administration Society Annual Conference, Sheffield

Davies, J.L. (1980a) *The Role of the University Rector in Policy Formation in the Contemporary Context of Steady State and Uncertainty* CRE New Series No. 51, Third Quarter

Davies, J.L. (1980b) *Political and Organizational Aspects of Institutional Evauation* Paper presented on OECD—IMHE Touring Seminars of Australia and New Zealand

Dresch, S. (1975) Education saturation: a demographic-economic model *AAUP Bulletin* Autumn 1975 pp.239-247

Edelman, M. (1964 *The Symbolic Uses of Politics* University of Illinois Press

Enderud, H.G. (1977) *Four Faces of Leadership in the Academic Organisation* Copenhagen: Nyt. Nordisk Forlag

Fenker, R.M. (1977) The incentive structure of a university *Journal of Higher Education* XLIII (4) July/August

Fielden, J. and Lockwood, G. (1973) *Planning and Management in Universities* Chatto and Windus

Frances, C. (1980) Planning for the 1980s: apocalyptic vs. strategic planning *Change* July/August pp.39-44

Glenny, L.A. et al. (1976) *Presidents Confront Reality* San Fransico: Jossey-Bass
Glenny, L.A. and Bowen, F.M. (1980b) *Signals for Change: Stress Indicators for Colleges and Universities* A Report to the California Postsecondary Education Commission, Sacramento, California
Hickson, D.J., Hinings, C.R., Lee, C.A., Schneck, R.E. and Pennings, J.M. (1971) A strategic contingencies theory of interorganisational power *Administrative Science Quarterly* June pp.216-229
Hills, F.S. and Mahoney, T.A. (1978) University budgets and organisational decision making *Administrative Science Quarterly* September pp.454-465
Hirschman, A.O. (1970) *Exit, Voice and Loyalty Responses to Decline in Firms, Organizations, and States* Cambridge, Mass: Harvard University Press
Johnson, M.D. and Mortimer, K.P. (1977) *Faculty Bargaining and the Politics of Retrenchment in the Pennsylvania State Colleges, 1971-1976* University Park, Pennsylvania: Centre for the Study of Higher Education, Pennsylvania State University
Krier, J.E. and Ursin, E. (1977) *Pollution and Policy* Berkeley: University of California Press
Kipnis, D., Schmidt, S.M. and Wilkinson, I. (1980) *Intraorganisational Influence Tactics Faculty Working Papers* School of Business Administration, Temple University, Philadelphia
Lindblom, C.E. (1959) The science of muddling through *Washington Public Administration Review*
Mayhew, L.B. (1979) *Surviving the Eighties* San Francisco: Jossey-Bass
Millett, J. (1962) *The Academic Community* New York: McGraw Hill
Mix, M.C. (1978) *Tenure and Termination in Financial Exigency* Washington DC: American Association for Higher Education
Moodie, G.C. and Eustace, R. (1974) *Power and Authority in British Universities* Allen and Unwin
Natchez, P. and Bupp, I.C. (1973) Policy and priority in the budgetary process *American Political Science Review* September pp.951-963
Olsen, J.P. and March, J.G. (1976) *Ambiguity and Choice in Organisations* Bergan Universitets for Laget
Parsons, T. and Platt, G.M. (1973) *The American University* Cambridge Mass: Harvard University Press
Pfeffer, J. and Salancik, G.R. (1974) Organisational decision making as a political process: the case of a university budget *Administrative Science Quarterly* June pp.135-151
Pfeffer, J. and Salancik, G.R. (1978) *The External Control of Organizations* New York: Harper
Pfeffer, J. and Moore, W. (1980) Power in university budgeting: a replication and extension *Administrative Science Quarterly* December pp.637-653

Pressman, J.L. and Wildavsky, A. (1973) *Implementation* Berkeley: University of California Press

Rubin, I. (1980) Universities in stress: decision making under conditions of reduced resources. In Levine, Charles H. (Editor) *Managing Fiscal Stress* Chatham, New Jersey: Chatham House Publishers, Inc.

Richman, B.M. and Farmer, R.N. (1974) *Leadership, Goals and Power in Higher Education* San Francisco: Jossey-Bass

Salancik, G.R. and Pfeffer, J. (1974) The bases and uses of power in organizational decision making: the case of a university *Administrative Science Quarterly* December pp.453-472

Shirley, R.C. and Volkwein, J.F. (1978) Establishing academic priorities *Journal of Higher Education* (5)

Sizer, J. (1980) *Institutional Performance Assessment under Conditions of Changing Needs* Paper presented to Fifth Conference of the Programme on Institutional Management in Higher Education, OECD—CERI, Paris

Sizer, J. (1982) In Wagner, L. (Editor) *Agenda for Institutional Change in Higher Education* Guildford: SRHE

Times Higher Education Supplement (1981) 1 May

University of California (1980) *Long Range Academic Plan Statement, 1980-85* Berkeley: University of California

Thompson, J.D. (1967) *Organisations in Action* New York: McGraw Hill

Trow, M. (1975) The public & private lives of higher education *Daedalus* Winter pp.113-127

Volpe, E.L. (1977) Retrenchment. The case of CUNY. In Heyns Roger, W. (Editor) *Leadership for Higher Education* Washington DC: American Council on Education

Weber, M. (1947) *The Theory of Social and Economic Organisation* New York: Free Press

Wildavsky, A. (1979) *Speaking Truth to Power: The Art and Craft of Policy Analysis* Boston: Little, Brown and Co.

Willey, M.W. (1977) *Depression, Recovery and Higher Education* A Report of Committee Y of the American Association of University Professors. New York: Arno Press (originally published in 1937)

9

A CROSS-NATIONAL VIEW

by Burton R. Clark

As a system of higher education develops, it builds its own sources of continuity and change.[1] The system nearly always grows larger and definitely becomes complex. It acquires structures of work, belief, and authority. Budgets are fixed, personnel entrenched in categories, physical plants turned into sunk costs. Institutions and sectors become major interests with their own traditions and rationales. System hegemony[2] develops: administrators and professors tune to their own norms; insiders have heavy influence, outsiders have great trouble in finding handles. In an age of bureaucracy and profession, to say that an academic system is deeply institutionalized is to mean that constraints upon change and imperatives for change are located in the system.

Thus it matters not whether we are examining the most polity-driven system, such as that of the USSR, or the most market-driven, such as the American. If we want to start at the right place for examining change, we start within the system. And if we want to start at the right end of the system, we start at the bottom. Academic systems, in common, are bottom-heavy. They are based on disciplines and combinations thereof, and organized around operating units, such as the department, that are individually authoritative.[3] Systems of higher education are the most loosely-coupled of those organized social entities that are conglomerate or amalgamated in nature while parading under unitary labels. If we do not grasp the distinctive nature of the operating levels, and take it from there, we simply go up the wrong road, thinking we are looking at structures that will resemble parts of a public bureau or business firm and then wondering why everything is strange or distorted.

To seek the effects of academic forms on change, we can begin with key differences among national systems in their division of work. With footing on this foundation we can then move to differences in authority and integration. Throughout, the analysis will not focus on problems of higher education in the United Kingdom during the next decade. But perhaps the international perspective can add a spot of sophistication, some different shading to the thinking of those who have to stand up to policy and decision. International comparisons at least encourage a certain backing-off from the burning problems of this year and next, helping us to keep the long-run in view and hopefully at least sensitizing us to some boomerang effects that will later disillusion us all and cause our descendants to curse our efforts.

STRUCTURES OF WORK
Within universities and colleges, academic work can be divided horizontally and vertically, in sections and tiers. Among institutions, such divisions can be seen as sectors and hierarchies.

Section Effects
In determining change, it makes a great deal of difference whether a system traditionally has had a chair or department structure at the operating level. The adaptive capacity of the chair is restrained by the capacity and inclination of a single chief, providing a narrow base for comprehending and managing a modern discipline. As chairs multiply to accommodate larger bundles of knowledge and larger clienteles, they fragment and balkanize disciplines as well as faculties and universities. A common characteristic of chair systems undergoing expansion in modern times is that the chairs become too burdened, responsible for more programmes, assistants and students than a single person can supervise effectively. Overload is the operational dynamic that undermines the legitimacy of the chair and gives increasing credibility to the argument that chair power is dysfunctional as well as undemocratic (Clark 1977 pp.126-28).

Because of such failure of form, an evolution from chair to department organization has been taking place during the last two decades in European systems (Van de Graaff 1980). The Swedish system, while retaining chairs, strengthened its departmental organization and has increasingly manipulated task assignments by altering the purposes and domains of the departments (Premfors and Östergren 1978 pp.36-37). The French system, following the 1968 crisis, has sought to group academic personnel, senior and junior alike, in department-like units of teaching and research (unités d'enseignement et de recherche — UERs) (Van de Graaff and Furth 1978 pp.57-58). Notably, the system in the German Democratic Republic went through wholesale top-down reform in the 1960s which, in the universities, replaced a large number of chairs and institutes with a fewer number of departments (Giles 1976 p.10):

> 'The traditional German subdivision of the university into a handful of Faculties (eg Philology, Mathematics and Natural Sciences, Medicine, Law and Economics, Theology) was reshaped into more manageable units known as *Sektiones* comparable to the departments of British and American universities. The innumerable institutes, built around a professional chairholder and often unhealthy centres of patronage and sycophancy, were abolished and merged into departments. In round numbers, some 190 departments (in the entire national system) took the place of 960 institutes. Berlin's Humboldt University, for example, now has 26 departments where formerly it comprised 169 institutes and 7 faculty.'

This was no minor change: 'the introduction of the *Sektion* was the most radical reform to take place in any of the Eastern European systems of higher education. It was also one of the most successful, and attempts to imitate the East German innovation have been detectable in the universities of other Socialist countries' (Giles 1976 p.12).

As a general form, the department has not been under such pressure. It has been assaulted mainly by general-education or liberal-education proponents, chiefly in the United States, who see it as a narrow base for broader programmes (McHenry 1977). The chief weakness of the department lies precisely in this direction. College organization, as typified in Oxford and Cambridge, is more successful in the support of undergraduate education that is something more than disciplinary specialization. Efforts to compensate for the weakness of departments in this respect lead towards matrix organization within which various types of interdisciplinary units co-exist with departments, in each of which both faculty and students participate; eg departments and undergraduate residential colleges at Yale, residential colleges and disciplinary boards at the University of California, Santa Cruz.

Everywhere the sections of universities expand in number. Departments, institutes and chairs multiply to keep up with the increased specialization of knowledge. Ironically, the counter-trend of promoting interdisciplinary programmes and problem-centred units produces additional units of specialized commitment: a child-study centre for example, or an energy research group. Thus the horizontal base of universities and higher education systems becomes wider with every passing decade. Departments may soak up the parochialism of chairs and provide more suitable coverage of disciplines, but the proliferation of departments and counterpart units fragments the base of the enterprise to an ever greater degree. As institutions and systems grapple with this problem, usually in an incoherent fashion, two responses are common: to increase the administrative capacity of the university or college to co-ordinate itself, with more oversight and formal linkage; and to elaborate levels of education and training within and across the many sections. Which brings us to tiers.

Tier Effects
The characteristic form of academic system around the world has provided essentially one organizational tier devoted to the work of the first professional or academic degree, with more advanced work consisting of students staying on with a professor to do research and write papers and dissertations. In contrast, the deviant US model stumbled upon a vertical differentiation in the last quarter of the nineteenth century in which a second major tier of professional schools and a graduate school in the arts and sciences sits on top of the undergraduate college.

The two-tier form has proven that it has greater adaptive capacity. The second tier, as exemplified in the US structure, is a bypass mechanism for the incorporation of new interests. The old-time professor — Mr Chips in the extreme — could retain his students through the undergraduate years, time enough to offer them an education defined as general or liberal while guaranteeing that type of academic a clientele, a curriculum, and a domain of jobs. The new professional training, and advanced research, did not directly intrude upon and compete for this time and space. Instead, operating somewhat in a world of its own, it became particularly responsive to emerging professions and would-be professions. As put by Robert H. Wiebe, an American historian, (1967 p.121. Emphasis added) the US universities did not simply respond to emerging professions but helped to initiate them.

'The universities played a crucial role in almost all of these professional movements. *Since the emergence of the modern graduate school in the seventies* (1870s), the best universities had been serving as outposts of professional self-consciousness, frankly preparing young men for professions that as yet did not exist. By 1900 they held an unquestioned power to legitimize, for no new profession felt complete — or scientific — without its distinct academic curriculum; they provided centres for philosophizing and propagandizing; and they inculcated apprentices with the proper values and goals. Considering the potential of the universities for frustration, it was extremely important that higher education permissively, even indiscriminately, welcomed each of the new groups in turn.'

Thus the second tier expanded, 'permissively, even indiscriminately,' to include an unusually wide range of professions, overcoming 'the potential of the universities for frustration.' In contrast, the British system, much more undergraduate-centred, apparently has difficulty in supporting advanced work. Becher and Kogan (1980 pp.118-119) have noted that 'postgraduates are another group who, although they apparently enjoy at least the limited participatory rights of students, are marginal to the enterprise in much the way that we have observed full-time contract researchers to be. . . . the institutional provision for doctoral students is much more limited than that for undergraduates. . . . This state of affairs is a relic. . . .' Perhaps the question can be raised, if it has not been already, of what price is paid for the emphasis in Britain on the first degree level and not the PhD.

Because multiple levels provide a more flexible and adaptive structure for varied tasks and changing demands than does a single one, we can predict increased vertical differentiation in national systems towards as many as four and five levels as marked by degrees. As a single tier buckles under the burdens of expansion, systems innovate with first, second, and third 'cycles', as in France, or new national testing devices, as in West Germany, or various other ways of establishing new hierarchies of sequence and selection, to cope with the tensions of mass entry and selective training, general and specialized education, teaching and research. However reluctantly, separate organizational levels are created to underpin the added programmes and degrees. For example, during the 1970s, the Japanese system has sought to create more graduate schools.

Helping to stimulate the development of tiers is the growth and proliferation of sections specified earlier. A more general first tier offers some integration within and across disciplines. In the new French model the first cycle attempts a more general approach to a discipline or profession, an introductory bridging of sub-specialities that offers some possibility of a reintegrated foundation for later specialization. In short, the expansion of tiers permits some consolidation of subjects, thus serving as a partial counter-force to the separation of academic specialities.

Sector Effects

The principle that diversified structures facilitate change applies even more strongly to the division of labour among institutions. National systems vary from single institutional type under single state authority to many types under market conditions. On the whole, the multiple-type systems have been more adaptable, and the direction of change is away from homogeneity. A single sector of nationalized public universities cannot zig and zag in the many different directions given by increasing heterogeneity of function. The form becomes overloaded; it does not adapt well to new types of students, new connections to labour markets, new academic fields; the hand of the past, fixed in faculty structure, is heavy to the point of rigidity. Many groups then develop an interest in new or partially-new forms that bypass the old. And so they chip away. If they are prevented from adding new enterprises and new sectors, they find a way to add a department here and an institute there, under regional or municipal sponsorship or private support, especially as the rigidity of the old nationalized system weakens its capacity to prevent such initiatives from taking place. Tightly-bounded, simplified systems lose legitimacy through repeated failures of response.

Separation of sectors is a critical issue that will not go away. The search for fair shares on the part of institutions and their staffs, and for equality of treatment and outcomes for students, pushes systems to be rid of binary, tripartite, and other multiple-sector arrangements. Thus national systems still actively seek a way to *de*differentiate. The label of university is generously passed around, as in many American states. New definitions tell the public there is going to be only one type of institution, the comprehensive university, with everything made a part of it, as in the Federal Republic of Germany and Sweden. Then the all-embracing unit must be exceedingly diverse internally, acting as a holding company that blesses everything with a single name while allowing fundamentally different enterprises within it to have different clienteles and different types of faculty, even to serve different levels of higher education and to give different types of degrees. The modern comprehensive university in some countries is an effort to have it both ways, to allow for differentiation of major parts while assigning a formal equality that will, it is hoped, keep down invidious distinctions. But this latent form appears unstable, especially in large systems, as the more prestigious parts resist the lumping of everyone together and as attentive publics as well as insiders perceive real differences and attach different values to the parts. Thus the German effort in the 1970s to develop completely new comprehensive universities and fashion ones that brought together technological schools with old universities has not been well received by university professors, whose resistance alone appears capable of stalling or severely attenuating the development of the form. Explicit sectors thus seem to be the chief answer to the macro-organization of an evermore extended division of academic labour.

Hierarchy Effects
Institutional hierarchy ranges from dominance by one or two universities, or a relatively small, élite sector, to modestly steep but open institutional ranking, to little or no difference in prestige. The forms of hierarchy have great persistence. The peaks of the French, Japanese, and British systems have exhibited great capacity to maintain their standing and dominance, to the dismay of reformers in general and egalitarian-minded ones in particular. The modest and somewhat open hierarchy of the US system also sustains itself, never, on the one hand, making any significant move towards the hierarchical form nor, on the other hand, moving towards total parity of esteem. Research universities remain the dominant sector. Within that sector (and each of the other sectors) some institutional mobility is noticeable: for example, Stanford University and the University of California, Los Angeles (UCLA) moved upward in the status hierarchy in the three decades between 1950 and 1980. But individual position is typically sticky, with strength begetting strength and with weakness developing into a vicious circle, in the long as well as the short run. And the formal institutional equality characteristic of the university component of the German system and all of the Italian one also persists well, without any rapid movement towards greater hierarchy.

The most hierarchical systems continue to serve relatively well in selecting and training talented people for public administration, their grand historical contribution. But against growing claims for equality and fair treatment they increasingly appear to be cases of failure of form, to be not sufficiently adaptive, and hence they face mounting pressure to change. Clienteles are joined by have-not sectors and second-best institutions in pressing for more equitable shares and less invidious distinctions. And as certain enterprises strive to become better, and do become better, as in many cases in Britain, they become attractive alternatives in some fields to the peak institutions. Leading private universities in Japan have become known increasingly for their quality, overlapping from almost the top the prestige rankings of the public universities. Even in France, the small and narrow peak comes under increasing criticism and more universities have entered the status competition. The move into more accessible higher education erodes the legitimacy of an extreme degree of concentration.

But the other two forms of modest and low hierarchy are also under pressure to change in character. The middle ground of hierarchy is also challenged on grounds of privilege, since, as in the United States, it exhibits important differences in job placement and life chances, correlates with social-class differences in access, and contains large differences in financial support. A relatively flat hierarchy such as the Italian structure, in contrast, is challenged for *its* deficiencies: an inability to differentiate and support 'non-university' forms of education and training; the lack of institutional focus for the selection and preparation of competent civil servants. Minimal differentiation means that centres of excellence are missing, and systems attempting to move towards greater institutional equality are forced sooner or later to face the growing problem of thereby maintaining or creating such concentrations of resources, personnel, and student talent.

In general, across sections, tiers, sectors, and hierarchies, simple arrangements constrain change while complicated arrangements facilitate it. By design or unplanned adaptation, national systems move along all four of these dimensions towards variety.

STRUCTURES OF AUTHORITY AND MODES OF INTEGRATION
Turning directly to forms of authority and integration, the contest between 'forces' of non-change and 'forces' of change is complex indeed. But certain predispositions are clearly evident.

For example, following Margaret Archer (1979), we may say that centralized structures of authority tend to remain centralized, and decentralized ones decentralized. There may be some drifting of each upon the other, but convergence can be readily exaggerated as we observe in the short run the efforts of some centralized systems to decentralize and decentralized ones to unify. We have every reason to expect that the French educational structure, let alone that of the USSR, will remain centralized. 'Bureaucratic indispensibility', as Ezra N. Suleiman (1979) has shown, remains extremely high in French government generally. In the most highly bureaucratized state among the Western democracies, power remains with, and keeps rebounding back to, the central bureaucratic élite whose members invariably attended a grade école prior to recruitment into one of the grands corps. The French institutions of centralization have great stability and endurance. They are even immune to shifts in power among political parties since the parties are composed of nearly identical bureaucratic elements. And such mildly decentralized systems as the British, and radically decentralized as the American, are not going to approximate to the French let alone the Communist model, even as they become more centralized. Too much power, with related traditions, is fixed at lower levels. The hands of history that are felt in present-day arrangements will hold British universities away from central ministerial control in a way that is qualitatively different from the French mode. Much of the funding of US institutions clearly will remain at the level of the individual states, protected by state power and long-standing traditions and understandings. Private institutions will continue to be highly resistive as corporate entities to control by central officials, even as slices of their operations become government-dependent in ways not to be imagined in the centralized mode. Here again we must be impressed by the constraint side of structural predisposition.

But a balanced account must leave the matter open and look also at the inducements for change, which lie in part in failure of form. Each national mode of authority distribution contains weaknesses that will stimulate compensating effort. Thus, in the European mode, reform has sought to pull authority from the top and the bottom to strengthen the historically weak middle levels of administration, at regional and institutional levels. In the German federal variant of this mode, reform has also been attempting to move authority upward to an explicit national level of co-ordination, while simultaneously strengthening co-ordination below the Länder ministries. In the British mode, reform has sought to develop a superstructure responsive to politically and bureaucratically determined central policy, to strengthen the top level of co-ordination in what was previously, in formal terms, a nonsystem of autonomous institutions. Similarly, in the American mode, the name of reform has been more administered order, in a complicated arrangement of at least three levels of co-ordination (multicampus, state, national), to strengthen co-ordination and direction in the largest laissez-faire system ever developed in the history of higher education. In Japan, authority has been drifting upward to the national level, with the huge sprawling private sector coming under greater governmental direction as the price of public financial assistance.

In short, in mature academic systems (a) the historically-established distribution of authority will tend to perpetuate itself, convergence among national systems will be limited; but (b) each national authority structure will contain weaknesses calling for compensating effort and thereby helping to set the direction of conscious reform and unconscious adaptation.

Within these broad patterns of authority, we can observe at least four major ways in which parts are co-ordinated, linked together to form what we call a national system. These are the bureaucratic, the oligarchic, the political and the market (Clark 1979). Each type of integration has its own ways of constraining and facilitating change. Bureaucracy can effect change through planning and hierarchical control. But it typically bogs down in institutionalized procedure, administrative struggle, and official efforts to effect uniformity and prevent deviation. Oligarchy — control by senior professors — can facilitate change via personal initiative and collegial planning. But it also typically constructs heavy constraints as personal privilege becomes entrenched, unresponsive, and even irresponsible, and the structure of work and authority is overloaded. Political intervention can break through the crust of bureaucratic and oligarchic resistance to change, altering the interplay of power and interest while supporting new programmes. But it becomes heavily resistant to change as ideologies of party and regime become system-wide doctrines and as political groups enlarge the web of entrenched interests, guarding occupied territory and vetoing any re-allocation of resources and initiation of new progammes. The market facilitates change by means of decentralized action and forced competition among enterprises. But it becomes a great stationary force when institutions settle into a mutually-acceptable division of labour or voluntarily become fixated on one rewarding model.

The problem of facilitating change is then partly a problem of balancing such forms of linkage. No one form alone apparently will give even satisfactory results, let alone outstanding ones, despite the claims of partisans of each. Much further study is needed of the way these forms operate in combination and under the various conditions that we observe in different countries, including finally the special features of history and context that make each national system unique and turn purported generalizations into tendencies and possibilities rather than iron laws. One likelihood is that the effect of each major form of order upon change will vary over time, facilitating in one period and constraining in another. The market form appears least susceptible to such variation, hence the form most likely to keep a system open to change and adaptable to new environmental demands. But the matter is hardly settled, since we can observe how much established academic enterprises voluntarily settle down, subject to their own internal processes of institutionalization and the tendency to leave well alone when the payroll is being met.

To reason about the constraint of change brought about by these various major forms of integration is to suspect that they need to balance one another over time. When central state authority has been in the saddle, then the opening up of the system to change may depend on some combination of incrementally adjusting that authority internally, devolving some power to lower levels, and strengthening the market-like interactions of students, professors and institutions. Alternatively, when market aspects have predominated and have caused stagnation, then political and bureaucratic interventions can indeed be vehicles of change. To know that no one form is forever dependable, for either the conservation or renovation of such an important public good, is to encourage an evolutionary perspective — and to make us realize that the hero of one period in history may be the goat in the next, for co-ordinating structures as much as individuals.

THE GROWING IMPORTANCE OF FEDERAL ORGANIZATION

The organization of academic workers around multifarious bundles of knowledge gives an academic system a low threshold in tolerating centralized government. Yet this large lesson seems almost beside the point in the short run as the aggregate responses of so many groups in and outside the system to pressing problems move the educational structure towards greater central influence. Despite the Archer dictum that decentralized systems tend to remain decentralized, many observers and participants in Britian and the United States will continue to worry about how much that decentralization will give way. And those in centralized systems, as in Sweden and France, who are promoting decentralization, are seeking to understand the pros and cons of greater provincial and institutional control. I propose that the clarification and assertion of an old doctrine will help: federalism or something like it is a necessary framework for a modern adaptive academic system, one that can be simultaneously spontaneous and purposively led.

In higher education, a division of academic power is the principal basis for guaranteeing diversity in all other respects. The university itself can be seen as a federal system: the semi-autonomous, discipline-centred departments pursuing self-interests distinctive from the authority of the whole. Collegial and bureaucratic structures provide dual authority at the several organizational levels. Halsey and Trow (1971 pp.111-12) commented in the early 1970s that

'it is not too fanciful to see the modern university as a federation of departments each facing outwards toward the research councils for research funds and toward schools and other universities for students and staff while at the same time living together on a campus with faculty boards and the Senate as mechanisms for negotiation and arbitration of their divergent interests.'

A few years later, Moodie and Eustace (1974 p.61) further note that 'there is an important sense (in the English university) in which the "higher" bodies seek validation from the "lower". Whatever the precise boundaries of departmental autonomy, its existence makes of every university a "federal" structure rather than a strongly centralized system.'

In turn, the higher education system as a whole requires the federal principle. Control should be patchwork control — a little here and a little there, in an unsteady state. But systems that are quite disordered are tidied up: patchwork gives way to some perceivable coherence. In the drive towards structural integration, how then are checks and balances to be maintained? A middle ground has two essential features: all levels of the system should in themselves be pluralistic; and intermediate bodies should mediate between the central authorities and the many levels of the understructure, buffering one from the ungainly ways of the other.

Agency pluralism at the top of a higher education system is the first line of defence against the monumental error of a monopoly of power. Such pluralism generally evolves from the natural pursuit of agency self-interest: rare is the national system in which all matters of research and higher education are handled in a single ministry or department. Even in relatively simple systems, ministries of agriculture, departments of defence, bureaus of mining, institutes of health, etc. support universities, colleges, and research centres in whole or in part and have their own academic constituencies out in the field units. Each headquarters office is then the representative at the centre of a particular set of operational interests, struggling for their welfare. In very complex large systems, as in the US, the division of academic control within the top layers can be extreme indeed, as dozens of agencies, for reasons of their own, become involved. Considering their typically intense need for highly-trained experts, and for the upgrading and retraining of professional personnel, *and* for the pleasing of constituencies, governmental agencies across the board can hardly stay away from higher education. Thus, agency conflict at the top is natural (Clark 1981). It should be expected, *and* encouraged. But there are strong inclinations to discourage it. The main battle cry in governmental reform is for the elimination of overlap and duplication, in the name of economy and efficiency. Conventional wisdom views monopolies in the public sector as good, overlooking the need for pluralism within the governmental structure itself, in the governance of such a complicated and basic function as higher education. The dictum is: create and maintain segments at each level and especially at the top.

Equally important is the buffering of control provided by intermediary bodies and forms. Levels of organization can and do check one another: when the Swedes inserted a regional level of governmental supervision during the 1970s, they created a possible counterforce to central direction as well as to university self-control. Different forms of authority also can and do balance one another: trusteeship, institutional bureaucracy, and faculty collegial control balance off against state bureaucracy and legitimate political control. The central idea is to have forms that will offer different compositions of interest and expertise at successively higher or lower levels. In its golden age (1920-1965), the British University Grants Committee came closest to the ideal. The processes of resource allocation at the top and the bottom were influenced by different mixes of interests and expertise. Holding intermediate powers between the university people and the governmental officials, the UGC clearly protected one from the other. There are many informal features of trust and friendship, and common background among political, administrative, and academic élites, that helped make the Committee work as well as it once did. But it is the form, the primary structure itself, that has been the most important invention in twentieth-century higher education in buffering central control by intermediate body. The dictum is: create and maintain forms and levels of power that mediate between the top and the bottom.

Surely our short-run thinking, affected so much by immediate problems, will cause us to err in one direction or the other. It is safer to err toward the mischief of factions that is entailed in excessive fragmentation and minimal overall control. For to err in the other direction is to ease toward the mischief of monopoly that is entailed in excessive order and strong integration. The latter is much the greater error, the one most likely to bring down the curses of those who must follow us.

NOTES
1   This chapter is drawn from Burton R. Clark, *The Higher Education System: Academic Organization in Cross-National Perspective* (tentative title: under preparation), Chapter 6, 'Change'.

2 'Certain areas of human activity have evolved their own action patterns: the world of science, or of painting. There is, in other words, such a thing as sectoral hegemony . . .' (Dahrendorf 1979 p.42).
3 'Underlying the status of the department is its crucial characteristic of being authoritative in its own field of learning' (Moodie and Eustace 1974 p.61).

REFERENCES

Archer, Margaret S. (1979) *Social Origins of Educational Systems* London: Sage Publications

Becher, Tony and Kogan, M. (1980) *Process and Structure in Higher Education* London: Heinemann

Clark, Burton R. (1977) *Academic Power in Italy: Bureaucracy and Oligarchy in a National University System* Chicago: The University of Chicago Press

Clark, Burton R. (1979) The many pathways of academic coordination *Higher Education* 8, 251-267

Clark, Burton R. (1981) *The Contradictions of Change in Academic Systems* Seminar paper presented at the Fifth International Conference on Higher Education, University of Lancaster, September 1-4, 1981

Dahrendorf, Ralf (1979) *Life Chances* Chicago: University of Chicago Press

Giles, Geoffrey J. (1976) *The Structure of Higher Education in the German Democratic Republic* Yale Higher Education Program Working Paper No. 12

Halsey, A.H and Trow, M.A. (1971) *The British Academics* Cambridge, Mass.: Harvard University Press

McHenry, Dean, et al. (1977) *Academic Departments: Problems, Variations, and Alternatives* San Francisco: Jossey-Bass

Moodie, Graeme C. and Eustace, R. (1974) *Power and Authority in British Universities* London: George Allen and Unwin

Premfors, Rune and Östergren, B. (1978) *Systems of Higher Education: Sweden* New York: International Council for Educational Development

Suleiman, Ezra N. (1979) *Elites in French Society: The Politics of Survival* Princeton: Princeton University Press

Van de Graaff, John H. and Furth, D. (1978) France. In Van de Graaff, John H. et al. *Academic Power: Patterns of Authority in Seven National Systems of Higher Education* New York: Praeger

Van de Graaff, John H. (1980) *Can Department Structures Replace a Chair System?: Comparative Perspectives* Yale Higher Education Research Group Working Paper No. 46

Wiebe, Robert H. (1976) *The Search for Order, 1877-1920* New York: Hill and Wang